MacARTHUR'S GHOST

P. F. KLUGE

MacARTHUR'S GHOST

ARBOR HOUSE
NEW YORK

Manufactured in the United States of America

10 9 8 7 6 5 4 3 2 1

Library of Congress Cataloging in Publication Data

Kluge, P. F. (Paul Frederick), 1924–
MacArthur's ghost.

I. Title.
PS3561.L77M3   1987   813'.54   86-32219
ISBN: 0-87795-901-3

To Michael Carlisle

MacARTHUR'S
GHOST

Part One

★ ★ ★
★ ★

DECEMBER 1981:
FORTY YEARS AFTER

1

At dawn, I discovered Manila. I learned that Manila air was fog and sweat and steam, that it smelled of garbage fires and cooking and diesel fumes and, just possibly, the sea. I reconnoitered the world-class monoliths the Marcos government erected on landfill at the edge of the sea, expositions, exhibitions, theaters, convention centers, concert halls, hotels, all protected by sleepy security guards cradling rifles the way a kid holds a teddy bear. I nodded to what looked like a permanent encampment of taxi drivers in the parking lot of my 90 percent empty hotel. They cooked and spat, played chess, gossiped. They slept inside their cars. They hardly ever moved, a cargo cult waiting for planeloads of moneyed tourists to turn their hemorrhaging economy around. I trotted along Roxas Boulevard and saw squatters sleeping among palm trees, washing themselves in public fountains, like starlings splashing in birdbaths. I caught the eye of a woman who stood holding her baby up and out, as if to ceremonially welcome the sunrise, till I noticed the baby was peeing into the morning tide. The woman turned and held the kid toward me, the catch of the day. I ran on. I was pursued. "Hey, Joe, give me a peso," cried the squatter boy who dogged my footsteps. I increased my pace and so treated the early morning traffic on Roxas Boulevard to a duel between an adult American in $50 running shoes and a barefoot beggar urchin, all sores and scars. I couldn't lose him. We raced past the U.S. embassy, through the morning crowd of visa applicants that clogged the sidewalk, past the marine guards. I turned, heading back to the hotel, and this maneuver surprised the kid. He stepped aside. Perhaps he feared a beating. But as soon as I passed him, the race was on again. "Hey, Joe. Hey, Joe." I couldn't lose him: he was a bad dream, guilty conscience, hangover. And he was loving it. So did everyone who was trapped in morning gridlock. They beeped their horns, they whistled, they laughed: office workers, taxi drivers, stevedores, and a whole busload of uniformed Lolitas headed to convent school. "Hey, Joe, very hungry. Hey, Joe, give me a peso." They picked up the chant. A corridor of sound, a gamut. At last I reached the hotel. Sanctuary. Rattan furniture, marble floors. Advertisements for tours and folklore shows. Air conditioning. Baby Maria and the Soul Titans nightly in the Tropical Shack. I stood inside, gasping, looking out. He was a cocky, scrappy, guttersnipe kid, the kind who tagged along with G.I.'s in the old war movies and wound up showing them the back entrance to enemy headquarters. He stood out there, hands on his hips, staring right back in at me. Not begging, just staring. One of the hotel doormen, dressed as a Spanish conquistador or something, watched him closely. I gestured for the kid to stay, went up to my room for my wallet. By the time I got back downstairs, he was gone.

2

"Hey, George," Clifford Lerner shouted. "You still in the business?"

They had been drinking for a while when Griffin found them in a cocktail lounge just off the Manila Hotel's main lobby, a party of friends, colleagues, competitors, fellow sufferers and sinners convening to celebrate the fortieth anniversary of World War II and feeling no pain. Just sitting around the Manila Hotel, it was hard not to believe that your life had worked out very well, landing you in a place of white marble floors, dark wood, high ceilings, a place of tropical plants and comfortable chairs, service with a smile, and the buoyant faith that with money all things were possible.

"Of course I'm still in the business," Griffin replied. He shook hands with Lerner, a sharp-tongued hack who ran half a dozen strings for magazines in Canada, New Zealand, and his native Australia.

"I heard you were running out of gas," Lerner said.

"That's what I heard too," Hugh Elliot said. "Had any fun here yet?"

"I got chased by a beggar when I went jogging this morning," Griffin volunteered. "He stayed with me all the way back to the hotel."

"You should see what chased me last night," Lerner said. "Caught up with me, too."

"Was she good?" Hugh Elliot asked. He was an L.A.-based freelancer who wrote mostly for men's magazines.

"Not she, Elliot."

"He?"

"They. . . . Two. Count 'em. Two. Mama-san told me, 'Take two, they're small.' "

"Oh, my God!" groaned Elliot.

Clifford Lerner liked being known as a lecher. Even now his attention strayed across the room to where a prim and handsome Filipina wheeled a cart to a table of Japanese businessmen, one of whom had evidently requested a cigar. The woman offered the man a choice of smokes, letting him select the appropriate thickness, length, and color. Already the sexual entendre was clear. "Heart be still," Lerner sighed.

The Filipina lifted the cigar, examined it, scanned it from end to end, the consistency and heft, with particular attention to the veins in the wrapper leaf. She spun the cigar, she stroked it, she snipped it, all her expert procedures accomplished with a clinical detachment that made the performance doubly exciting. Finally, she doused the cigar in brandy, toasted and lit it, and bowed as she presented the corona to a giddy, beet-red Japanese.

"You think they're here for the fortieth anniversary of World War Two?" Elliot asked.

"They won't be laying wreaths tonight," Lerner said. "You know how the Japanese set it up, Hugh? This is beautiful. You're in Tokyo. You have a lifetime contract with Mitsubishi and a wife at home and kids studying for exams and you want to get away. So you sign up for a certain kind of tour, and you get this mail, this catalog, this damn near yearbook and it's all women, wall to wall. And you just pick the one you want. Let your fingers do the walking! You fly into Manila, there she is, waiting for you in your hotel room."

"So is this what it's come to, Clifford?" Griffin asked. "Drooling over Japanese sex tours? Is that your lead for a piece on World War Two's fortieth birthday party?"

"Come on, Griffin," Lerner protested. "You ought to know by now. There's the stories you write. And . . ."

A glance at the Filipina cigar girl, wheeling past on new missions of mercy in the cocktail lounge. "And there's the stories you live."

Griffin, Lerner, and Elliot were some of more than a hundred "travel industry media professionals" whom the government of President Ferdinand Marcos had induced to visit Manila, so they could better describe the destination appeal of this stable, friendly, peace-loving, and pro-American nation. Timed to coincide with the fortieth anniversary of the outbreak of the Pacific War, the week-long public relations orgy included seminars, receptions, and tours. There were tours of Spanish Manila, its fortresses and cathedrals and centuries-old universities; tours of American Manila, its elite housing, monuments, and shopping centers, although it was granted that America's finest legacy was the gift—intangible though it might be—of democracy. There were tours of Marcos-era Manila, not omitting the leader's dynamic achievements in imposing "revolution from above": land reform, public housing, health and welfare. There were scenic excursions also: waterfalls, volcanoes, rice terraces, hot springs, battlefields, aboriginal tribes, golf courses, beaches. These were stories to write. But what George Griffin had come to Manila to find was what had evaded him so far: what Clifford Lerner called the story you lived.

From the start, Griffin had no illusions about his newspaper columns, the Faraway Places/Backyard Adventures tandem with which he serviced about eighty newspapers. No illusions, either, about the airline magazines, the annual reports, the travel guides that rounded out his income. But he had always believed that, somewhere along the way, the world would open for him. Tossing off his columns with cynical dispatch, he would nonetheless accumulate a store of experience that would lead to something finer. A book. The book. Through all his travels, he kept accumulating notes. He'd once heard that a writer was a man on whom nothing was lost. He worked hard to be such a man. Nothing, or very little, was lost on him. But—and this was the caveat that time imposed—if nothing was lost, everything was wasted. Though undiminished in volume, Griffin's note taking had become mordant and despairing, less an investment in future success than a narrative of continuing frustration. Still, Griffin kept scribbling, compiling the tale of his paper chase around a world he had circled so many times he could feel the very mountains eroding beneath him, old trails indistinguishable from new, endings and beginnings all tangled together.

*   *   *

"Jet lag?" Clifford Lerner was peering down at him. Griffin had drifted off. Now he saw that most of the people in the lounge were headed down a corridor to a gala dinner given by their Filipino hosts.

"Just thinking."

"You want to talk about it?" No doubt Lerner was willing to listen. Maybe he saw something in Griffin that recalled his own hopeful, younger self. Certainly the reverse was true. Griffin saw his future in Lerner: alcoholic, amoral, anecdotal proprietor of a thousand pungent stories he would never write. An old hand. A character. Lerner scared him.

"No thanks, Clifford."

"Well, come on then. Dinner's on. They fly you halfway around the world, put you up in a five-star hotel, the least you can do is eat with them."

In the Champagne Room were candlelight and violins and chafing dishes and crystal and a seating order from which there was no hope of escape. The table was for six and Griffin stood by his chair, waiting for his partners to arrive. The first were Mr. and Mrs. Ernesto Torres, operators of a resort in Batangas Province, where Griffin was quickly invited to laze, bathe, golf, and ride horseback. "We have some wonderful horseback riding," Torres offered with a wink, "four-legged and two." Mrs. Torres informed Griffin they had five children, three "already in California."

"George Griffin."

Someone had picked up the name tag he had left sitting on his plate. Griffin looked up and saw an American woman, a black. That was unusual. So were her freckles. And her green eyes.

"Hi," she said. "I'm Susan Hayes." She introduced herself to the Torreses and sat down across from Griffin.

"Two more to go," Griffin said, nodding toward the remaining empty seats. "No place markers. What does that mean?"

"It depends," she said. "Either a very important couple or very unimportant."

The issue was settled quickly. A head waiter approached from across the room, leading a white-haired gentleman, an aristocratic pipe smoker, who tapped shoulders and shook hands as he passed, like a host acknowledging a room of satisfied guests.

He was the sort of man who had to be somebody because the woman on his arm would certainly never be seen with anyone who didn't matter.

"Important?" Griffin asked.

"Very important," Susan Hayes replied. "Jun and Birdy Villanueva. Jun Villanueva is a lawyer who is one of the most respected leaders of the anti-Marcos opposition, the legal opposition . . ."

"Legal?"

"Yes. The people who ran things before Marcos took power. Reputable people, businessmen, intellectuals, professionals, old families—that's the legal opposition."

"They don't carry guns?"

"No. That's the other opposition."

"Nice people around!" cried Torres, the resort owner, chuckling at a joke that Griffin didn't get.

"Nice people around," Susan Hayes explained. "NPA. New Peoples Army. Communists."

"Are there many of them?"

"For years, the estimate was that they numbered about six thousand and were a source of concern, but no immediate threat. Lately, they say ten thousand. Still a source of concern but no immediate threat."

"Is that Villanueva's daughter?"

"His wife," said Susan Hayes, wincing a little at his directness. "They're respectable, important people. They always have been."

"But what are they doing here? They're oppositionists. And this is a Marcos party."

"They're all Filipinos," Hayes answered. Before Griffin could ask more, she rose from her chair—maybe five seconds before it was strictly necessary to do so. "Hello, Jun. Hello, Birdy."

Jun Villanueva was the image of an elder statesman, cordial, likable, and slightly vacant. He thought he recognized Griffin's name, he said, in fact he was almost sure, and he thought that a man must be very fortunate, or very talented, to travel so widely and be paid for it. So much for Jun Villanueva, Griffin thought: he's on automatic pilot. But Birdy Villanueva was something else again.

"Such a carnival!" she said, glancing around the room. The first lady of the opposition—only a bullet or (this being the legal opposition) a heartbeat away from power—was all in white: a knee-length white skirt, a kind of less-is-more singlet topped by a showy jacket that was gossamer and flouncy. "Will you tell your readers, Mr. Griffin, that they should come and have fun in the lap of this dictatorship?"

"Not if you think they should stay home . . ."

"No, no," Birdy said. "If they have a taste for scandal, tell them to come, by all means. Tell them to come to Imelda's film festival. The more the merrier. Let them . . . let us all eat cake together . . ."

"My wife speaks out," Jun Villanueva intervened, "but is never outspoken."

"I can see that," Griffin said. But Birdy's attention had wandered. She searched the room, taking names for the revolution or maybe checking to see who else had gone shopping overseas lately. Griffin turned to Susan Hayes.

"Where are you from?"

"Florida."

"Oh."

"Disney World!" Torres interjected. "I have to see that place. Have you visited there, Mr. Griffin?"

"Yes. In the line of duty."

"I hear you can spend many days there and not see all of it."

"I guess so," Griffin agreed. "Then again, I saw plenty in thirty-six hours."

Torres was all ears, waiting for more, but Griffin decided to keep his memories of that drunken weekend in Orlando to himself: his rudeness throughout the press tour, his wisecrack during the visit to the audioanimatronic display of walking, talking U.S. presidents ("We're one up on Lenin's tomb!"), his snide theorizing that Howard Hughes, J. Edgar Hoover, and Walt Disney all favored Mormon employees, which somehow led to the old joke about the three most overrated things in life being home cooking, home screwing, and the FBI. Clifford Lerner was right, and the word was out: Griffin was running out of gas.

"Where do you work?" he asked Susan Hayes.

"At the U.S. embassy."

"Doing what?"

"She processes applications for people who want to go to Disneyland." Birdy Villanueva had struck again and everybody was amused. "But we have our Disneyland here, already!"

"But Birdy . . ." Resort owner Torres did not approve. "You give our guest the wrong idea."

"Hardly!" Birdy brushed him aside. "We have Fantasyland. Frontierland. Pirates. Jungle Adventure. We have it all. A cartoon king and a cartoon queen and a whole cast of dwarves and elves and clowns."

"Mr. Griffin is here to promote travel," Jun Villanueva reminded his wife. "Now if he listens to you, dear, everyone will stay at home. Where would that leave us?"

"It would leave us in a position to settle our own problems in our own way. At least we would have to stop blaming outsiders for what was wrong and that would be a relief!" She turned to Griffin and it felt flattering, to have her focusing on him. He doubted her attention rested anywhere for very long. "How subversive I must sound! Mr. Griffin, the twin pillars of our national faith are the desirability of Americans being here and of Filipinos being there . . . in America. If everyone stayed home, we might be a nation. Now we are . . . a place."

"Darling, I have an idea," Jun Villanueva ventured. It was his role to calm Birdy down. "Perhaps Mr. Griffin can join us Thursday evening."

"It's just a discussion group," Birdy said. "A seance in memory of free speech. If you wish . . ."

"May I bring a guest?"

"Certainly."

"Be my guest, Miss Hayes?"

"How can she say no?" Birdy said. Then she glanced across the room. "Attention, everyone! Now begins the fashion show."

There was a surge of applause and music and a blitz of flashbulbs as the First Lady of the Philippines, Imelda Marcos, made her entrance. Griffin had to admit that the effect was stunning: a white dress, floor length, with only black hair and diamonds for contrast. Queen of the Catholic Prom, appointed for life. Time had puffed and coarsened her, turning the one-time beauty queen into something of a matron. Still, the sense of past beauty, melding with current power, made her unforgettable.

She presided at the head table and, while some Ministry of Tourism official went into a lengthy and obsequious introduction—as if the audience needed to be clued in to her identity —the First Lady surveyed the room. Wherever her gaze alit, there were smiles and waves, followers marked present. It was like some tropical Camelot, Griffin thought, with knights, retainers, ladies in waiting, a close attention to dress, fashion, seating order, nuances of personal appearance, whispers, expressions. Camelot. And Camelot lasted until the First Lady arose to make her speech.

"The Philippines," Imelda Marcos began, "is east and west, right and left, rich and poor. We are neither here nor there."

Sometimes, at a movie, even before the credits finish, you know it's all a mistake; it's not going to work. Griffin had that sinking feeling now. Turning, he saw Clifford Lerner roll his eyes, place a finger at his temple, and discharge an invisible revolver. It wasn't a speech so much as an hour-long impromptu monologue. There was the First Lady's philosophy of tourism, her strategy for grass-roots economic development, her defense of high and mass culture, her plans for bringing the world to the Philippines, the Philippines to the world. There was an enthusiastic account of plans for the upcoming Manila International Film Festival, a world-class conference that would enrich and ennoble the humblest citizen of this struggling yet dynamic archipelago. There were those who criticized the cost of projects like the film festival—the parties and receptions, travel and hotel rooms, and most of all, the massive Parthenon-scale Film Center, which heroic construction crews were struggling round the clock to complete. What justification, they asked, for such an edifice in such an impoverished land? But there was always need—in fact, there was special need—for beauty amidst poverty. Reason not the need! Was there not poverty in Athens when the first Parthenon was built? Was India a land of plenty when Shah Jahan dreamed of the Taj Mahal? No, a thousand times! Reason not the need! Man did not live by bread alone! Or rice!

But what about some coffee? Griffin wondered. The First Lady was only warming up and Griffin badly needed coffee. He'd tried staring at waiters. He'd waved his hands in the air, as if guiding a crippled fighter onto a pitching aircraft carrier

flight deck. In vain. Shit! He recognized some of his Disney
World anger coming out again, recklessness and despair. Two
kinds of contempt, for himself and for his world, leapfrogging
toward disaster. He pushed his chair out, ready to arise and
lurch across the ballroom, empty coffee cup in hand. Maybe
he'd hold the cup in one hand and a pencil in another, imitating
a beggar. . . . Then he felt someone's hand on his arm. It was
Susan Hayes, motioning for him to lean toward her.

"Don't," she whispered.

He waited for more and, while he waited, he enjoyed the
appearance of intimacy, being so close to an attractive woman
in a dark room.

"Don't?" he asked.

"Don't," she repeated and to Griffin it meant, don't do what
you've done before in other places, don't do what you would do
here, now, without me.

"Okay," he said, regretting the withdrawal of her hand and
tamely sitting up to catch every word of Imelda Marcos's
speech. When historians looked back on these days, the First
Lady reflected, they would not confine themselves to food production. They would not be wholly preoccupied with sacks of
rice and tons of fish, with pigs or poultry, though in all these
categories there were statistics to demonstrate that the New
Society had scored impressive and underpublicized gains. But
no! There was food for the belly. But there was also food for the
eyes, the heart, and the immortal spirit!

Suddenly, abruptly, she sat down. Everyone else stood up, a
standing ovation that continued while the First Lady and her
entourage made an exit. Griffin stood too, stretching, yawning.

"Well, Mr. Griffin," Torres, the resort owner, asked as soon as
they were back in their seats, "Did you enjoy the First Lady's
speech?"

"Only one complaint," he answered cheerfully. "It was too
short."

Birdy Villanueva laughed a laugh that was public and derisive.
"Did you like that account of the Parthenon? *Our* Parthenon?"

"Unforgettable."

"Our Parthenon collapsed a few weeks ago. Several floors of
fresh cement crashed down. The government says only six
workers died. Others counted dozens of bodies."

"I'm sorry to hear that."

"Even now there are cracks in the foundation. Structural problems. Some questions as to whether the landfill below has completely settled. What nonsense! That absurd woman!"

"Athens wasn't built in a day," Jun Villanueva offered brightly.

"Or for a film festival!" Birdy retorted. "In time for the visit of George Hamilton and Virna Lisi, Franco Nero, Barbara Carrera."

"This is not fair, Birdy," Torres protested. "You think we should live our lives under corrugated metal roofs? Should we project our movies on bed sheets? You would laugh at us then. And yet, when we aspire to match the best in the world, you laugh again. That is not fair. We are a hospitable people. We go out of our way for strangers. The whole world knows this. And when some of our people give their lives—six or sixty, I don't know—so we can give foreigners a party, you laugh at us. That is very unfair."

Torres's wife patted his hand to calm him. The room darkened and a slide show depicting the natural wonders of the Philippines, not stinting certain recent improvements instigated by the leader, his wife, and offspring, began. People started leaving right away, the Villanuevas among the first to go. But while other people ducked out under cover of darkness, Birdy Villanueva walked right through the stream of light from the projector, her queenly silhouette shadowing a picture of Mrs. Marcos tiptoeing through fields of miracle rice. Perfect timing or coincidence?

"Hey, George," Clifford Lerner came by to whisper. "Night out on the town. Meet you outside . . ."

"Can I offer you a drink?" Griffin asked Susan Hayes.

"I don't think so," she said. "I'll see you Thursday night, though."

"I'm sorry if I cornered you. If you can't come, which is my quaint way of saying if you don't want to come, you can always phone in sick."

"No, no, it's fine."

"Any advice for me . . . about tonight?"

"None you'd keep. Off you go, Mr. Backyard Faraway."

3

Five travel writers, some with a history of junkets dating back to Ciudad Trujillo, set out together that December night. They were rich foreigners partying in a city that was poor, so Manila came at them, offering itself in any way it could, tempting, smiling, testing to see how, and how much, the distance between rich and poor could be eroded in a single foolish evening. When Griffin thought about it later, it reminded him of one of those war movies that begins with a half dozen character actors patrolling treacherous country, forcing strongpoints, fording rivers, fighting skirmish after skirmish, and dying along the way.

They began by reconnoitering del Pilar Street, a carnal, carnival avenue lined by bars, massage parlors, boardinghouses, souvenir shops, V.D. clinics. Surprise was not on their side: their approach was hailed by doormen, shoeshine boys, money changers. They started at the Firehouse, loudest and largest of the go-go emporia. The Firehouse was a theme bar. There were pictures of fire trucks and hose companies on the flame-colored walls; there were sirens, alarms, axes, helmets on display. Onstage there were firehouse poles, and fire truck lights were overhead. And everywhere, onstage, along the bar, at tables, on the dance floor, were the women who did what was needed to extinguish fires, wherever they combusted. It was hard to tell, with smoke and flashing lights and constant shifting, but George Griffin guessed there were fifty women around the Firehouse. At any time, half a dozen of them were onstage, dancing, curling themselves around firehouse poles, sliding up and down, writhing on the floor, high-kicking toward the audience. Yet it was oddly sexless, like a dressing room for teenage girls who had just opened a care package from Frederick's of Hollywood and decided to throw a naughty, spur-of-the-moment pajama party, posing, modeling, staring at themselves in mirrors, constantly pulling at one end of a garment, tugging at another, inspecting each other and themselves, then yielding to a new group and circulating among the customers, to see if anybody took them seriously. For the most part the dancers were small and girlish; Griffin understood Clifford Lerner's "Take two, they're small." They were very young; not quite so young that a customer would feel perverse, but still young. "Old enough to bleed, old enough to butcher," Lerner said.

On Mabini Street, the travel writers were ushered through a ground-floor bar, upstairs, into the "VIP Mezzanine," a dark, moldy loft where they were urged to recline on low-lying sofas, and the girls who descended upon them, disposing of blouses as champagne arrived, made clear that fellatio was the specialty of the house. That was where they lost Hugh Elliot. He lay prostrate on a couch, pants down around his ankles, hairy belly gasping, arms flung wide in agony or ecstasy, it was hard to say, but what George Griffin remembered was the three girls who knelt around him, one on each side, one between his legs, a triple fellatio, each taking turns, the movement of their heads, rising, falling, like a trio of oil derricks pumping liquid treasure from deep out of the earth. "And then," George Griffin said, "there were four."

Dapper, literary Willis Ownby was the next to go, damned as soon as they stopped in a little club near the cemetery, a gay bar where some of the boys—for they were always boys and girls, never men and women, and though this should have made things morally worse, the effect was somehow otherwise, for it gave to everything the quality of play, of youthful frolic, whether it was the naughty posing of girls at the Firehouse or the innocent nudity of boys here, the boys who had taken plastic fibers, mostly blue fibers out of some cheap plastic washline, fibers they had inserted crosswise through their foreskins, the result being a kind of permanent French tickler, and this was a piece of handicraft that Willis Ownby could not forego. Now they were three.

The next place, back on the del Pilar strip, had a large red apple emblazoned in neon over the door, a ripe and shiny

MacIntosh. This was the Lost Eden, a fancier and more formal place, where a floor show featured classical skits in which statues came to life and danced before dreaming artists who committed suicide on waking, and shipwrecked maidens hallucinated about elephantine lovers, and the final skit featured audience participation. The skit was simple. An old-fashioned circular bathtub was placed onstage and then the most beautiful woman any of them had seen in Manila, clad in panties and T-shirt, stepped onstage, into the tub. The master of ceremonies invited a few members of the audience to come up onstage, to pour water on the kneeling and obeisant beauty, and then to soap and wash her. The first few customers willingly obliged, paying particular attention to the beauty's breasts and buttocks.

That was when Griffin saw trouble coming. You couldn't blame Lerner. Most of the women Griffin had seen were cheerfully delinquent teenagers, grabbers and gigglers, but the woman in the bathtub was different: olive-skinned, straight Castilian nose, dark winning eyes. She was taller than average, formed and tapered and, what was best of all, she made no contact with the people who watched her, the Japanese tour group, the gamy Americans, the affluent Filipinos who for once shed their macho nonchalance and assumed an attitude of protectiveness toward the woman in the tub. To all this, she seemed impervious. This was not a performance, Griffin thought, it was an epiphany, which someone was now preparing to defile. Clifford Lerner rolled up his sleeves, as though he were going into surgery, but the emcee ignored him. Lerner was more and more inflamed by the beauty in the tub. Who wouldn't be? She was cleanliness and debauchery, sex and hygiene, and when it seemed the show was ending, lights coming up, the girl arising, Lerner lurched to his feet, upended a table of San Miguels, dove forward, tripping over the edge of the stage, smashing his forehead against the side of the tub, where he was tackled by the master of ceremonies, who helped him up, held him tightly, never failed to call him sir, and forced him out the door. Griffin settled a ridiculously inflated bill and found Lerner and a rookie named Gibbins waiting outside.

"You're bleeding, Clifford," Griffin said, pointing to a nasty gash on Lerner's forehead. "You may need stitches."

"Just a flesh wound," Lerner countered, wiping at the wound and coming away with a blood-smeared hand. "Where to next?"

"You'd better have that looked at, really."

"Oh, Christ, Griffin, you're no fun at all anymore. What's the matter with you?"

"It's not me, Lerner. You're the one who's bleeding."

"So superior," Lerner said. "Only you're not superior, George. Just younger. Think about it."

Diving through a convoy of jeepneys, Lerner staggered down the other side of the street, weaving through beggars and peddlers, skipping over satay grills, finally stopping outside a place called the G-Spot, where a half dozen girls ushered the wounded writer inside. He waved good-bye: no hard feelings.

Thomas Gibbins, the other survivor, had behaved impeccably, a model of the thoughtful traveler. He asked questions about the Marcos regime, about the U.S. Military Bases Agreement, the distribution of wealth and poverty in Manila. At the start, when a girl at the Firehouse dumped herself in his lap and started trifling with his zipper, he wondered aloud about the most recent charges leveled against Marcos by Amnesty International.

"What are you going to say about Manila?" he asked now. They had stopped for Irish coffees at the Club Tennessee, a monstrous nightclub with colonnades, pillars, nymphs, fountains, and a sign that advertised an "Ivy League College Girl Fashion Show."

"I don't know," Griffin said. "Manila as bargain capital?"

"You'd recommend the place? After a night like this? The whole town's a brothel. I don't believe it. And I don't believe in it. I've never paid for it."

"Good for you."

"I'll be glad to go. I'm on a swing through New Zealand. Two weeks on the South Island. I'm hiking the Milford Track. Where are you headed?"

"I don't know. I thought I might stay around."

"Why would you want to do that?" Gibbins asked. "This whole place is rotten. Jesus, I've never seen anything like it, the way they come at you here. It's Catholic, it's macho, it's dictatorial, it's small, it's hot, it's poor, it's . . . evil."

"So much for the good news."

"Always a joke, huh, Griffin? Well, the bad news is that it's American."

"Used to be."

"Come off it, George. So what if they print their own postage stamps? We run this place like the Russians run Poland. We prop up the boss man. Arm the army. Siphon off the opposition. And hold onto our beloved military bases for dear life."

"You may be right."

"Why hang around then?"

"For all the reasons you mentioned."

"I don't get you." Curiosity mingled with loathing in the way Gibbins looked at him, and it startled Griffin to realize that was probably the way he himself looked at Clifford Lerner: *watch out, that's what I'll become.*

"Get me out of here," Gibbins said. He got out of his chair unsteadily. In spite—no, because of his intention to remain faithful to his bride—he'd been drinking while the others were playing. Now he was drunk. Griffin threw some money on the table, took him by the elbow, and guided him across the dance floor toward the door. He was feeling protective about young Gibbins. It was nice to meet a journalist who cared about his work. Suddenly Gibbins jerked away from him.

"What in the world is that?" he asked. He was looking through a window that ran full length down one side of the room, a one-way window that enabled Gibbins to gaze in at dozens of women available for his selection. They were a merry company, unself-conscious, trying on makeup, reading movie magazines, dancing to cassettes.

"You coming, Tom?" asked Griffin.

"Boy, oh, boy." He leaned forward, his forehead against the glass, despondent, defeated. Sad. But when Griffin reached out to take his elbow again, he refused to budge. He was like a leashed dog, transfixed by some ecstatic scent.

"I've only been married a year," he said, already confessing. "See that one by the TV? That's the one. The hair!"

There were several girls watching an old "Let's Make a Deal." The girl with the hair was hard to miss, though, a cascade of straight black hair, a raven waterfall that plunged down to her buttocks. Dressed in an innocent white shift, she was like a teenager up past her bedtime, ready to dive under sheets as soon as she heard her parents' car come up the driveway. She was striking, almost as memorable as the girl in the tub, and Griffin reckoned there was hope for everyone in the discovery —Manila discovery—that sin did not necessarily defile, or virtue beautify. Gibbins signaled to a female attendant to bring out the long-haired girl. "Got to be," he said.

The door opened and in a moment the girl emerged, walking directly to where Gibbins stood waiting for her. She leaned against him and slipped her hand around his arm: they made an intimate and ideal couple already. Gibbins was bewitched; he ran a hand over her hair, beginning at the top of her head, down the back of her neck, over her shoulders and back, over her buttocks, down as far as his hand could reach, and the hair streamed on. The girl smiled, looked at Gibbins, and said, "Hello, Joe," and Griffin knew that World War II had not been fought in vain.

4

Griffin wrapped a towel around his middle and pushed aside the sliding door to the terrace. The chair he sat in was still wet with dew, the concrete floor damp and cool beneath his feet. It felt good to preside over the city, half naked, from ten floors up, sober and alone.

Manila Bay was dotted by dozens of ships. Far beyond was the Bataan peninsula, a hefty shoulder of mountains pushing into the sea. Corregidor would be out there somewhere too, he guessed. Right below was the Cultural Plaza, the Marcos showcase. To one side was the Coconut Palace, a guesthouse for foreign dignitaries, built out of all-native materials; the Pope had declined to stay there. To the other side was Mrs. Marcos's Parthenon, the Film Center. Behind it was an artificial lagoon, complete with transplanted palms and trucked-in sand, a place for starlets and producers to cavort during the coming film festival. Easy for a certain kind of writer, Paul Theroux or one of those snotty Naipauls, to be strenuously droll about all this: another comical little hot-weather country, gobbling aid and gulling the masses while the postcolonial elite went California dreamin'. Manila was a feast for ironists. But that wasn't Griffin's trade.

FARAWAY PLACES

by George Griffin

It is a dream, a very old dream at that, so old a dream we hesitate to confess it. In short, a cliché: the vision of an island, a palm-fringed island set in a vast blue sea. We've seen it in shipwreck cartoons, in soft-drink ads, in television shows and . . .

And in my last column from Fiji, Griffin thought, yanking the paper out of his typewriter, crumpling it in a ball that, nonetheless, expanded in midflight and landed well short of the wicker wastepaper basket across the room. A miss at the beginning, a miss at the end. Very well then. Try again, old whore, for the perfect position. Tickle those keys . . .

FARAWAY PLACES

by George Griffin

It is time—high time—the budget-wary traveler with a taste for something different takes a look at the Philippines, a friendly, stable, eager-to-please country that combines the exotic appeal of the Far East with the beachcombing Bali Hai charm of the blue Pacific. What's more, English is spoken, dollars are welcome, and Americans are greeted as friends . . .

. . . in this rickety, senile dictatorship, which deserves a Garcia Marquez to chronicle its vain excesses, its terminal spasms, its rococo conspiracies, but what it gets is George Griffin, who is having a harder and harder time separating the words he hides from the ones he sells, but if you are going to break down it might as well be here, far from home, in a city of dreams—bad, good, and wet. But come now, once more upon the mattress, the old proficiency. The eyes of the Sun Belt are upon you . . .

FARAWAY PLACES

by George Griffin

We think of ourselves as a nation of winners and yet we cherish the memory of our defeats. That is why we revere our Valley Forge and make the Alamo a shrine. That is why we remember the *Maine,* remember Pearl Harbor. And that is why, forty years later, a handful of Americans, middle-aged and older, are making a pilgrimage halfway around the world to that certain island I can barely glimpse outside my hotel window, out beyond the shimmering blue horizon of Manila Bay . . .

Now you've got it, Griffin thought, now you've hit the G-spot, better than anyone who's faster, and faster than anyone who's better. Look, ma, no hands!

> It's a tiny island, rocky, nondescript, with no hotels, no shops, no beaches to speak of, No Bali Hai, no Waikiki. It was never fashionable, it is not in season. Honor and memory, not pleasure, bring us here. In the company of men who gave much more, we give a little of our time to the island called Corregidor . . .

Got it! With the lead paragraph in place, the rest was easy. His audience, his loyal readers would be well-served. He often pictured them. He pictured them reading his columns during Sunday football games, or around a breakfast table piled high with store-bought donuts. Sometimes, traveling, he glimpsed them holding his guidebooks, checking his clippings. On the flight to Hawaii for instance: three and a half hundred of his faithful, blinding him with their flashbulbs and white shoes, crossing the Pacific watching *Saturday Night Fever,* spilling rainbow-colored drinks that looked as if they were mixed off a barber's shelf, staggering over crushed macadamia nuts toward lavatories where the return-to-seat sign never dimmed. Pausing a day while waiting for the flight to Manila, Griffin had infiltrated groups of readers in Waikiki: sunburns and souvenir pineapples, monkey pods and muu-muus. They were his people, he their envoy. They were faithful savers in small accounts, fervent dreamers of cautious dreams, admirers of tropical flowers and goldfish ponds, tasters of tropical fruit and juice. On the beach, they waded in shallow, warm waters, tickled to death, and they limped arm in arm along the sea, while pagan surfers cavorted where the high waves broke. Many were old, many had waited too long. There were lots of widows, doing what *he* would have wanted me to do. At hotel-sponsored luaus they sat at long tables, accepting a sliver of mahi-mahi, a dab of poi, a paper cup of roast pork, all of it topped off with a hula lesson for the young at heart. And Griffin never knew whether to laugh or cry. He'd never decided. But he knew that his crumby columns dealt in dreams. Not his dreams, though. Then the phone rang.

"So how's the budding author?" someone shouted. "I saw

your name in the paper, in the list of travel writers in town for
. . . for whatever they flew you in for."

"Who is this?"

"I say, I got that famous writer his first job, back on the
Newark News. It's Eddie Richter."

"Eddie?"

"How long's it been? . . . Your mother's funeral, I guess. How
long ago was that?"

"Fifteen years."

"That long? Damn, sometimes I look at myself and I say, what
the hell are you still doing here, anyway?"

"What *are* you doing here?"

"I'll come by and tell you. Hour from now, down in the lobby.
And Georgie, I may have something for you. Something special."

"What's that, Eddie?"

"Same thing I got for you a million years ago, back in the
Garden State. A job!"

Griffin sat at his typewriter, staring at the phone. Eddie Richter, calling him as though childhood were yesterday, Manila an
easy drive down the Garden State Parkway, in the general direction of Atlantic City. Richter was a flack. Not a PR man, not a
public relations counsel, not even a press agent. He called himself a flack. An acquaintance of Griffin's father, he had been an
endless source of tickets for baseball games, circuses, ice capades.
"How's the budding author?" he would ask whenever they met.
Griffin hadn't thought of Eddie Richter for years. But mulling it
over now, he felt guilty about having left the man behind. For
there had been a time when Eddie was crucial, the time when
George was chafing to set out in a writing career, and Eddie had
made a phone call to a newspaper in Newark and arranged for a
summer job as a reporter, and that was the beginning of everything. Eddie reminded him of the times of early promise, summer jobs, first bylines, when being a sharp student led to being a
reporter, which led to being a writer. Just like that.

"George. Over here!"

Eddie Richter looked as if he'd just flown in from Miami:
cherry slacks, white shoes and belt, pink T-shirt, and topping it

all, a mesh-and-plastic golf hat that advertised something called
PALM TREE PRODUCTIONS. Walking to him across the lobby,
George saw familiar things: hairy arms, shrewd eyes, smell of
cigars. That sense of being in on things, the inside track, the
ground floor, the straight poop.

"Boy, did you get old!" Eddie Richter exclaimed. "How old
did you get?"

"I'm thirty-six now."

"Me, I'm closing in on seventy. Or seventy's closing in on
me." And then as Griffin stuck out his hand, Eddie pulled him
into a hug. "You carry me back, Georgie. You really do. So how's
the budding author?"

"You know, if you read the papers. Where have *you* been
these past years?"

"I did what everybody else who makes sixty-two and six does,
Georgie. I closed up shop and I moved to Florida. To South
Miami Beach, if you can believe that. Where the garment mak-
ers and candy store owners and kosher butchers go to die. The
longest six months of my life. Sitting around watching the foun-
tain outside a hotel isn't for me, kid, and eating supper at four
o'clock so you can get the early bird special, complete dinner
half price, choice of rice pudding or Jell-o for dessert . . . No,
lucky I found out about this movie deal."

"Movie deal?"

"Come on, kid," Eddie said, urging him toward where a car
and driver waited. "We'll take a spin. We'll talk. We got a lot of
catching up to do. Catching up and moving on." As he walked
across the driveway, he reached up and tweaked George's ear.
That was another trademark. He was one of the generation that
nudged shoulders, patted heads, chucked chins, was always
throwing imaginary haymakers and uppercuts. Remnants of a
time when all things were possible.

"Manila is my kind of town," Eddie announced as soon as they
were under way. "I been to these other places you write about. Not
for me. Hong Kong is banks and insurance companies, way over
my head. Microchips. And Singapore is just a high-rise shopping mall dressed up as a country. No place for me. But here . . ."

He gestured out the car window. They were in the Ermita

district, along del Pilar, scene of last night's debauch, and it was quieter by daylight but just as crowded: money changers, labor recruiters for the Arab world, armed guards, tourists. The bar girls sat out on the sidewalk in hair curlers and bathrobes. Manila by day: dripping air conditioners and movie magazines and rock and roll. If America conquered the world it would look like this.

"Being here," Eddie said, "I feel like I'm a character in an old movie."

"What kind?"

"Sometimes I think it's a western, with shoot-outs and robberies and outlaws. Other times, you read about what goes on in the provinces, it's like one of those moat-and-castle jobbies, with princes and robber barons and dungeons. Or a western, with posses and guns for hire, hanging judges, that stuff. But mostly it's like one of those old private eye things that had hookers and detectives and goons and bodyguards and bar girls and shoeshine boys and weird rich people and crooked cops and a plot that nobody could follow."

"And you like it?"

"Like it? Hey, George, I'm as happy as . . . I don't know . . . a horse in clover? A pig in shit? An outhouse rat? Anyway, I'm glad to be back."

"When were you here before?"

"Forty years ago," Eddie answered. "A bunch of us—"

"Come off it! You? You waded ashore with Douglas MacArthur?"

"Not me. I was onshore waiting for him."

"Christ!" It was amazing. Eddie Richter just didn't figure to have a war record. He was more the sort of man you sent out to entertain the troops. Even now, he looked as though he ought to be filling out a card table with Mickey Rooney, George Burns, and Red Buttons at some golden-age resort. "So you were a guerrilla?"

"I still am, kiddo. Which brings me to this job I got in mind for you. You're not doing anything tomorrow are you?"

"No."

"Okay. Now tell me this. Ever hear of MacArthur's Ghost?"

5

The veterans wore pastel jump suits, or shorts and polo shirts. Their wives wore polyester slacks and drip-dry blouses. They fussed with cameras, compared sunscreens, checked itineraries. They were Griffin's people all right, K-Mart shoppers. They traveled heavy and they traveled scared and they traveled mostly to confirm that there was no place like home. Still, they intimidated him, this December morning. They had traveled someplace Griffin had never been: a war. Any other place, he could feel superior to them. No ticket they bought, he couldn't get for free. But this was different. The war: that stopped him.

A hovercraft cut across the bay, trailing spray and waves, turned into the harbor, where it cut speed, losing the pillow of air it raced on. It sagged into warm and oily water and bumped against the pilings. Crew members jumped onto the dock, warning passengers to watch their step as they came aboard. Was there any irony in being so gently ushered toward a battlefield?

The Marcos shoreline of hotels and theaters disappeared. So did the polluted air, the eternal haze, the pall of sun-warmed smoke and fumes that covered Manila. Suddenly, the world came out in Technicolor, a true blue sky, water to match, everything clean and clear and endless. Far ahead they saw the green slopes of Mount Mariveles, the Bataan peninsula. Every minute it became more massive and more brightly green. Pretty soon there would be—would have to be—Corregidor.

"You want my egg?"

"Do I . . ." Griffin was facing one of the veterans, wearing a name card that identified him as WALTER FEDEROVICH of Harrisburg, Pennsylvania. Walter was a narrow, wiry Slav, with thinning black hair combed straight back. His nose was prominent, his skin cratered with blackheads he would take to his grave. His arms were hairy and muscular and you could see the sleeveless undershirt he wore beneath an aloha shirt. Next to him his wife was massive and patient; her muu-muu fit her heavyweight body like the tarps exterminators heave around houses before they throw in the termite poison.

"You want my egg?" he asked again.

"Thanks," Griffin said. Around him, the veterans and their wives were belaboring the box lunches that came with their tour. Poking straws into paper cartons of orange drink, they looked like a class trip headed across New York harbor to the Statue of Liberty. Griffin tried to peel the egg, pulling away a tiny fragment of shell. Walter Federovich took the egg back, rapped it against his knee, removed the remaining shell in one piece, and returned the egg to Griffin. "There you go."

"I guess you were here before," Griffin said.

"Yeah," Federovich answered and left it at that. Amazing, Griffin thought. A man like Walter Federovich liked boasting he could make it from Harrisburg to Miami in twenty hours. Maybe he wondered if California was all it was cracked up to be. But here he was, halfway around the world, not once but twice, scanning across the water, spotting a swelling just above the horizon, something that might turn out to be clouds, or heat waves, or nothing at all, except Federovich knew better. He winced and turned away.

"Seen much of Manila?" Griffin asked. "This time around?"

"Nope," Federovich answered. "The hotel. Some shops and things for her."

He gestured toward his wife—Vera, by her name tag—and Griffin could see that she was worried about her husband. The color was draining from his face. He was nervously rubbing his sweaty hands on his knees.

"It's stuffy in here," Griffin sympathized.

"Yeah," Federovich said, talking fast, as if he were searching for an alibi. "I forgot that. I thought I remembered . . . it all. Everything. But when I stepped off the plane . . . that whooosh of hot air . . . that sun. Comes up hot, goes down hot, we used to say. Nothing nice about the edges of the day. No dawn, no twilight."

He checked out the window and no doubt about it, there was Corregidor, a brown, rocky coast, cliffs and slopes, green knobby hills. Federovich stared, looked harder, looked away, as if he had recognized someone he didn't want to meet and was hoping that they could pass each other by.

"You'll be fine, Walter," his wife assured him. "It's just an island now. Another place, is all."

"Sure!" He glared at her, resenting her having gone public with his distress. Then the anger passed and he patted her on the knee, as if apologizing for all the things that he could never tell her.

The hydrofoil reduced speed as it came in to shore, dropping down into the water, so that what had been almost an airplane was now something less than a boat. Inside, passengers were stirring, anxious to leave. Some of them were already pointing out landmarks. Cameras were clicking.

"This place," Walter Federovich said. He hadn't budged. The first veterans were already onshore, clambering onto tourist buses.

"Walter, we'll miss the tour," his wife warned.

"What a tragedy that would be," Federovich snapped. His tongue was sharp. He just couldn't move. That was all.

"This place gives me the willies," he said. "Always will."

"You've got nothing to be ashamed of," Griffin said.

"How the hell would you know?" Federovich snapped back at him.

"Walter!"

"You get out, Mother. I'll be along."

Vera Federovich climbed up the steps, onto the wooden dock. Griffin could see her pacing back and forth. He glimpsed the hem of her muu-muu, swishing back and forth outside the porthole.

"I'm sorry, Mr. . . . ."

"Griffin. . . . That's all right. I understand."

"The hell you do," Federovich responded. There it was again, something stirring. What was it? A wound? An infection? A memory?

"I guess I'm ready to show my face," Federovich said, arising quickly, as though determined to get through with whatever punishment Corregidor had saved for him. "That's what all this is—"

"What's that?"

"Showing your face in a place you used to be. Saying to the place, well, you're still here, and so am I, so hello again and good-bye . . ."

It was an extraordinary moment, Griffin felt, like a glimpse through water, choppy, sun-splashed water that suddenly calmed and opened to reveal what was sunk and lost below. And before he could fully observe it, let alone describe it, the moment was gone. Federovich was climbing aboard a tour bus.

6

There were big doings on Corregidor this December morning. There were more boats coming across Manila Bay, an invasion flotilla, and there were helicopters, one of which had brought Eddie Richter to the island ahead of Griffin. Now he sat waiting behind the wheel of a war surplus jeep that was spattered red, white, and blue.

"So how was the boat ride? Okay?"

"Better than that."

"Sorry I couldn't get you on the helicopter. You don't work for us yet and there was something about insurance. Hop in."

"Is this thing safe?" Griffin asked, glancing at the rotted out flooring, which let him look down at the road.

"Safe? It's indestructible. Tell you something, George, once you've driven a jeep, everything else is near beer."

They raced down alleys that were cut through second-growth forest, brushy saplings that took over when the original jungle had been bombed and burned. There were shadowy side trails leading to concrete bunkers, rusting warehouses, gun emplacements. There were bombed-out barracks, shattered concrete dangling from twisted metal rods, like broken fingers pointing accusations at the sky. There was Malinta Tunnel, once MacArthur's headquarters, but Eddie had no time for history. He slammed to a halt on the other side of the tunnel and rushed George through a yard swarming with the people and equipment, the odd combination of chaos and punctilio that marks a film crew. At the rear of the yard, some people were sitting at a picnic table on a grassy knoll.

"Well, here he is," Eddie announced. "Introductions are in order. You know George. I told you all about him. Now—"

31

"I'll take care of this," someone interrupted. He was a burly, Texas-looking fellow, an athlete gone to seed with beer and barbecue. "My name is Hugh Beaumont. I'm from Houston. I have a couple little businesses there. Drilling equipment and such. This here's Larry Wingfield . . ."

A tall, blond fraternity boy, readying a blackball. He seemed at home on Corregidor, though he was way too young to be a veteran.

"Larry lives in Pacific Palisades, California, and here, and Hong Kong. He's a lawyer, the kind that never shows his face in court. He specializes in movie financing. There's lots more. His family—"

"Let's not waste any more of Mr. Griffin's time," Wingfield interrupted, but it sounded like he was the one who didn't want to waste his time: on Griffin.

"And this—saving best for last—is Cecilia Santos." A Filipina princess, no doubt about it, well turned out in white puffy pantaloons and blouse, and a wide red sash around her tiny waist. Last night's women were local products in a crowded local market. Cecilia Santos was private stock, wrapped in tissue, marked for export.

"Miss Santos is our liaison with the Philippine government," Beaumont said. "And with some local investors. What we have here is a coproduction, a partnership. Has Eddie put you in the picture yet, what we're doing here?"

"I thought I'd leave that for you," Eddie said.

"Okay. Larry and I have a connection with a World War Two guerrilla outfit headed by Colonel Harry Roberts Harding, who was known as 'MacArthur's Ghost.' Maybe you've heard about him."

"I think so," Griffin said. "First the war, now the movie?"

"That's it, yes. But don't think it's just a bunch of buddies getting sentimental. Hell, we are sentimental. And we've all got other ways of making money. But this is a go project. We expect to spend a lot and make a lot. And do some good besides."

"The script?"

"That's all taken care of," Wingfield said. "A fast-paced adventure with lots of action, mystery, romance. And something else. Patriotism. We're going back to a time when America stood for something."

"I see," Griffin said. "So . . . a World War Two movie set here
in the islands . . . and patriotic."

"I know what you're thinking," Wingfield said. "It's been
done before. All those bloody epics Hollywood turned out during and right after the war. *Bataan. Back to Bataan. An American Guerrilla in the Philippines.* Blood and guts and old glory.
It's the kind of thing that got unfashionable during the sixties.
We were the villains then. But there's a new spirit in America.
We're winners again. We like winning. It's terrific being Number One. We're tired of flagellating ourselves. Tired of apologizing for what we've done, or tried to do. That's the spirit of the
country and that's the spirit of the film. That's the spirit, too, of
everyone who's on board this project."

"Aren't we getting ahead of ourselves with Mr. Griffin?"
Cecilia Santos interrupted.

"I reckon we are," Beaumont seconded.

"Sorry," Wingfield said. "It's just that what we don't need
around this project is cynicism."

"The thing of it is," Beaumont said, "the key part is the role
of Colonel Harry Roberts Harding, MacArthur's Ghost. Now
after the war, Harry Harding kind of disappeared."

"Until now," Wingfield resumed. "We had to look for him. In
this business you never know. He might have come back at us
after the movie was in the can."

"Come back?" Griffin asked. "You mean that you were afraid
he'd sue you?"

"It's happened before," Wingfield said. "This is a movie after
all. Not a documentary. So we take liberties."

"Our hero has to get in someone's pants," Beaumont said,
blushing when he remembered Cecilia Santos was sitting at the
table. She was unperturbed.

"Our concern was that he might object to these necessary
. . . infidelities . . . in the script, that he'd embarrass us . . . so we
looked," Wingfield said. "But he hadn't kept in touch with anyone we knew. We tried the Veterans Administration. Veterans
groups. We placed ads in newspapers and magazines. I'll be
frank. Whether or not we found him, we wanted to be able to
demonstrate that we had made a good-faith effort, what in law
is known as 'diligent search.' "

"You'd have just as soon not found him, I take it," Griffin said.

"Well, anyway we did," Beaumont said. "Eddie found him down in Florida. Owned a motel. We sent Eddie down to talk to him."

"He wanted *in,*" Wingfield said. "He wanted to come back here, he said he'd been thinking about it. He wanted to knock around some, look up old places, old faces. That's how he put it. Old places, old faces. The money part was easy: a flat fee in exchange for a legal release, plus a point in the profits of the film. He took what we offered him. But he wanted to be here. We're going to have him on our hands a while and that's a problem."

"Why?" Griffin asked.

"It's like this," Beaumont explained. "He was a tremendous man. No film could tell the half of it. But we don't want him sitting around a movie set for two months. That's asking for trouble."

"That's where I come in," Eddie Richter said. "My idea was maybe we could turn a minus into a plus. We'd find us a writer to accompany Colonel Harding as he visits old haunts, wartime comrades, movie locations. His story was never told."

"And," Beaumont added, "if we're right in thinking that the time has come for a stand-up-and-be-proud movie like this, then the time is also right for a book that would tie in with the movie. So that's pretty much it."

"I'm flattered."

"Don't be too flattered," Wingfield warned. "My nomination was William Manchester. He's unavailable though."

"I was thinking about Richard Tregaskis myself," Hugh Beaumont said. "Wrote *Guadalcanal Diary.* Only he's dead."

"I'm your third choice, then?"

"Well . . ." Beaumont hesitated, glanced at Eddie. "Should I tell him?"

"Go ahead. Sure."

"We were thinking about Eddie for this job. Only he says we need a real writer."

Griffin looked at Eddie. He couldn't help wondering how it happened that the same man who'd gotten him into newspaper work years before should rescue him from newspapers now.

"Thanks, Eddie."

"Does that mean you're interested?" asked Beaumont.

"I could be."

"He's wondering about the money," Wingfield announced.

"Forgive me," Griffin said. "It's part of the new spirit in the land. How much?"

"It's simple," said Wingfield. "You travel with Colonel Harding at our expense. All expenses—reasonable expenses—we pick up. Whatever you write, you write. And whatever it makes, you keep."

"Could be a best seller, what with the movie coming out," Hugh Beaumont said.

"Two hundred dollars a day for sixty days," Griffin responded.

"What's that?" asked Wingfield.

"My fee."

"I think we can settle this right here and now," Larry Wingfield said, with the tone of a man who had heard just about enough. "Would you mind taking a stroll, Mr. Griffin? Thanks. Won't take long."

"Thank you," Griffin answered. He walked away from the table, through the lot, out to the road, and found himself confronting Malinta Tunnel. Looking back, he could see the film people in conference. He didn't want to be seen hovering eagerly around the edges. He stepped into the tunnel.

This was MacArthur's fortified stronghold, the innermost keep of the first great American defeat. It was a short tunnel, 1,400 feet, so that you were always aware of the light outside. That must have been a paradox: it was supposed to make you feel good, seeing the light at the end of the tunnel. But here in Malinta it must have been the other way around, knowing that the enemy owned the world outside, the sky and the sea and the green mountains, the whole daylit world. Griffin walked the tunnel, studying the laterals that branched off from either side. Some had ceased to exist: a pile of rock and broken concrete marked where entrances had been. Others were still in place, dark burrows where generals and politicians, nurses and wounded, all the detritus of a lost cause, had assembled. MacArthur's ghosts.

There were people at one end of the tunnel. Griffin walked toward them, until he heard them speaking Japanese. He stood there and savored the moment, fear and irony together. They were tourists posing with their guide, taking turns photographing each other, still in uniform: white short-sleeved shirts, dark suits with boxy trousers and flapping jackets. They carried their cameras like weapons and the ground around them was littered with discarded Polaroid sheets, like so much spent ammunition.

"Hey, George." Eddie had come up behind him.

"Why do you think they come back?" George asked.

"I don't know. Couple thousand of them died in here when we retook the island. Blew themselves up."

"They come back for the same reason we do. Because this is where they got their asses kicked."

"Could be," Eddie said. "Could be." George was disappointed he hadn't been asked to defend his statement. He felt he was onto something. Victories were clichés. Everything about them was conventional: the rhetoric, the statuary, the hagiography, the literature and music. Victories were temporary. Defeats lasted forever. And that was why, if you had a defeat in your life, and you survived, you kept coming back to it, picking at the memory, because the memory picked at you. You would never let go of it.

". . . made it harder on yourself," Eddie was saying. "You hurt yourself with Wingfield. He says you're a 'media smart-ass.'"

"I'm sorry."

"Are you really?"

"Yes."

"You don't want to go back to your regular work?"

"No," Griffin said. He couldn't face it: more Faraway Places and Backyard Adventures. And it bothered him that he might have missed out; odd, after all the years of waiting, of telling himself he'd be ready when his chance came, he hadn't been ready at all, because he wasn't the person he had been when he started waiting.

"Here," Eddie said. "The script. The cast. The shooting schedule. I'm your guardian angel, kid. You start right away."

"Right away?"

"What do you think we're doing here? Harry Roberts Harding is due at noon."

7

Happiness, Griffin liked to say, was a sometime thing. And—he liked to add—it had been some time since he'd been happy. But on Corregidor, the few hours before Harding came, he was as happy as he'd been in years. It had something to do with his new job, with beginnings and endings he sensed in himself. And something to do with Eddie Richter, his guardian angel. And it had a lot to do with the jeep, the rusted-out red-white-and-blue wonder with which Griffin spent two glorious hours conquering Corregidor. Speed, liberty, and good roads: what couldn't they cure?

The island had three levels. Shore level was "Bottomside." "Middleside" was next. "Topside" was the crown of the island, a high, grassy plateau. Battles had ended there. So did tours, among the ruins of the American headquarters: a colonial-looking stone building, the command post MacArthur had abandoned when he burrowed into Malinta Tunnel, and the nearby parade grounds, where the American flag had flown and fallen. On a bluff overlooking the sea was the Pacific War Memorial, a marble arcade that listed all the battles and campaigns of the war; out beyond was the Pacific itself, mute witness to all of it, and when Griffin stood there he had a nice feeling for the continuity of things, the linkage of then and now, the connection between those battles, which were names carved in stone, and that ocean down below: this was where they touched.

He lingered at the memorial until the place started filling up with tour groups. Harry Roberts Harding's return was something of an event, it seemed, not only for the American vets, and the small contingent of Japanese, but for dozens of Filipino veterans also. They had their own style. Whatever they had been, they still were, in bits and pieces of old uniforms, shirts, jackets, caps, medals. How odd it was! The Americans had rushed, willy-nilly, into peacetime. The Japanese marched off into civilian life, trading one uniform for another. But the Filipinos held on to what they had been: fighters, soldiers. Griffin passed among the veterans looking for Walter Federovich. He wanted him to know that the man who wrote columns that Vera Federovich clipped out of her Sunday supplement was becoming something else. But Federovich was nowhere to be seen. Griffin retreated to the Topside Barracks, the massive mile-long ruin. He stepped inside, through broken plaster, over rusted pipes and pools of water. Geckos ran for cover in vines that reached through windows. He walked up one flight of steps, then another, and out onto what was left of the roof. He sat down and pulled out the script that Eddie had given him.

"MacArthur's Ghost" was the title. As for the rest: three Americans, a polo-playing upper-class rogue, a sardonic, street-wise bartender, and a southern missionary's son meet and compete and romp through the streets, playing fields, clubs, and plantations of sleepy, charming prewar Manila. These three—the rich boy, the poor boy, and the choirboy—live and love and brawl, but their lives lack purpose. The Japanese attack. Purpose is amply provided. The fall of Manila, the disaster of Bataan. The siege and surrender of Corregidor. While thousands of comrades are marched into captivity, the three Americans decide to fight behind enemy lines. What adventures! With polo horses from a Manila country club, they lead a cavalry charge against a Japanese camp. They forage on Bataan for abandoned weapons and ammunition. They stage daring raids in occupied Manila. They contend with Japanese, with Filipino collaborators, with loyal villagers, and they become known as MacArthur's Ghosts. They prepare for MacArthur's return, but their campaigns don't end with the liberation of Manila. The love of a woman held captive by the Japanese, the desire to avenge a massacred village, the rumor of a treasure hoard of gold—Yamashita's gold—draw them into the northern mountains of Luzon, into the final Japanese redoubt, where the woman is rescued, the dead are avenged, the treasure found—and lost. Sequel anyone?

So that was it: a patriotic stand-up-and-be-counted movie that was going to make money and do good; Griffin was convinced it would do both, or either, or neither. It might be a hackneyed clunker or it might be a shrewd mélange of wartime action and romance, with more than a touch of *Raiders of the Lost Ark.* He'd seen—and paid to see—lots worse, and some of what he'd paid to see he'd liked. Who knew? It might even be a classic American movie.

The movie people were at the edge of the parade ground, with the veterans—a couple of hundred by now—behind them. Americans, Filipinos, Japanese.

"Well, I guess you read the script," Hugh Beaumont said.

"Yes sir, I did," Griffin answered manfully.

"Come on now, what'd you think of it?"

"Well, I don't know how to put it exactly . . ."

"Then put it approximately," Wingfield prodded him, "and we'll take it from there."

"Well . . ." Griffin looked around, as if he feared being overheard. Everybody was listening, Beaumont, Cecilia Santos, Wingfield. Even Eddie.

"It's a pisser," he said.

"A pisser?"

"You heard me."

"A pisser?" Beaumont asked.

"What does that mean?" Cecilia Santos asked. "A pisser?"

Suddenly, Beaumont was laughing, clapping him on the shoulder. They were all laughing. No doubt about it, everyone seemed to agree, it was a pisser. They were still laughing when they saw the helicopter circling overhead, its shadow crossing over them, once and once again: MacArthur's Ghost returning.

As soon as the helicopter landed, a military band launched into "Halls of Montezuma." The veterans of three nations stood at salute. The helicopter door opened and two men stood there, each urging the other to go first. "You go." "No, you." "Please." "No, I insist." It went on that way, an amusing little tableau, till the men agreed to squeeze through the door together and, awkward as it might be, walk down the steps side by side, arm in arm, the tall, spindly, red-haired American who was Harry

Roberts Harding and the genial, suave, aging Filipino who was Ferdinand Marcos.

"This is terrific!" Wingfield exclaimed. "Was this your doing, Cecilia?"

"I passed the information along," Cecilia Santos said, but she stopped short of taking credit for Marcos's presence on Corregidor.

"What about it, Hugh? You put in a word someplace?"

"Not me," Beaumont answered.

"Well, we owe thanks to somebody," Wingfield maintained.

"Maybe not," Eddie said. "Could be, nobody pulled strings or dropped a name, or made a phone call, or called in a favor. Maybe it just happened. Because that's Harry Roberts Harding out there. MacArthur's Ghost is back."

Marcos and Harding walked across the parade ground. Marcos was relaxed and lively, pointing out the Topside Barracks, the flagpole, the jungle. He was the picture of a host who was enjoying himself as much as his guest. Harry Roberts Harding nodded at Marcos's comments, looked wherever Marcos pointed. The band stopped playing when the two of the men came up to where the veterans were standing, and now the silence was nearly absolute. There were no color guards, no bodyguards. It was just a couple of men walking across a field to where another group of men was standing. When they came close they stopped and stared. When you haven't seen someone for half a lifetime, you have the right to stare. You offer yourself to them, they to you, and you conjugate your lives: here I am, there you are, here we are. And then you go into tenses, what you were, and are, and will be. That was what happened now. Harding stood there, scanning up and down the line, front ranks and rear, sorting out faces and memories. No rush about it. Then, Harding glanced at Marcos and made a little nod, which was answered by a little bow and they marched toward the Pacific War Memorial, camera crews and photographers scuttling around, ahead and behind. When Harding had gone fifty feet he stopped and turned back toward the vets, who were still standing quietly.

"Come on," he said. It wasn't a command, it was more like an invitation: come on, come along with me, there's history somewhere down the road, we'll make ourselves at home there, you'll see.

Ferdinand Marcos was a charmer. He opened lightheartedly, joking about how, though the years had thinned the ranks, there were certain veterans who had thickened mightily. Then he turned serious. Whatever has happened to us between now and then, whatever we have done or failed to do, nothing can change what happened here. Nothing. He paused and surveyed the crowd, cocky, defiant, daring anyone to contradict him. Like a priest at a wedding he waited for someone to say why this ceremony should not proceed and he must have enjoyed the perfect quiet. The world was so full of complaints. Banners flapping in the breeze, the smell of jungle and the glare of heat: he seemed at home here, and Griffin had no problem believing that he had come because he wanted to. Next he launched into an affectionate, rambling introduction of Harry Roberts Harding. Someone once told him, he said, that the classic American hero was the tall, quiet, rugged man like Gary Cooper or Jimmy Stewart. They were right and wrong. The description was correct, but the names were the names of movie actors who, no matter whom they portrayed, remained actors. He knew the real thing, the authentic hero. Then he turned to Harry Roberts Harding. "Welcome home, my friend," he said. And saluted him, a salute that Harding returned. Harding extended his hand for Marcos to shake. Marcos took the hand and pulled the taller man toward him, into an embrace.

"Wet hankies all around," someone said. Griffin turned and there was Clifford Lerner, with Thomas Gibbins beside him.

"Hello there," George said. "Tom, I thought you were off to New Zealand by now. The Milford Track."

"Fucking beats hiking, he's decided," Lerner said. "He's in love or something. May never leave."

Gibbins stood there, avoiding Griffin's eyes.

"The one with the long hair?"

"Yes."

"It was all I could manage to drag him off to Corregidor today," Lerner said. "Nice show, though. Beers, anyone?"

"Shh," George said. Harry Roberts Harding was fussing with the microphone, trying to raise it. "I have to hear this."

"Why?"

"I'm doing a book on him."

"On *Harding*? Oh, my God, you must be joking. They don't do books on war heroes anymore, George. Haven't you heard? This is the age of the Strong Female Character. Not your line, boy."

"Shut up, Clifford."

"Come on then, Tommy," Lerner said, acting hurt. "We'll drink to your recovery, George."

When Harding finished adjusting the microphone, he pulled a sheet of paper out of his pocket. Everyone assumed it was a speech that had been prepared for him, although Griffin wondered if it wasn't just a piece of paper, a pretend speech that he was going to discard. In any case, Harding glanced at it, folded it neatly, and shoved it back into his pocket.

"I can't lie to you people," he said. "Not to you. I can't even bullshit."

A round of cheers and laughter, Marcos enjoying it enormously, a performer sensing he was in for a performance.

"Well," Harding said. "I'm back. I was going to say 'I have returned,' but I hear that line's been used. I forget who by."

More laughter. Everyone relaxing. Just folks. No harm in a little irreverence at MacArthur's expense.

"When I heard they were making a movie out here and wondering if I'd be interested, my instinct was to say no thanks, I'll wait till it shows up on television, and that's the night I'll kick off my shoes and pop open a beer and try to convince myself that I used to be as good-looking as—what's the name of the guy they're paying to play me?"

Amusement on the speaker's platform. No one seemed to know, till Eddie Richter whispered something to one of the Filipino cameramen who whispered it to someone else who whispered it to Marcos.

"Tom Selleck," Marcos said.

"Who?" Harding leaned forward, as if he were a little hard of hearing or maybe it was to force Marcos to speak a little louder and thus prolong the joke.

"Tom Selleck!" Marcos shouted.

"He good-looking?" Harding asked. The president of the Philippines shrugged and passed the question back down the line, security man to cameraman to Eddie and back the answer came.

"Yes, very handsome," Marcos said, mimicking the obliging eager-to-please manner Filipinos took with foreigners.

"Very handsome?"

"Yes," Marcos said. And then the punch line. "Maybe."

"Very handsome, maybe," Harding pondered. "Well, Gary Cooper's dead. And I'm not getting any younger. That's why I came back. The more I thought about it, I couldn't stand the idea of growing old and dying and not seeing this place, not being here, again, ever."

Now he had them, every one. Laughing at his jokes, suffering his pauses and stumbles, his momentary awkwardness, ready to follow.

"The older you get, the more you look back. You look back because what's behind you is an awful lot livelier than what's in front. So I've been looking back and thinking about the past, not in a bragging way, but deeper. I've been wondering about what went right and what went wrong and how things turned out the way they did. I've been thinking about heroes. All kinds of heroes. The public heroes and the secret heroes. The liberation guerrillas."

If Harding had not paused just then—whether by design or simply to give himself a rest—Griffin would have missed the look of puzzlement that crossed over Marcos's face and the slight gasp of surprise from Cecilia Santos, just beside him.

"I've been thinking, maybe more than's good for me," Harding said. "About Roque Ablan and Jesus Villamor and Walter Cushing and Juan Olmos and Felipe Olmos and Felipa Cualala and my old friend Nestor Contreras. I think about him all the time. There were heroes whose chests were all covered with medals and there were heroes who were covered with nothing but earth. So I decided to come back and look around and see what I could find out about what was left of them and . . . left of me. I came back to keep some promises I made a long while ago. It's time I kept them."

He stopped, looking left and right, groping. There was a sense of loneliness about him, something forlorn, that made everybody root for him. He was a veteran among veterans and there wasn't one of them who wouldn't claim him. But there was also something separate. It wasn't just that he had been a leader—the loneliness of command—and that his name resonated while others were forgotten. Harry Roberts Harding put himself apart.

"I guess I'll wind this up now," Harding said. "I hear the movie company's got some cold beer in the shade and they wouldn't mind if we drank some. Just one more thing. When that helicopter landed and I saw you and I saw your faces, which some I knew right off and others I kind of knew and some others God forgive me for not knowing . . . when I saw you standing there, well, nothing on earth could have moved me more. Thanks."

The Marcos party left immediately after Harding's speech and when Griffin joined the movie people inside their hospitality tent, he gathered that the abrupt departure bothered them.

"He made a goddamn beeline for the chopper," Wingfield complained. "You'd've thought he was being evacuated or something."

"What'd they say?" Hugh Beaumont asked.

"Press of duty, demanding schedule, et cetera," Eddie Richter answered. "Could be true."

"Does that mean you believe it?" Beaumont asked.

"I didn't say that," Richter answered.

"I think they feel they got boobytrapped," Beaumont said. "I think they were annoyed."

"And I can't blame them," Wingfield said. "We've got a problem."

Puzzled, Griffin looked around the room for help. He'd thought Harding's speech was great—way beyond the expected patriotic boilerplate.

"I guess you liked the speech, huh, Griffin?" Wingfield said.

"As a matter of fact—"

"May I have a moment?" Cecilia Santos asked. Griffin liked the way she took over. He'd underestimated her, he guessed, mostly wondering who—or what—it would take to get her to do something carnal. You couldn't help wondering: her looks, her style, her whole manner encouraged it. But the mistake was thinking that was all there was. That was her doing. But it was his mistake.

"The Marcos government has gone—and can show it has gone —far out of its way in support of this project," she said. "Your production will be featured at the film festival. You have unlimited choice of locations. You have the support, behind and in front of cameras, of the Philippine Armed Forces. This is generous treatment in a nation with many other problems on its agenda . . ."

"You're right, Cecilia," Beaumont said, as if to avert whatever was coming next.

"There is more," Cecilia Santos continued. "The First Lady's enthusiasm for cinema is well known. When you came, she welcomed you. And she induced her husband to welcome you as well, though, as you may know, he does not always share her enthusiasms. In return we ask very little: that you behave responsibly, all of you."

"Responsibly?"

"That you not embarrass yourselves—or your hosts."

"You're right," Beaumont said. "I don't like it but you're right. . . . Damn it, we've got a loose cannon on deck."

"Loose cannon?" Griffin asked. "What's going on here? I don't get it."

"Later," Wingfield said, dismissing Griffin's interest and turning to Eddie. "Is there any way we could send him back?" Wingfield asked. "We paid him to come. What if we doubled the money and asked him to leave? Let him do his damn book in Florida. And take his writer with him."

"No way," Eddie said. "He's here. We have to stay with our original plan."

"Where's Harding now?" Wingfield asked.

"Outside, with the old-timers," Eddie answered.

"All right," Wingfield said, arising. "Let's mix and mingle for an hour. And then get the hell off of this rock."

Corregidor was lovely late that afternoon. The sun slanted in from the west, burnishing the barracks, flushing out the last brightness in the grass and trees and sea below as if, what with night coming on, you might never see them again that green, that blue. Harry Roberts Harding was sitting at a picnic table, drinking beer and saying good-bye to his old comrades forever, no doubt: too late for exchanging addresses and making Christmas card lists.

"Hello, Eddie," Harding said. "Are you done working for the day?"

"I wish," Eddie answered, sitting down beside him. Griffin studied Harding closely. His height was the first thing you noticed. He was at least six foot two. The thinness was next. Words like gangly and lanky came to mind, western-sounding words that put you well on the way to thinking of him as the sort of frontier hero Marcos had evoked. There was more: the dark, swarthy skin, the kind of in-deep tan you don't get on vacation, and the face, which was creased and leathery and outdoors-looking, western skin, western face. The eyes though were post-frontier, watery blue and red-rimmed by beer, or jet lag, or emotions. Wary eyes that were looking up at George Griffin and wondering, what now?

"This is George Griffin," Eddie said, and Griffin looked at Harding as Harding looked at him. It was a dishonest exercise, thought Griffin, asking yourself whether someone looked like what you already knew he was. Sure, you could see the lineaments of a hero in Harry Roberts Harding. But you saw the same features pumping gas along interstates, or hitchhiking between small towns.

"I'm pleased to meet you, sir," said Harding.

"Likewise," Griffin said.

"So how about the speech?" Harding asked Eddie. "I hope it wasn't too bad."

"Too bad?" Eddie exclaimed. "The speech was just fine, Colonel."

"I didn't want to disappoint anybody . . ."

"When you speak the way you did—from the heart—you can't let anybody down."

"Everybody liked it then?"

"Oh, sure, they were pleased as punch," Eddie responded. "Colonel, I forget if I mentioned it before or not, but I had this idea about your coming back here. That business about thinking things over, how everything turned out, trying to make sense of things, it sounded like you meant that."

"Sure I meant it," Harding said.

"The idea is, we'd get someone to tag along with you in the Philippines, and while you go around, he could write it all down —what happened back then, your memories, and what you're thinking now and how it all adds up."

"A writer, you mean . . ."

"That's exactly what I mean," Eddie said. "And George Griffin here is the writer that I have in mind."

The tables were turned now. Griffin had looked at Harding and seen a man who might have been a hero. What did Harding see? What was he looking for? Someone he could use, command, confide in? Was he looking for a friend? An ear? An arm? A shoulder?

"What kind of write-up did you have in mind, Mr. Griffin?"

"A book."

"A book. I see. Have you ever written a book, Mr. Griffin?"

"George is known mostly as a travel writer," Eddie volunteered. "He does a column that's in lots of newspapers, Faraway Places, Backyard Adventures, you probably've seen it . . ."

"I'm not sure."

"And he's done travel books galore. Guides that you take along. Where to shop and eat and the right hotels to stay in and side trips so you can get to know a country."

"No," Griffin said. The more he heard, the worse it sounded. "No, Colonel, I haven't written a book. Those guides aren't books. They're confetti."

"Confetti, compared to what he's going to do with you," Eddie said. "I think he could do a good job for you, Colonel."

"Ever been here before? In the Philippines."

"No."

"Ever been in the service?"

"No."

"Wrong age?"

"Wrong war."

"Well," Harding said. "I don't know. I'm not saying yes and I'm not saying no. I want to think about it. Eddie, do you have anything scheduled for me tomorrow morning?"

"No sir, you're clear till noon. There's that ceremony out at the cemetery."

"Another speech?"

"No, just a wreath."

"Okay, Mr. George Griffin," Harding said. "Suppose we get together tomorrow morning at my hotel. Around the middle of the morning."

"We'll be there," Eddie said.

"No," Harding corrected. "Just Mr. Griffin and me. Manila Hotel. The MacArthur Suite."

8

"Who the hell are you?"

An American stood in the entrance of the MacArthur Suite, a middle-aged, red-necked sloven in wrinkled khakis and a Snoopy T-shirt. If he was a civilian, it was in name only. His crewcut testified you never knew when you might be called up, even though the astonishing beer gut that sagged across his cowboy belt was hoping it wouldn't be soon. He was the sort of man who could fight like hell for two minutes. He'd be finished after that, but the first two minutes would be lethal.

"George Griffin. The colonel is expecting me."

"It's okay, Charley, he can come in."

Harry Roberts Harding was sitting in an armchair placed on the verandah that overlooked the park below. Another chair had been occupied by Charley. Between them was a table with a dozen empty San Miguel bottles. It looked as if they'd been playing chess with beer bottles, and Charley had won big.

"Say hello to Charley Camper, George."

"Hello."

"Want a beer?" asked Camper. He smelled of sweat and beer, this Sunday morning.

"I don't drink before dark."

"Beer's not drinking," Camper said, beheading a San Miguel.

"Better take it, George," advised Harding.

"Thanks."

A ripple of laughter sounded from another room. Griffin turned and found he was looking into Harding's bedroom. It wouldn't have passed inspection, what with the mussed-up bed and yesterday's clothing tossed over the back of a chair, a collection of bottles and pills on the night table and, if that were not

49

enough, two cute Filipinas sitting in front of the television set,
tuned into a disco dance show. Was that what happened in the
MacArthur Suite: a pair of nubile little hookers to welcome
home the hero? Had the girls watched TV while the old-timers
rutted on top of them? It was hard for Griffin to picture. Hard
for Charley Camper, too.

"Those are my daughters," he said.

"Your wife's—"

"From here."

"Charley Camper never left," Harding said. "One continuous
tour from 1940 until now. You should do his story, not mine. He
lives in Olongapo, raises kids and chickens . . ."

"Both of which need feeding," Camper said. He stuck a finger
in his mouth and whistled, a piercing alarm that wrenched his
daughters right away from the television set. "You gonna come
see me, Colonel?"

"Count on it, Charley."

"We'll throw a couple of dead chickens on the barbecue,
drink some beer. You come too, Griffin. You ought to see Subic
Bay."

Camper nodded to his daughters, who kissed Harding good-
bye and shyly shook hands with Griffin. A moment ago he
guessed they were prostitutes. That was impossible now. They
were Charley's daughters.

Harding stepped out on the balcony and, waving good-bye,
watched the Campers clamber into a pickup truck loaded with
sacks of feed and crates of chickens and a half dozen Filipinos.
They looked like a tribe of Okies who had missed California and
kept heading west. Security guards and doormen gasped as the
truck belched a cloud of smoke, emitted a wolf-whistle howl
that must have rattled glasses in the Champagne Room, and
lurched out of the curving driveway of the Manila Hotel.

"I still haven't decided about this book thing," Harding said.

"Is there any way I can put your mind at ease?" Griffin asked,
wondering what it would be: tape recordings versus written
notes? Authorship credits? Control of the manuscript? A share
of the advance? A piece of the royalties? What was going to be
the crunch?

"There's no way you can put my mind at ease," Harding said.
"But you can answer a question."

"What's that?"

"Are you proud to be an American?"

"Am I what?"

"You heard me, Griffin. Are you proud to be an American, yes or no?"

"Is this a loyalty oath?"

"Don't go getting your back up. Just a simple question . . ."

"It is not a simple question."

"Well, okay, take your time." Harding got out of his chair and walked across the room. People knew he'd returned to Manila, all right. There were flowers along the walls and baskets of tropical fruit, and whiskey bottles with ribbons and calling cards around their necks.

"Listen, Colonel. I like America. I get into arguments all the time with people who knock it. But you want simple answers like yes or no and I don't suppose that satisfies you."

Even as he spoke, Griffin recoiled at his own stubbornness. Couldn't he make allowance for the years that separated them? Harding was the Victory-at-Sea generation. Why not hum a few bars?

"Okay," Harding said, turning to shake hands.

"Okay? I thought . . . I didn't give the right answer, did I?"

"There is no right answer," Harding said. "Not in my book. Only wrong answers. Two of them."

"Which are?"

"Yes and no," Harding replied. He stood there, smiling at Griffin, and Griffin smiled back, wondering what kind of strange campaign they were starting on.

"It's not what you expect," Harding said. "It's not your standard story."

"That's all right, Colonel," Griffin said. "I've had it with standard stories."

"And it's not like the movie either. I can tell you that right now."

The Filipino servant came to say that Mr. Richter was waiting down in the lobby.

"It's a memorial service out at the cemetery," Harding explained. "Eddie said no speeches. Still you never know. You want to come, just in case?"

"Sure."

Harding went into his bedroom to shower and dress. While the servant removed the empty bottles Charley Camper had left behind, Griffin wandered into the foyer. Even in the time he'd been visiting, the place had filled with still more gifts welcoming Harding back to Manila: fruit, flowers, whiskey, dress shirts, baskets, wood carvings, velvet paintings of martial scenes. It felt like a trade fair, a hospital sickroom. And a funeral.

"Amazing, isn't it?" said Harding as he emerged from the bedroom. He plucked a card off a basket of fruit: "Manila Branch, Defenders of Bataan and Corregidor." Another card, on a yard-high carving that showed a G.I. and guerrilla shaking hands. "Baguio American Legion," Harding read.

He reached inside a white box that had some shreds of wrapping paper and ribbon still taped to its sides. Out came a picture, obviously a wartime group portrait, dozens of guerrillas, one row kneeling, one row standing, the men who had come out of the jungle forty years ago.

"Can you find me?" Harding asked.

Griffin scanned the ranks. Ancient faces, daring you to guess what became of them.

"Women . . ."

"Yes. Some."

"This isn't easy. . . . I thought you'd stick right out. Here?"

This was Harding, at the height of his power and fame. He belonged in a picture like this, a black-and-white. He was from the time before wars were in Technicolor. He was a hick with a bad haircut, an awkward fellow who looked as though he'd been dragged into the picture: Charles Lindbergh, Will Rogers, Clyde Barrow, Lou Gehrig, Lincoln.

"That was before the second Battle of San Leandro," Harding said. "Did you ever hear about that battle?"

"No . . ."

"I didn't think so. It's your final chapter. We'll go there together. I'll tell you how it was and I want you to take it all down."

"That sounds fine," Griffin said, still poring over the picture Harding had handed him. It was out of a time when men at war posed for group pictures, like sports teams, faces forward, staring out into history, taking their chances on tomorrow.

"You must have felt like you owned the world back then,"
Griffin said.

"For a little while, we did."

Eddie Richter and Cecilia Santos were waiting in the lobby,
ready to escort them to the military cemetery in Makati. Eddie
had dressed for the occasion: his aloha shirt was black and white.
Santos wore a basic black dress: whether it was the color or the
dress that was basic, Griffin wasn't sure, but Cecilia Santos was
a traffic stopper.

"How are you gents doing?" Eddie asked.

"I think it's going to work out fine," Harding assured him.

"That's great," Eddie said. "I had a feeling about you
two . . ."

"It's not too early to thank you for putting us together," Harding continued.

"Do you believe you can write a book, Mr. Griffin?" Cecilia
Santos asked.

"Yes, Miss Santos," Griffin answered, wondering what she was
getting at.

"And who, besides yourself, checks this book to verify its
accuracy?"

"Who beside myself will verify the book's accuracy?" He repeated the question thoughtfully, as if this were a novel question, worthy of his most careful consideration. This had to come
up, he thought, but he'd expected it would be from Wingfield,
and much later.

"Yes . . . who will verify your work?"

"Who wants to verify it?" Griffin responded. "Anybody
who wants to talk to me, I'll be more than happy to meet
with . . ."

"That's not the point," Santos said. "Talking to you is not the
point."

"Sorry," Griffin said.

"Who, finally, *controls* the book? Who owns it? Who does the
story belong to? Does it belong to the Philippines government?
To the investors in the film?"

"It sounds to me," Griffin said, "that something is bothering you. I'd like to answer your question, but it would help me if you told me what your concern is."

"That's right," Eddie chimed in. "Any problems you have . . ."

"I'm not sure it's my problem," Cecilia Santos said. "It may be your problem." She looked hard at Griffin and her look told him that his act hadn't fooled her: the sincerity, the ingenuousness, the apparent puzzlement. I know you, her look said. I know what's in your head and in your heart, what's in your wallet and between your legs. And I am not impressed. "The government approved this film on the basis of a script that was submitted. That script was read . . . very carefully. Certain revisions were suggested. All of them were made. Now we have this so-called book . . ."

She's really pushing it, Griffin thought, staring out the window so she wouldn't see his anger. They were on the so-called superhighway from Manila to Makati, passing through a zone of slums. For some reason—beautification, security, who could tell?—a wall of concrete blocks fenced the slums. But wherever there was a road, the wall opened, and people on the superhighway had a glimpse of the Third World, a Malthusian vista of tin roofs and tired wood, potholes and puddles, garbage piles and cooking fires and wash lines. Families of nine. Could this island contain them? Could the world?

"Anyone who knows the Philippines," Cecilia Santos was saying, "knows that the war years were a complicated time. There were difficult issues. Collaboration. Coexistence. Resistance . . ."

"I know," Harding said. "I was here."

"I was in the neighborhood myself," Eddie Richter added.

"But you've been away, both of you. And you have no way of knowing how alive these questions are. You have no way of knowing how, not long ago, an opposition weekly published an analysis of the war record of no less than President Marcos himself. The article—written by a Filipino living abroad— claimed that the exploits in Marcos's memoirs were exaggerated, that many of his medals were frauds. Well, gentlemen, the magazine was closed and the staff placed under house arrest, pending trial for slander and subversion."

"I guess somebody hit a nerve," Eddie said.

"Exactly. And Colonel Harding hit a nerve when he made his speech on Corregidor. Just one example. He—"

"He?" Harding spoke up. "Me."

"Very well sir . . . you . . . you referred to liberation guerrillas. Do you remember that?"

"Sure."

"Guerrillas at the moment of victory: I'm sure that's what you meant. But here a liberation guerrilla is someone who started to fight only when the battle was over. What you would call a Johnny-Come-Lately, more interested in back paychecks than in freedom. In short, an opportunist."

"That so? You have people like that?" Griffin saw a tiny smile cross Harding's face.

"You see my point. This is not history. This is not movies. Reputations are at stake. The Philippines government does not want to be embarrassed. It deserves to know who this book belongs to."

"Well, lady, it's my story," Harding said.

"But the issue—"

"My damn story," Harding repeated, as if that settled everything. Cecilia Santos waited for more. When nothing came, she retreated, but in good order.

"I see," she said. "You wouldn't object if I take this matter up with Mr. Wingfield?"

"No, I don't care," Harding said. "The movie company paid my way out. I understand they're picking up George's fee. Well, tell Larry, if he's worried about his investment, I'll refund the ticket and I'll hire George myself. You game, George?"

"That'd be fine," Griffin said.

"Hope I can afford you."

"You can afford me."

"So that's that," Harding said. "It's up to you. I'm here and I'm staying, movie or no. I guess you could revoke my visa or something, but I can't imagine that. Not after the boss hugs me on Corregidor and welcomes me home, I don't believe he'll run me out of here, out of these islands, which are famous for their hospitality. So, it's like the man said."

"What man?" Cecilia Santos asked.

"I have returned . . ."

9

Relaxed and nonchalant, like a gardener strolling among his roses, Harry Roberts Harding led a party of veterans out into a field of crosses. There was nothing sad about this little walk; it was as if the buried dead had arrived early at a place where all of them would camp eventually. Harding walked up to the monument, deposited a wreath and stood still for a moment, as though to give everyone a chance to remember him. Then he rejoined his comrades for the walk back across the cemetery.

Griffin thought it was wonderful. It was the feeling of Corregidor all over again. While he stayed behind with people who took notes and exposed film, the man out there had touched, or been touched, by something special. It was lucky he'd tapped into MacArthur's Ghost, who was going to take him somewhere he had never traveled: the story you lived.

"Is that all?" Cecilia Santos asked. She'd expected more, it seemed, standing there with pen and paper, ready to file a report, but the paper was creamy blank.

"Tabula rasa, Cecilia?" Griffin asked.

"What's that?" Eddie asked.

"It means blank tablet, unwritten page," Cecilia Santos said. "Latin."

"Tabula rasa," Eddie repeated. "Sounds like the name of an exotic dancer."

"I was impressed," Griffin said. "I'm glad I came. How about you, Miss Santos? Was it worth your time?"

"I'm happy it went well," she admitted.

"I'll tell you one thing," Eddie said. "It won't be too many more years us old fossils will be showing up like this. Every year, there's a few more underground and a few fewer upstairs. I can remember when—"

"What's that?" Cecilia Santos interrupted sharply. Eddie peered over in the direction she indicated, to where Harding had come out of the cemetery and stood near the administration building.

"I don't know," Eddie said. "The deal was, he was supposed to sign the visitors' book and pose for pictures and that's all."

"He's giving a press conference!" Cecilia Santos cried, rushing toward the group that had formed around Harding. When Griffin started to follow, Eddie held him by the elbow, gesturing for him to stay where he was.

"I love it," Eddie said. "He's MacArthur's Ghost again."

"She doesn't love it," Griffin said, gesturing to Cecilia Santos. But Eddie wasn't worried.

"Did I tell you about Florida?" he asked.

"Florida?"

"He was running a motel halfway down the coast, on the Gulf side. A ten-cabin mom-and-pop operation filled up with senior citizens who go soak their bodies in some mineral springs down the road. The place was all canes and bathrobes, ace bandages and herb teas, and Harry Roberts Harding is their gofer, running errands all day long and babysitting at night. That's where he was at. Sitting out front, not sleeping, just sitting, watching moths dance around a neon vacancy sign and thinking God knows what. That's how he was, the night that I drove up. And I said, 'Colonel, you're going back in.' "

"And he knew what you meant?"

"He knew, all right," Eddie answered. "Now look at him. MacArthur's Ghost. It tickles me."

The impromptu press conference had broken up, it seemed, and Cecilia Santos walked briskly back toward them, reading out of her notebook.

"Your simple, straightforward American hero," she said, "your honest-to-God veteran of the last good war, your legendary guerrilla leader . . ." She struggled to control herself, rustling through her notes, inflamed by what she found. "Hints, threats, promises. He said he will have secrets to tell, heroes who were betrayed, victories that were defeats. That's not all. He mentioned Yamashita's treasure."

"What did he say?" George asked. The treasure had appeared in the screenplay, he recalled. It was a trove of gold supposedly hidden by Tomoyuki Yamashita, the "Tiger of Malaya," who had defended the Philippines, retreated to the mountains of northern Luzon, and been hanged for war crimes in 1946. But Griffin had assumed that the treasure was a scriptwriter's device, something to give purpose—otherwise in short supply—to a conventional thriller.

"Yamashita's treasure," Eddie explained, "is the oldest, hoariest, hardiest . . ."

"Most discredited," Cecilia Santos added.

"Yeah, most discredited wild goose of a treasure yarn to come out of the war, right up there with Amelia Earhart or with Hitler in the Amazon. Did he say there was a treasure?"

"Oh, he's no fool, your colonel. Do we want to find out what really happened? Do we want to know who the real heroes were? Or where the treasure lies? Where do we go?"

Eddie and George traded glances, but neither of them saw it coming.

"To your book!" she said. "Everything will be in the book he is preparing with the celebrated American writer, Mr. George Griffin!"

Part Two

★ ★ ★
★ ★

HARDING'S FIRST CHAPTER

10

The Reverend Elbert Hubbard Harding believed that there was order in the world and so might have been consoled by the fact that he died on December 8, 1941 (Manila time), when Japanese planes swept into Pearl Harbor and ended forever the colonial America that had made him a king in the remote mountains of northern Luzon. Reverend Harding did not believe in coincidences. He believed in patterns: death and the Japanese came riding in together, end of life and end of an era.

Reverend Harding and his wife, Dorothy, had come to the Philippines at the turn of the century, not long after Admiral Dewey sailed into Manila Bay. Public health officials, doctors, teachers, swarmed into the conquered archipelago, determined to demonstrate America's ability to transform what it had captured. Many stayed in Manila, a city Harding despised. To him, Manila was a feudal, popish place, where Catholicism had festered for four centuries, where *illustrados,* the Hispanic elite, all lace and rosary, sent their offspring to Madrid to marry, and where businessmen now rushed to proclaim themselves Americanistas, vowing to serve the newcomers with the same obsequious zeal they had bestowed upon the Spaniards. Harding made his way north, into the mountains of the central Cordillera. Here, among primitive tribes, Igorots, he found a place more to his liking. Many Americans were attracted to the mountains, cool, green realms, underpopulated, unmapped, un-Catholic, Indian country, really. A doctor, a miner, a botanist, anthropologist, or missionary could make his mark here. He settled in Sagada, a collection of mountain huts, winding lanes, shady pine groves, flowered meadows, rice paddies: a Shangrila. Harry Roberts Harding was born in Sagada in 1923. He still thought of it as home. "I was born in the mountains," he said.

What would you call the impulse that sends a man who already dwells in an isolated mountain village on months-long solitary treks even farther into the Cordillera? Was he aloof? Was he lonely? Proud? Shy? Did Elbert Hubbard Harding choose to be what he was, or did he have no choice? He occupied himself with a series of monographs on the natural history of the mountain provinces, monographs he published locally at his own expense, cheap watery printing on paper that was worse than newsprint, bound with covers that looked like shopping bags.

Luckily, Hubbard was the first missionary to Sagada. The Igorots had no basis for comparison or complaint. They accepted this distant eccentric as the very model of what a missionary should be: a cordial, distant, nocturnal creature.

Dorothy Harding saved the situation. She was the one who learned local languages; organized native weavers, carvers, farmers; opened a school, dispensary, and guest house; operated the radio that linked Sagada to Manila and the world. Her husband was American mysticism and spiritual loneliness. She was American ingenuity, improvisation, hustle and bustle.

In 1937, Dorothy Harding accompanied her son back to Georgia, where he was enrolled in a private preparatory school outside of Savannah, his mother's hometown. It was a wrenching change, from the hills of never-never land to the pranks and discipline of a military-oriented boarding school. Harding felt as if he was being punished for he didn't know what, unless it was the happiness of Sagada. He thought about that. Maybe happiness was something that had to be paid for by punishment. More punishment than expected: he had been in school a month when his mother was killed in an automobile accident.

Elbert Hubbard Harding's wife had lain underground all winter before the first letter came from Sagada, a note penciled on the cheap paper that reminded him of home, a note replete with the same pro-forma pieties his father dispensed—though only when forced to—in funerals at Sagada. No, his father wasn't coming to the rescue, that much was clear. He'd have laughed at the idea of rescue, he'd ask what it meant, how it was defined, if anyone really believed such a thing was possible and then, when his son was all tangled up and tongue-tied, he'd have gone for a walk someplace. So Harry Roberts Harding resolved to be the architect of his own deliverance, beating the military school at its own game, finishing in three years what was meant for four. On the way home, on the train across America, the Pan Am Clipper to Manila, the car to Baguio, the hitchhike truck to Bontoc, the hike up the trail from the Chico River to Sagada, he pictured his confrontation with his father. Then came the end of the climb, the trail curving into pine groves, the first glimpse of the rice terraces that fed the village, centuries-old dikes and pools that took his breath away and told him he was home. And then: the first incredulous waves from the people who remembered him, woodcutters, weavers, farmers who waded out of the fields, kids who trailed him, shouting and cheering through the village to the gate, the garden, the home that was empty. His father, as usual, was someplace else.

Young Harding camped out in dust, dead plants, fallen-apart furniture, and filthy kitchen. His father appeared to have confined himself to his laboratory. Here, at least, there were signs of life: pencil shavings, pipe cleaners, clothing that was soaking—no, marinating—in buckets. These were his welcome home. In a few days, his nature—and his mother's—asserted itself. The house was cleaned, the roof fixed, the garden weeded and watered. The villagers noticed. Before long, they were stopping by with the same problems they had brought his mother, the same rotted-out teeth, skin infections, letters that needed writing, shipments to and from the market down at Bontoc. It was on coming back from Bontoc, laden with powdered milk and razor blades, bottles of aspirin and bolts of cloth, that he saw his father. The old man must have just come back from wherever he had been. Pick and knapsack on his back, he was looking around the yard his son had recaptured from the wilderness, less pleased than puzzled, as though he might have gotten his home address wrong.

"So," said Elbert Hubbard Harding. "You're back."

"Yes," Harry replied. He had thought this would be a moment to remember. He was wrong.

"I saw . . ." the elder Harding remarked, gesturing toward the garden. "I let things go. Couldn't seem to find the time for gardening."

"Or writing," Harry charged.

"Yes," he conceded. "That too."

"You got the letter I sent. I know that. It's inside. You didn't answer."

"No, sorry. It's how I am. That's all."

No, Harding thought, the moment he'd been hoping for would never come. He wanted it. Love or hate, it didn't matter. But love had a way of tumbling into affection, familiarity, and hate into mere disappointment. His father reached out a hand, a weak ecclesiastical handshake.

"Nice to have you back, son. Shall we go in?"

"Where have you been?"

"Up in the mountains. You know. One of my walks . . ."

"I mean . . ." A last stab at meaning. "Where have you been all these years?"

"Oh. That." He took the question seriously, turned it over some. And when the answer came it was a surprise to both of them, a bona fide discovery. "Up in the mountains."

"Could I go with you sometime?"

"Of course," his father said. "But don't they need you here at the mission?"

"They can spare me. They spared you."

"Spared me?" The old missionary was taken aback. He'd never looked at things that way, never evaluated his performance. "Why, yes . . ."

He was laughing. It was the first time Harry Harding had seen his father laugh.

"Why, yes . . . I suppose they have."

In the end, his father was a mystery he never solved. The old man fussed with plans for what he called, ironically perhaps, "the father-and-son expedition." Sometimes he seemed to take it seriously, poring over maps, marking trails, springs, campsites, and such. Those maps were his father's finest works, Harding saw: hand-drawn, carefully marked and annotated, with comments front and back. But the father-and-son expedition was canceled.

"I'm not getting up," Elbert Hubbard Harding announced

one morning. He was on a cot in his laboratory. During the night, he'd moved his writing table, his smoking tools, his wash-basin and bucket closer to the bed, which was covered with books and maps.

"You're not getting up today?"

"Or tomorrow."

"Why?"

"Because I can't move my legs. That's why. Or feel them."

"The doctor down in Bontoc—"

"Don't waste his time. I'm staying here. That's final."

"You want me to radio Manila, at least?" Mission headquar-ters was in Manila. A nightly radio net linked various Episcopal outposts.

"They've got better things to do in Manila," he said. "At least they think they have. Let's not disturb them."

Harding looked up at his son. He was surprised to see frustra-tion and hurt. And mourning.

"They'll never take me alive," he joked, patting his son's hand.

The old man sank steadily during the next two weeks, declining food, shunning what few medical palliatives the mission offered. He slept a lot. "Testing the waters on the other side," he called it. "Practicing oblivion." Meanwhile, the nightly broadcasts from Manila crackled with tension between America and Japan. Young Harding thought that America might have to teach the Japanese a lesson, sooner or later. "Take them down a notch or two." He said as much one night and was irritated by his father's silence. If the prospect of a war did not concern him, what would?

"Do you think there'll be a war?" he pressed. His father had had a good day, which meant he had died at a slower rate today than yesterday. It was like watching him go down a flight of steps, some large, some small. Sometimes he took them two at a time, sometimes he paused and looked around. He thought about his father a few years later, at dawn, at a place called Los Banos, when he watched General Tomoyuki Yamashita go up the steps to the gallows where his life was ended.

"A war?"

"Yes, damn it, a war!"

Old Harding had been working on his maps, transferring comments from recent journals to the map margins, updating his cartography of a world he'd never see again.

"A war." It sounded as if someone had asked him about the weather. It even looked that way: the old man glanced outside, as if he could find his answer in the stars.

"Do you think we'll win?"

"Who's we? This 'we' you're talking about."

"Our side. The Americans and Filipinos. Why do you always force me to define terms?"

"It's a good exercise for you. Knowing who *I* is. And *we*. And *they*. Think about it."

"Every question I ask, the ones that I wait for years to ask, they come out sounding stupid. You're going to die. . . . And we're going to be strangers."

"Yes." It seemed like a perfectly normal proposition to the old man! Yes, of course he was dying. Yes, they were strangers. Everything in natural order. But some of his son's frustration must have touched him, because he put aside his maps and looked at him carefully.

"You'll get to know me, Harry."

"What? When you're dead?"

"Exactly. You'll see. You know who I've been thinking about as I've been lying here? Or who comes to me in dreams these nights? My father. I'm here in a mountain village in the middle of a country that's going to war, and I'm thinking about someone who died in 1918. My father. I didn't know him. At least I thought I didn't. Just like you. It runs in the family, I suppose. But here I am. All full of him. I wouldn't call it a miracle. But it's remarkable. The company of the dead . . ."

"What about me?"

"You'll think of me, years from now. The oddest things will bring me back to you. I don't know, the smell of wood fires, or something you do while shaving, or the sound of someone whistling. It's the way lives overlap."

"I might not live that long."

His father picked up his maps. "That's what I've been working on . . ."

They buried him the way they buried all the village people: not at all. The Igorots came to the mission with a coffin that had been carved out of a tree trunk. They lifted his father inside, closed the top, wrapped some rope around, and carried him out the mission gate. In the front garden, the American flag was flying on a pole set in a bed of roses his mother had planted. It hung limp and motionless like an inverted mop. Harding unfastened the guide ropes and brought the flag down. On the road the Igorots watched carefully: a housekeeping chore suddenly became a ceremony. Harding grasped the flag by its ends, careful that it didn't touch the ground. Then, with a military-school flourish, he folded it over and again, crisp deft folds that resulted in a three-cornered tricolor, which he exhibited to the people of Sagada, then tucked inside his knapsack. Thus ended forty years of American stewardship in the mountains. He wondered what it would be like for whoever came next, following in his father's footsteps. No act could be a hard act to follow.

The whole village marched off the road, down a steep and slippery trail that led toward the burial caves. Everyone was there, Harding saw, the pious converts, the "rice Christians," the die-hard animists. That surprised him. His mother was the one who saved lives, yet his father—the world's worst missionary—was the one they revered. ("Why haven't we got more Episcopalians?" a no-nonsense inspector had asked. "They wouldn't like it," the old man replied.)

Now they wrestled his coffin down into a limestone ravine, pallbearers sliding through mud, tripping over roots, scraping against rock outcrops, and then, at bottom, struggling upward toward the dark mouth of the cave, as if forcing a morsel of food up into the jaw of an unwilling monster, pressing the coffin between its stalactite incisors, among rotted out coffins, broken bones, the detritus of other lives, past feedings. At the front of the cave, the pallbearers stopped, maybe just to rest, but it felt like another one of those awkward moments that Harding was expected to fill with words and rituals. He stepped over toward the coffin and stood beside it, his hand on the wood. After a moment, he dropped his hand and stepped away. A meaningless gesture, but everyone else who was there stepped forward, put a hand on the coffin, stood silent, and moved on.

They could have left the coffin near the mouth of the cave, where other recent coffins had been deposited, but they clambered onto a ledge that led farther in. The dead were all around them now. Some coffins had opened, revealing curled, dessicated remains, their posture in the coffin the same as in the womb. Did they believe, did anyone, that they would rise and walk again, here or somewhere else? They left his father on the highest, inmost corner of the cave.

Harding walked back through the village, past the mission, out of Sagada, through rice fields and wildflower meadows, through bamboo thickets and mountain streams, uphill into forests of teak and banyan, and when he came to the end of what he knew, he found a trail his father had marked for him, and he followed it into the mountains, toward Baguio and a man named Harrison Wingfield.

11

Harrison Wingfield had come to the Philippines right after mustering out of the American Expeditionary Force in France. His superior, General Pershing, had cut his teeth fighting Moslem rebels in the Philippines and Wingfield credited the general with "pointing me in the right direction." The direction—as always, with Americans—was west, far past the borders of the closed frontier, eight thousand miles across the Pacific, to a place Wingfield nonetheless regarded as part of America. Not a commonwealth, not a colony, but "territory." His territory, and America's. He'd done well out in the watery west. He owned gold mines in the mountains, rice plantations down below. He sat on the board of a half dozen companies that brewed beer, repaired ships, printed schoolbooks, assembled radios.

Baguio was his headquarters. That made sense. Believing he was still in America, he lived as if he had never left home, in that part of the Philippines that most resembled the country he had left behind, the cool, piney summer capital where like-minded Americans had built a town almost from scratch, with good roads named after presidents, and sensible buildings that could have fit a midwestern county seat, and a municipal park that Daniel Burnham, architect of Chicago's Midway, had designed. From the lecture halls and dormitories of the Philippine Military Academy—"our West Point"—to the barracks and officers club of Camp John Hay, Baguio was an American place, Harrison Wingfield its first citizen. But he thought of himself, or at least encouraged others to think of him, as plain old Uncle Harrison. His polished verandah was just a front porch, his sloping lawns a mighty good place for Easter egg hunts, his gleaming banisters a playground slide. "He's got his countries wrong, he's got his centuries wrong," Harding's father had said, "but he gets his numbers right, your Uncle Harrison."

They were not related. Harrison Wingfield was everybody's uncle. But it had always seemed to Harding that Wingfield took a particular interest in him. Wingfield always arranged for the missionary boy to visit Baguio twice a year, several weeks at a time. For a while, Harding suspected Wingfield might be interested in his mother, who accompanied him. In a way, he courted her. But the jealous son was courted also, and before long he came to believe that his mother's flowers were like his own horseback rides, free-will gifts. If anyone was Wingfield's target it was the ever-absent Elbert Hubbard Harding. Uncle Harrison had taken it upon himself to make up for all the missionary's faults and defaults. Elbert Harding was someone he strove to atone for.

Baguio days. That was how Harding thought of them, and always would. A special time, Christmas and summer vacation combined. Baguio days were scented, carefree, companionable days. Baguio days meant wide porches and polished floors, carpets of lawn, lemonade gazebos swarming with hibiscus, swims in hot springs and horseback rides to gold mines and trips to the market with Uncle Harrison, where piles of strawberries were his for the asking. Leathery libraries and dark wood and warm blankets at night and white uniformed servants and rides with Uncle Harrison in a 1934 white convertible Packard roadster that was the twin of President Quezon's. Baguio days. Childhood and peacetime. Over now.

"Mr. Harding, sir," the servant announced.

"That you, Elbert?" Wingfield asked, peering outward. The sun was setting behind where Harding stood, dropping into the Lingayen Gulf. The Japanese navy was there, where the sun was setting, and though it was only the sunset that made Wingfield raise his hand to shield his eyes, it looked as though he was warding off an attack from the west.

"Harry Harding, sir," he said, stepping farther into the room. "Uncle Harrison, my father died last week."

Wingfield's hands pushed into the mess of paper on his desk, burying themselves to the wrists, then withdrawing. "I see."

He lifted himself out of his chair, which sighed in relief, even as the floorboard groaned in pain. The big man walked toward him. White suit, white shirt, black shoes, black tie. Smell of sweat, cologne, tobacco.

"I'm sorry," Wingfield said, shaking his hand. "He was one of the originals. What a sense of timing!"

"He told me I should come here. You'd know what was happening, he said. And you'd know what to do."

"It's remarkable what an expert I've become lately. Come on, son, let's have a walk."

"I'm not taking you from your work, Uncle Harrison?"

"Hah!" Wingfield laughed. He padded over to his desk, gave the offending paperwork a fierce shove into the corner. "Confederate money, my boy. And this is the fall of Atlanta. Come along."

Wingfield gestured to the servant. "You might as well drink. There'll be time enough for teetotaling."

"What are you having?"

"These chilly nights . . ." Harrison Wingfield loved the nip in the Baguio air. It meant fireplaces, sweaters. Home. To him, a shiver was a sensuous pleasure. It was hard to shiver in the tropics, hard to grow roses, hard to stage a credible Christmas party. These became important rituals. "I believe a brandy would go down nicely. . . . Attack the most expensive bottles first, that's my policy. Scorched earth, empty bottle, so forth and so on . . ."

"I'll have brandy too."

"You know, I thought you were in Georgia someplace, son. It shocked me seeing you in my office. I thought of you as one of the people who'd be coming to our rescue sometime. Not as one of the trapped. Come on, let's walk."

Wingfield took him by the arm and ushered him out of the office, across the porch.

"Shouldn't we wait for our brandies?" Harding reminded him.

"The servant will find us."

"Oh . . ." Harding felt stupid, not knowing what servants were for. They went down the steps and out across the lawn. Behind the house, the property ended at a precipice, where there was a flagstone patio set in the rose garden. The 1941 Christmas tree was already in place. Maybe Uncle Harrison was an optimist. Or his servants hadn't been told the war news.

"How'd you get here, Harry?" Wingfield asked. "I hear it's bad along the main roads. They're bombing everything that moves."

"I didn't come along the roads," Harding said. "I walked through the mountains."

"You what?" Wingfield gestured at the dark ridges beyond, the ranges upon which he'd feasted, pulling gold out of the ground.

"My father drew a map. It's a map that—"

"Shh!" The servant approached with brandy, glasses, and a box of cigars. "Thanks, Nemy," Wingfield said. "That'll do for tonight."

"Yes, sir." The white-jacketed figure disappeared across the grass.

"You have to watch what you say," Wingfield said.

"You don't trust—"

"We're talking about people who lived three hundred years with the Spanish. Then they had us for fifty years. Maybe they like us as much as they say they do. Maybe they love us. But your Filipino is a fellow who's adaptable."

"But Nemy's been here since—"

"I like these people, son. I like them a lot. But liking's one thing. Trusting's something else. That makes me the opposite of your late father. He didn't like anybody, but he trusted everyone. He lived, but he was lucky. I'm not counting on luck. You shouldn't either."

"Before he died, we had this—I guess you'd call it—argument," Harding said. It was easy, talking to Uncle Harrison Wingfield. He adopted everyone he met, plopped them down in a chair, made time for them, never rushed himself or anyone. Words came easy, out here in the dark, Baguio twinkling down below. "I asked him whether he thought we'd win the war. He asked me who *we* was. He said that was one of the most important things, knowing the meaning of *I* and *we* and *they*. He told me to think about it."

"God forbid I should ever agree with your father," Wingfield said. He swirled the brandy around in his glass, inhaled, swallowed it. It all came together, the way he did it, touch, smell, and taste. Harding admired that.

"I know who *I* am," Wingfield said. "I'm sorting out the *we* and the *they.*"

"Someone's in the kitchen with Dinah, strumming on the old banjo . . ."

The next morning Harding awakened and wondered if the war had gone away. He was like a terminally ill patient who surfaces from a night's deep sleep and, for the shortest moment, can't quite remember why he's sleeping in a hospital bed.

"and singing fee fie fiddly eye oh, fee fie fiddly eye oh oh oh . . ."

Uncle Harrison was preparing his famous lumberjack breakfast, a meal too important to be left to servants, who had learned to steer clear of shattering eggshells, clattering pots, spattering bacon and batter. Harding lay back in bed and savored the morning. The first rays of sun infiltrating the rose garden, glittering on the morning dew, marching toward fog that sulked among the pines.

"Five minutes, missionary boy!" Wingfield shouted up the stairs. "There's a war on, you know."

Harding wondered what happened while he was sleeping. How many had died? What was lost? A few more miles of coast? A stretch of road that led to Manila? Maybe it had been a good night, when the disease that was working its way through the American commonwealth rested and trifled, but Harding knew about good nights from watching his father die. He knew that every night, good or bad, brought him closer to the end.

He wondered what Uncle Harrison had in mind. It was hard to picture him waiting for the Japanese. Internment camp? Execution? Life in hiding? For himself, Harding was remarkably placid. If worst came to worst, there were always the mountains. He was convinced he could live forever in the mountains. He was young and healthy. He could shoot, fish, forage, ride. More than that, he had his father's maps, which he believed in completely. Every time he studied the maps, he found something new, a notation, a connection, a pattern. Was there water in the mountains? There were springs, hot and cold, pools and lakes, rivers above and underground. Was there food? There were fish, and fish traps. He knew where. There were fowl. He knew where they swarmed and when they nested. He knew bees and honey and where the hives were. Coconuts and bananas, soursop, durian, mango. Were there friends? His father had marked down every visit to every tribe, hostile, hospitable, good village and bad, chiefs and headmen, herbalists and midwives, and half the villages were places that he alone had visited. Were there hiding places? There were caves, clearings, abandoned farms, played-out gold mines, campsites of his father's own devising, some far in the mountains, others within a hundred yards of main highways. The curtain was coming down on America in the Philippines, a world was crumbling, and Harry Roberts Harding, heading downstairs, never felt better in his life.

Uncle Harrison was at the stove. Sometimes he missed his flapjacks altogether. Sometimes they clung on the edge of his frying pan before plummeting to the burners. A few he caught perfectly, and these were eaten.

"Good morning," Uncle Harrison said. He gestured toward a kitchen table, where four Americans were seated. "Say hello to all that stands between you and the Army of the Emperor of Japan."

There were just four of them, packing away Uncle Harrison's pancakes like so many hungry boarders. Harding said hello.

"Howdy," one of them responded, a brawny red-faced chap who was blowing onto a cup of hot coffee. "I'm Charley Camper."

"Charley's head of the men who got left behind to look after Camp John Hay," Uncle Harrison said. "A skeleton crew, not that you could prove it now."

"That fellow with his face in a plate is 'Mean' Meade," Camper said. Meade was a country boy, athletic, laconic, and single-minded about feeding. He was spooning marmalade into his mouth, emptying a whole jar as if it were a can of pork and beans.

"And the movie star's name is Sudul. Hold onto your wallet and lock up your daughter when he's around."

"Heard all about you," Sudul said. Harding recognized his type from military school days: he was the kid who hid cigarettes and found drinks and claimed to know about women.

"What's left over is named Polshanski," Camper said, nodding toward a tall, slight, stoop-shouldered man with a narrow face and dark, melancholy eyes. A worried man, permanently displaced. That sad aspect made what he did surprising: he looked up from his pancakes and he winked.

"Delighted," Polshanski said. "Misery loves company."

"I have some news for all of you," Uncle Harrison said. "The Japanese'll be here tomorrow night."

"That's not news," Polshanski said. "That's weather."

"Are you sure?" Camper asked.

"Absolutely," Uncle Harrison said. He pulled over a stool and sat in front of them, a barefoot millionaire in a Chinese bathrobe. "It's over here."

"Well, Sudul, looks like you win the pool," Camper said, wiping off his mouth and giving off a belch that sounded like a depth charge.

"We were hoping it'd be longer," Polshanski explained to Harding. "We made bets."

"Christmas, maybe, or even New Year's," Meade added. "Sudul knew better, of course."

"Don't blame me," Sudul said. "Somebody had to win the bet."

"We lose the war, he wins the pool," Polshanski sighed. "You don't even have time to spend the fifty bucks."

"Want to bet?" Sudul rejoindered.

"What's our plan?" Camper asked Uncle Harrison.

"For today, business as usual."

12

Charley Camper—Sergeant Charley Camper—was a truck driver, a horn-blowing, down-shifting, double-clutching race-truck driver who treated the Baguio roads as his personal grand prix. He was a sweating, farting, belching concatenation of bodily functions, whose personal gas tank, engine, transmission, and exhaust pipe perfectly matched the empty troop carrier he guided around the doomed resort city.

In a bigger country, someone like Charley Camper would already have made his getaway. But this was an island, a small island turning smaller, with time running out and no running away, so you drove faster and faster on the roads that were still open. They stopped at a stone gateway. Beyond, a white crushed-coral driveway curved off through ranks of evenly spaced royal palms.

"This the Pineda house?" Charley asked. A couple of Filipinos sat in front of a crushed-coral driveway that curved off through ranks of evenly spaced royal palms. They were squatting on their haunches, hunkered down. Harding had seen Igorots hold that position for hours, eating, waiting for game, sitting out a storm.

"Yes, sir," one of them answered.

"Are you the guys?"

"Yes, sir, we're the guys."

"You got names?"

"Yes, sir," the Filipino answered.

"Well, that's nice," Camper said. "What are your names?"

"His name is Serafin," the Filipino said, gesturing at his companion. White cotton slacks and shirts, wide-brimmed hats. "My name is Flash," he said. "Sir."

76

"Well hop in back," Camper said, turning into the estate. The driveway went on forever, curving over lawns, dipping into a wooded glen, then angling back up to the top of a hill.

"Uncle Harrison said you got raised in a mission," Camper said. "Then they shipped you off to military school."

"Yes, sir."

"You ever had any?"

"Any what?"

"You could die for your country before you get your first piece of ass. A virgin soldier's a hell of a thing. Wow! This is some cabin!"

On Sunday drives years before, Uncle Harrison delighted in showing Harding fragments of a country he had never seen. Baguio had hunting lodges from Michigan's Upper Peninsula, Victorian three-stories from the Midwest, and—as he now saw —a porticoed, pillared plantation house straight out of *Gone with the Wind*.

"I wonder how the hell they got their money," Charley Camper mused.

"Looks deserted," Harding said.

"It's okay," Camper said, reaching deep inside a pocket for a handful of coins, screws, washers, contraceptives, and several sets of keys. "Let's see. Pineda . . ."

He found the key, walked up the steps, and unlocked the door. "You go with Flash, cover the ground floor," Camper said. "I'll go upstairs with the other guy."

"I don't understand," Harding said. "What are we supposed to be doing?"

"It's simple. We're a moving and storage company. We take whatever's movable and worth moving and put it in the truck."

"Then what?"

"There's some mines back in the hills, way hell and gone. We've been putting the stuff there. We've emptied half a dozen places already. Just me and some of my boys, till today. Today's a rush job, so we got some help. Which, by the way, you want to keep your eyes on."

While Charley and Serafin rummaged around upstairs, Harding and Flash moved from room to room on the ground floor. The house turned them all into gawking peasants. Sometimes it

was the marble floors, the flowered wallpaper, the sunken bath-
tubs, but at other times it was the little things they noticed, like
soap that was shaped, colored, and scented like fruit. Equally
puzzled, Flash and Harding lifted and sniffed the soap.

"Banana," Flash said.

"Apple," Harding followed. They stepped over to a sink.
Harding turned on the tap, washed his hands. Flash did the
same with his banana. They raised their hands to their noses and
then they looked at each other and laughed.

"Hey, missionary boy!" Hefting a trunk full of paintings, Charley Camper stood in the doorway. Serafin was behind him, man-
handling a piano bench. "You wash up after we get done
working, not before. Come on, Serafin."

"Excuse me, sir," Flash shouted after them. "Why take the
piano bench if you cannot take the piano?"

"Because we can carry the piano bench," Charley retorted.
"Now stop washing your hands. Damn, missionary boy probably
flushes the toilet *before* he uses it!"

Flash and Harding worked well together, moving from room
to room, joking about their discoveries. An archery set. A Victrola that filled the house with tangos. Harding came across a
collection of pornographic postcards, which he regretted not
keeping. Forty years afterward, he could still describe the way
the woman on one of the postcards looked, not just her naked-
ness or sexuality, but the detached expression on her face, the
slight pout of her lips, the way she seemed to look at him as if
she were a little ahead of him on a road, wondering if he'd ever
catch up. A virgin soldier, Charley Camper had said, was a hell
of a thing. He tossed the postcard in a box, then joined Flash in
the library.

"I was looking at the books," Flash said. "Very many books.
Some new. Some very old."

He walked along the shelves, running his fingers along the
spines, as if reading the titles in Braille. Then he saw that Harding was waiting for him. "I'm sorry, sir."

"It's all right," Harding said.

He noticed the way Flash was studying him, as if he were
asking: what kind of American are you? Are you a man like
Harrison Wingfield, a patriarch businessman? Are you a cowboy

drinker like Charley Camper? Are you something else again?
Something unknown?

"I don't know what this is all about," Harding said. "Whether
we're helping these people, whoever they are, move out, or the
Japanese move in. It feels funny."

"The Pinedas are very wealthy," Flash said. "They have a
house in Manila. And a bank. And rice plantation in Tarlac. And
tobacco in the Cagayan Valley . . ."

"They have a lot to lose."

"Or much to keep . . ."

A horn sounded. "Let's get a move on," Camper shouted from
the truck. "There's a war on."

"Do you read books, Flash?" Well meant as it was, it sounded
as if he were asking if the man could read.

"I read books sir, yes," Flash replied. "I'm a printer. Not that
all printers can read but—"

"A printer? I thought you were off a plantation in Pampangas.
Charley said you'd come up to talk to Mr. Wingfield."

"I work with the farmers tenants union."

"But you don't have a farm."

"Neither do the farmers."

"What are you doing here?" Harding asked.

"I wanted to see this house," Flash said. "The Pinedas are
the wealthiest landowners in my province. I wanted to see
this . . ."

The horn honked outside. Charley Camper was getting rest-
less. "You guys don't hurry, we'll have to put this stuff back at
bayonet point."

"Why don't you take a few books with you," Harding offered.
"I saw Charley lift some bottles of whiskey . . ."

"Thank you, no," Flash said. "After the war . . ."

They stepped outside and, like that, their partnership dis-
solved. The two Filipinos hopped in back with the automatic
obedience, verging on enthusiasm, of hunting dogs. The Americans shared the front seat.

"That Flash is an intelligent man," Harding said.

"His union's been giving Uncle Harrison a pain in the ass,"
Camper said. "He says they're Communists."

Back in Baguio, Camper halted in front of the bombed-out

marketplace, a pile of charred wood, crumbly concrete walls and twisted, corrugated metal. The vendors had moved across the road, into Burnham Park, where the softball field was piled high with corn, cauliflower, beans, broccoli, strawberries, with cheap shoes, bolts of cloth, goats and chicken, coconuts, tobacco. It was tempting to think that these people were beneath the battle, that while war swept back and forth these poor folk, the scratchers and hagglers, kept on living. But the market, not the mansions, was where the Japanese bombs had fallen.

"Okay, boys," Camper said, shoving some pesos out the window into Serafin's hands. Serafin thanked him. Flash remained silent. When Harding glanced his way, their eyes met. Harding waved as they drove away and Flash smiled back. Then they disappeared into the crowd. Day laborers.

"Don't we need them to help us unload?" asked Harding.

"Security," Camper replied. "The fewer people who know where we leave this stuff, the better."

"Who knows?"

"Uncle Harrison. Me. You. My three men. All Americans. One of us better live, that's all I can say . . ."

They stashed the treasure in an abandoned mine shaft outside of town and returned to Camp John Hay at dusk. Harding had known John Hay since childhood. The green and white bungalows, the tennis courts, dining halls and gardens all reminded him of summer camps he'd seen in Georgia, resorts from which deer and duck and trout, not armies, were meant to be attacked. John Hay was a relaxed and playful place he'd roamed through freely, scooting past sentries who were no more menacing than school crossing guards. And now, with the army down on Bataan, with windows nailed shut, chairs folded and piled on verandahs, it felt as if the place had shut down for the season. The sadness of autumn, campfire counselors, storytellers, lifeguards all gone back to school, not to war.

Camper drove down a path that went past some cottages, through the golf course, to a barn and a corral full of horses.

"We've got everything we need. Guns, ammunition, medicine, food, a portable radio, though I don't know who there'll be to talk to."

"Where do you figure on riding to?" Harding asked.

"You know. The mountains. Uncle Harrison says you know your way around. You want to ride with us?"

"Is Uncle Harrison coming along too?"

"I don't know. It was you he wondered about. What do you say?"

"Okay."

Harding remembered that moment by the corral. It was one of those clarifying moments when the future opened and revealed itself, like when you came around a curve in the road and saw the land in front of you and you knew that this is where you were headed, this was where you were starting from, and these were the men who'd be going with you. And you looked at a man like Charley Camper and said to yourself, the same way you'd say it if you were introduced to the woman you were going to marry or the man who was going to kill you: so here you are. At last. And Charley Camper, looking at Harding, must have felt the same way too.

"We're going to go through a hell of a lot together, aren't we?" Charley asked.

"Yes."

Empty chairs and sheet music lingered on the bandstand, but the musicians were gone, and bartenders, cooks, and waitresses, and all the people whose dance contests, amateur theatricals, steak nights, raffles had turned the Baguio Officers Club into an American place.

"There they are!" Polshanski cried, hopping off a barstool when Camper and Harding arrived. "Now we can get started. What'll it be?"

"Your best scotch," Charley responded. "And, Polshanski?"

"Yeah?"

"The older it is, the better it gets. It's not like milk."

"Pick yourself," Polshanski answered, placing three bottles on the bar, and then a bucket of ice. "When you get done with these, we'll see about a refill."

Meade was at the piano, playing a barely acceptable "Now Is the Hour." He gave up as soon as he heard a truck pulling up in front. "Damn, it's Sudul!"

Three girls on each arm, Sudul entered the room where MacArthur, Pershing, and Quezon once had waltzed. He led the women into the middle of the dance floor, pivoted at the center of the line, and the six bewildered bar girls made a slow, debutantish circle.

"Party time," he announced. "It's Christmas, New Year's, and God Bless America. Thanks to my brains and your money, this party's been paid for in advance. Any questions?"

"Well, that's damn nice of you," Meade said, staring hungrily, A horny, healthy, single-minded farm boy. Where'd he learn to play the piano?

"I'll take the pretty ones," Polshanski said. "Drinks are over here."

"Hold it!" Camper shouted. "Damn it, Sudul, make some introductions."

"I thought everybody was pretty well acquainted," Sudul said.

"Well, you forgot yourself, Mr. Smooth Guy," Charley said. "Ladies, this is Harry Harding. A missionary boy. Harry gets first choice."

It was a joke, Harding thought, a bad joke. He waited for the others to laugh, but when no one laughed, when they all stood there, even the girls, waiting for him to make his selection, he faltered and blushed.

"Harry . . ."

"First choice for the dance?"

"Sure, that's what I mean," Camper said, winking broadly. "Where's that record player?"

Al Jolson singing "Avalon." A tune across the world, a relic of the past, a song that could be inexpressibly sad, when played in a colony about to be overrun. Harding had chosen the first girl he came to. The others were dancing too. Harding danced awkwardly, a mechanical box step, holding the puzzled Anita at arm's length, talking about Sagada.

"Listen, Harry," Camper whispered. "This is a dance, not a drill. And I could fire a howitzer between your cock and her crotch, and all I'd hit is air."

It took time for the party to start, but in an hour the fundamental sadness of the occasion was almost overcome. If people can celebrate at wakes, drink and brawl, there's no reason they can't dance at the funeral of a nation. And when they tired of dancing, the girls plopped themselves in easy chairs and clamored for a movie. Polshanski dug out the projector, which had been the heart of the club's imaginary life. They chose *The Westerner*, with Walter Brennan, but the problem was that whoever ran the projector was separated from the girl he'd paired off with. Harding volunteered. He'd remember that scene forever: the cavernous officers club, the small stream of light from the projector, like a flashlight or a searchlight, and the western stuff onscreen, racing horses and raw towns, a movie fantasy that flickered while Japanese moved through the night, and during the movies one couple or another crept off, a rustle, a moan and a giggle, the girls with their eyes on the screen while the soldiers mounted and moved. Harding leaned over to Anita, the puzzled, dutiful Anita.

"Watch the projector carefully," Harding whispered, and the smell of her hair almost made him change his mind. "I'll be back," he said.

13

Harrison Wingfield's house was lit up, a light in every window, lights on the verandah, lights shining out across the grass, so that the place resembled an ocean liner in night seas, the foundering *Titanic,* maybe, settling into the depths with staterooms aglow. And as Harding came closer that last night, it seemed there might be lifeboats huddling alongside, for he saw groups of Filipinos on the lawn, talking quietly, singing, spitting, peeing against trees, all the things that Filipinos seemed to do at night.

It was touching to see how the Filipinos rallied around a man like Uncle Harrison in his hour of need. He was sitting on a wicker chair that was like a throne, a half dozen Filipinos around him, like faithful servants who would carry the deposed king to safety someplace.

"Hello, Harry," Uncle Harrison greeted him. "I wasn't expecting you till later."

"I came back early," Harding replied. He nodded and smiled at the Filipinos. For the first time, he noticed they were armed, every one of them, not only with machetes but with pistols and rifles too, and he guessed these loyalists must be a part of some campaign Uncle Harrison had devised.

"Hello, everybody," Harding said. Flash, his partner in the morning, was on the verandah. "What's cooking? This is very impressive."

"Very impressive," Uncle Harrison repeated with a startling bitterness. Harding looked around, wondering what he'd missed. There was anger all through Uncle Harrison. You could see it in his eyes, the set of his mouth, the way he smoked, rather than savored, his cigar.

"These gentlemen," Uncle Harrison said, "are workers off my plantation in Pampangas. All members of a farmers union that

has been after me for years to give them forty, fifty, sixty percent of the rice harvest. The numbers keep changing, of course,
because whatever they get, they want more and in the final
analysis, the numbers don't matter, because the goal is one
hundred percent for them and zero for me. I know it and so do
they."

Uncle Harrison poured and drank some brandy. No smell, no
sip this time—he drank it. Harding sensed how wrong he had
been. The people who had rushed to be with Uncle Harrison
were his attackers, not defenders. Even the lights that shone
through the house had been turned on to discourage pilfering,
he later learned.

"Harry, you may wonder why anyone would want to negotiate a labor contract when there's a war. I wonder about it
myself. Why they come on this last night to press their case
against me . . ."

"Sir!" It was one of the Filipinos, darker than average, taller
too. He had been leaning against the verandah. Now he stood
up and prepared to speak and the speech was aimed at Harding.

"In war and peace. We grow rice. Americans or Japanese. We
grow rice. And—"

The man broke off. Was his lack of English stopping him? Or
his anger?

"Well, I won't negotiate," Harrison Wingfield said. "You can
all go home, as far as I'm concerned. Negotiate with the Japs."

"Sir." It was Flash.

"Who are you?"

"My name is Felipe Olmas," Flash replied. He pointed to the
previous speaker. "My brother, Juan."

"Well?"

"When the war is over, will you return?"

"Who said I was leaving?"

"I see," Flash nodded. "Sir, we are not leaving either. And
someday, sir, we'll talk."

Flash glanced at his brother, nodded, and the men on the
porch got up to leave, filing quietly down the steps, polite as so
many dismissed servants, except that Flash stopped and smiled
at Harding. Then he glanced at Uncle Harrison, heavy and
brooding. "Good-bye, sir," he said. "But not forever."

As the peasants were leaving, the servants moved through the house, turning off lights. The mansion went dark, room by room, and Uncle Harrison stayed in his chair. When he spoke it was some lines of poetry that sounded like a valediction, or a curse. Years later, Harry Roberts Harding committed the lines to memory.

The Assyrian came down like the wolf on the fold,
And his cohorts were gleaming in purple and gold,
And the sheen of their spears was like stars on the sea,
When the blue waves roll nightly on deep Galilee,
Like the leaves of the forest when summer is green,
That host with their banners at sunset were seen,
Like the leaves of the forest when Autumn hath blown,
That host on the morrow lay withered and strown
For the angel of Death spread his wings on the blast
And breathed in the face of the foe as he passed . . .

"What's that?" Harding asked.

"A poem. Part of one, anyway. 'The Destruction of Sennacherib.' It's by Lord Byron. I forget the rest. Did you see their guns?"

"Yes."

"They stormed the police station before they came here. Well, stormed might be a little strong, I admit. They walked in and took what they wanted. Let's put it that way. They say they want to be able to defend themselves against the Japanese. That's what they say."

"Why don't you talk to them?"

"Oh, Harry. Sometimes I hear your father's voice . . ." Relaxing, Uncle Harrison poured himself another brandy. "The last drop of the last bottle. Too bad we can't drink up our houses, our fields, our stocks. Our libraries. So at the end, you could pour it into a glass, all of it, and swallow. Why don't I negotiate? Someday you'll see. I hope you will. See that when you come to a place and spend your life in it and build something you're proud of you don't just give it away, you don't give it up, you don't give it back. To the Indians."

"The Indians?"

"To anybody. They didn't come to negotiate. Maybe some of

them thought they did. But that Olmos, the brothers, they came because they wanted to see the last of me. Well, I disappointed them. They'll remember me like this, sitting right here, sitting while they stood, and staying when they left, when I told them to leave, guns and all. That's what they'll remember. Am I right?"

"Yes, Uncle Harrison," Harding said. "I suppose you are."

An hour later, the Americans rode slowly up the driveway, like a funeral procession, hooves crunching on gravel. Harding looked hard for traces of the orgy at the Officers Club, red eyes or shaking hands. But Meade was stolid as ever. You'd think he was headed out to plow a field. Camper was red, robust, ready for action: first day of hunting season. Polshanski and Sudul were the same.

"The Japanese are here," Uncle Harrison said. "A group of local citizens met them on the road, to arrange the surrender of the city. It's all over here."

"We brought you a horse. And a rifle."

"That's changed. A letter came last week, and a radio code last night. From President Quezon, through General MacArthur. They consider me an important person. I don't think I am. But maybe I stand for some important things. Anyway, they don't want our visitors to capture me. They're sending a plane."

"A plane? Where to?"

"I'll show you . . ."

14

It was good-bye to everything, that last morning. Good-bye mansions, good-bye John Hay, good-bye golf course, divots of greensward bursting off their trail, good-bye to the polo field—did horses remember?—and then, down into the valley in back of Baguio, along well-marked equestrian trails that led to waterfalls and picnic grounds that attracted Sunday expeditions and then, finally, into the cordillera. As the trail twisted, Baguio would sometimes be in front of them, sometimes in back, high and low, so that it felt like the city was revolving around them, a sprinkling of lights just a little lower than the stars. And then, a little later, while they stepped downhill, farther into darkness, the first sun hit the city and they knew that, in Baguio, it was just another morning. It was like betrayal, such fine weather for the Japanese.

"Stop looking back, Harry," Wingfield whispered. "It's a bad habit, looking back."

"I just wanted to see how it looks."

"It looks like every other morning," Wingfield said. "Just as fine. Places don't acknowledge us. Neither do people. Unless we make them."

Uncle Harrison had a way of saying things that made Harding uncomfortable. With the soldiers, he bantered easily, but when he spoke to Harding his voice had an edge and his words had added weight.

"Why is it," Harding asked, "That there's a lesson for me in everything you say?"

"It's simple," Uncle Harrison snapped. "You've got a lot to learn."

"Unlearn, too, I'll bet."

"That could be," Wingfield acknowledged. "Listen, son, there are men you talk to and it's just talk. These men are like that. Food and fornication, whatever, 'Getting laid and getting paid.' You're different . . ."

"What have I done?"

"It's nothing you've done. I can assure you of that. It's what you'll do."

The road they came to began somewhere in the flat lands, the rice provinces that had already fallen. It wound upward, through hills and rain forests, it spanned bridges, clung to mountainsides and ended here, among Uncle Harrison's mines, with a river on one side and a chalky cliff on the other. Where it ended, it widened. That was the airstrip, which was called an airstrip because a plane had landed there once. It could also have been called a parking lot for mining equipment, or a dump. Or the end of the road. It most certainly was that.

"When's this bird due?" Meade asked.

"They didn't say, exactly," Uncle Harrison told him. The ride had been rough on the old man. He'd been slapped by branches, clawed by vines and creepers, tripped by roots: it seemed the land itself wanted to deny his bulky form escape.

"What do you care about the plane?" Sudul asked Meade. "They didn't request the honor of *your* presence on Corregidor."

"I noticed."

"So are we staying behind, or are we getting left behind?" Polshanski wondered. "You tell me."

"They're in my house now," Uncle Harrison said to Harding. "I can feel it."

"It'll probably go to someone who's important," Harding commiserated, though it seemed odd, worrying about a house. After all, this was war, and war was a time when everything was at stake. So why was a house above the battle? Was the house a prize that got passed intact from the powerful people on one side to the powerful people on the other?

"I'm not worried about the Japanese," Uncle Harrison said. "It's the Filipinos."

"It'll all be theirs someday anyway, won't it?" Harding said. "They become independent in 1946. That's the plan. So they get to run the country and . . . it's their country then."

"Is that so?" Uncle Harrison asked. There it was—that smile,

that chuckle. Shall I tell you about Santa Claus? The Easter
bunny? How babies are made? How countries become independent? "Well, we'll see. Come 1946, you look at the flagpole. See
what's flying. You might feel wonderful. Then stop by my house.
See who's living there . . ."

"Quiet!" Camper hissed.

Uncle Harrison was startled. But Camper didn't care about
that. "Lead the horses back into the trees, Meade. Now!" He
turned to Uncle Harrison. "It's the Japs. The Japs are coming up
the road."

Harding had wondered what the enemy would look like.
There was some part of him that hadn't quite believed in them.
The news on the radio, the bombing of Baguio notwithstanding,
he hadn't seen them and seeing was believing. Now he saw.
There were four men in a jeep, a driver and officer in front, two
men in back around a mounted gun. They sped down the airstrip and, when they reached the mining shacks at the north
end, they paused, turned, and stopped. The officer had binoculars and scanned the perimeters, cliffs, streams, forest. Then the
jeep began to move, very slowly, around the edges of the airstrip, a reconnaissance that would bring it to within a hundred
yards of where the Americans were hiding.

"Wait till I give the order," Camper said. "Harding, Sudul, go
for the machine gun. The rest shoot the ones in front."

The jeep came nearer and nearer, so slow, so confident it
looked like something that had been separated from a victory
parade. Harding saw the saucerlike helmets, cloth draped out
the back, the off-white uniforms, wrapped puttees. He saw the
officer, a white, heavy, unhealthy man, and the driver, swarthy
as a peasant. He saw the machine gunner was a cartoon Japanese—yellow skin, buck teeth, spectacles. His companion was
jabbering and smiling.

"What are you waiting for?" Meade urged.

"Shit!" Camper whispered. "Look!"

At the end of the airstrip, a truck lumbered forward, canvas
covered at the top, open at the sides, and loaded with Japanese.
The jeep and truck met at the center of the airstrip, then moved
together to the mining shack. A couple dozen Japanese soldiers
hopped out, formed up, and began a search of the area around
the old mine.

"What now?" Polshanski asked.

"We hope they leave," Camper said, sighing. "Soon."

The Japanese were staying. While some probed the area around the mine, others carried some wood out onto the airstrip and started a fire. Then a merry, whistling orderly ran across the airstrip with a cook pot. When he reached the river, the Americans could recognize him for what he was: the unit runt, gofer, mascot, the cuffed-around misfit who lived for a kind word. They watched him lower the pot into the stream, saw the surprise on his face when he felt the coldness of the water. They heard him slap the water on his face. He gasped with pleasure. They shared the moment he had, squatting at the side of the stream, scanning the mountains, watching clouds pass overhead, the sun dappling leaves in the forest where killers were concealed. Reluctantly, he picked up the pot, climbed up the bank, and headed back to safety.

"They're cooking," Camper said. "That must mean they're staying the night."

"That's it, then," Sudul said.

"How about it, Mr. Wingfield?" Camper asked.

"I don't want to keep you," Wingfield repeated.

"If we're going to do something, we should do it," Meade reasoned. "If we're not, we shouldn't be here."

"You're right," Harry Roberts Harding said. "Here's what we're going to do."

15

Thanks to the report Harrison Wingfield brought to Corregidor, which was conveyed from there to Australia and America, the events of that afternoon at an unnamed gravel airstrip in the mountains of northern Luzon put Harry Roberts Harding in a line of leadership, and legend, that went from Custer and J.E.B. Stuart back to Hannibal. For Harding had led what was acclaimed as "the last cavalry charge in the history of warfare." Years later, he repeated the phrase slowly: last cavalry charge in the history of warfare. Think about that, he said. A last cavalry charge had to happen in warfare. When else? And wars were part of history. What else? So drop the "history of warfare." That left you with "last cavalry charge." But of course there was no way of knowing that it was the last such charge. So when logic whittled away at headlines you were left with cavalry charge. But the men weren't cavalry, not really. So what you were left with was six men on six horses, five of them looking at Harding for a signal that might never come. He stood beside his horse, well back in the trees, Sudul and Uncle Harrison on his right, twenty feet apart, the others at similar intervals to his left. All of them were watching him.

"I hope, I hope, I hope," Harry Harding repeated. Hoped that the sense of easy victory would make the Japanese complacent and that the isolation would make them careless and that the weariness of the long hot day would settle over them, and that the orderly would tell them about the river, the cool and bubbling river, and thus lead the compulsively clean and fastidious Japanese to their deaths.

And late that afternoon they came, a relaxed and laughing company, led by the eager-to-please orderly, who pointed the way down the bank, showed them deep pools, stripped and plunged in ahead of the rest, as if to demonstrate that no harm could come to them here. And his reward was that they tossed his clothes in after him and laughed as he chased his undershirt downstream, wading from pool to pool, slipping over slick rocks.

Watching the Japanese climb out of their uniforms, stack their weapons, and clamber down to the water, Harding wondered if the war had ended. These men were off duty, at peace. They were civilians, more than civilians, they were children, naked kids at that. Most of them. At the top, where the airstrip was, three Japanese remained in uniform, rifles at hand, waiting their turn. Even they were more like lifeguards than sentries, smiling, pointing, commenting on bellies and penises. They would be the first to die.

Harding glanced left and right, raised his hand, pointed forward, and the Americans rode out from hiding, quietly, step by step, pausing between the last rank of trees. At that last moment, even as he raised his Springfield, Harding saw that it was left to the orderly to be the first to see them, to stand naked in a wading pool, shock on his face and a scream in his throat that was lost in gunfire by the time he delivered it.

Some of the Japanese dashed for their uniforms and were shot with one leg in their trousers, one leg out, sometimes both legs in but belt unbuckled, so they tumbled back down to the river like the victims of a lethal potato sack race. Others dashed naked up the hill, modesty be damned, going for their guns, and these were shot before they reached the top, so they lay on the grass, some still, others moving, like fresh-caught fish tossed on a bank. One or two stayed in the water, as if that would protect them. They ducked beneath the surface, holding their breath, but the river barely covered their backs. Harding saw Meade, the cruelest of the Americans, ride down to the river and train his gun at a Jap who'd hidden beneath the water. He could have shot him right away, but he waited for the man to surface, then he shot him in the arm, and the man went underwater again, to emerge and be shot again, this time in the leg, and as he went below a third time, into the pool his blood was turning red, there was no knowing how long Meade would have prolonged the torture if Harding hadn't shot the man. That was the first man he killed.

"The jeep!" Charley Camper shouted. "They started the jeep!"

A couple of Japanese had driven the jeep to the center of the strip where three survivors of the river rushed toward them and climbed aboard, wet, bleeding, naked, like shipwreck survivors jumping into a lifeboat. When they were on, the jeep raced off toward the far end of the airstrip. And stopped.

"What's that?" Harding asked. The Japanese were well out of range and none of the Americans were about to pursue a jeep down a winding mountain road.

"What are they up to?" Meade wondered. "Why are they stopping?"

"My God," Polshanski said. "I think they're coming back."

"They're *what*?"

"They're coming back at us."

The jeep came straight at the Americans, firing long before it was in range. What was it that drove the Japanese back into battle? Fear of retreat and defeat? Shame at having been ambushed by men on horseback? At leaving their dead comrades at the riverbank? Maybe it was anger. There was lots of anger that early in the war.

Harding told his men to scatter, some to one side, some to the other. All he meant to do was save them from being mowed down all at once, but what started as a safeguard turned into a strategy, a strategy in the oddest possible battle, an amalgam of every childhood game: cowboys and Indians, bullfight and bull, rodeo, polo, dodgeball, keep-away, and war. Once the Americans scattered, the Japanese spun and circled, rushing off in one direction, then the other, speeding, braking, firing wildly. How long did it last? Three minutes? Five? Ten? Jeep versus horse, wheeling around an airstrip. A rushing, milling, dusty fracas.

Harding wasn't the best shot. That was Meade, or maybe Camper. But he was by far the best rider and that was what he did, running circles around the jeep, turning and reversing and drawing fire because he knew that's what he was there for, and the Japanese knew it too, ignoring the others, exposing themselves, all for the sake of a shot at Harding, so that was what

Harry Harding remembered of the last cavalry charge in the history of warfare was trying to avoid a jeep manned by a squad of half-naked Japanese.

Then the jeep stopped at the center of the airstrip. Tires shredded, gas leaking, steam coming out of the engine, windshield riddled with bullet holes. The driver was hunched over the wheel, another man had collapsed next to the machine gun, a third was in the front seat, and suddenly it was quiet. A trick? Draw the Americans in to point-blank range? The horsemen advanced slowly, firing as they came, one shot for every forward step.

"It's over," Charley Camper shouted. "Hold your fire."

He trotted over to the jeep.

"God, is it over," he said.

They pushed the jeep, Japanese and all, over the edge of the airstrip. It rolled down to the river, half submerging. The truck went into the river too. Harding pictured what the place had been like half an hour before, the exhilaration and delight that both sides found there. Now bodies littered the riverbank and floated in shallows. Gas, blood, oil, all leaked away.

The plane came at dusk, a low, slow, furtive biplane, more like a crop duster than a warplane. They watched it land and turn. The pilot waved impatiently, engines idling, anxious to be on his way.

"He's not much for ceremony," Uncle Harrison said. "For that matter, neither am I."

"It's okay," Sudul said.

"But I wanted to say thank you," Uncle Harrison continued, "which is a word I rarely use."

"You're welcome," Camper said.

"Good luck," Meade echoed.

"I'll be back someday," Wingfield said. "If I didn't believe that, I wouldn't be going now."

"We know that," Camper said.

"I hope we meet again," Wingfield said, "when I come back."

"We'll be here," Harry Roberts Harding answered.

Part Three

★ ★ ★
★ ★

FAMOUS IN MANILA

16

TRAVEL WRITER GRIFFIN TABBED FOR WAR YARN and POT OF GOLD FOR COLUMNIST? and—best of the bunch—MACARTHUR'S GHOST'S GHOST. Suddenly George Griffin was famous, and his fame was of the purest, airiest kind: unearned. Phone messages piled up in his box, notes were slipped under his door. People wanted to interview, meet, get to know him, one-time guerrillas, unacknowledged heroes with tips, maps, names, with stories, scars, clippings, medal problems, medical problems, visa, immigration, and pension problems. And now he was sitting in a hotel bar with Susan Hayes, waiting for Birdy Villanueva's driver, and he had to believe that Susan, too, was part of his run of luck, the whole package of entitlement that flowed from his alliance with MacArthur's Ghost.

"Suddenly you're a celebrity," she was saying, with an irony that enhanced more than diminished the fact that what she said was true.

"At least in Manila."

"And all this happened since . . ." She stopped and laughed. "This sounds so portentous—the night we met. Sounds like a song cue."

"Speak quietly when you say that." Griffin pointed to where some flamenco troubadours surrounded a navy man and his date. "They'll be over here. Quick, what'll it be? 'Red Necks, White Sox, Blue Ribbon Beer'?"

"Try 'Hole in the Bottom of the Sea.' That usually stops them. Say, Mr. Backyard Faraway, how did it go that night? Your first night out in the city where all things are possible?"

"My God," Griffin sighed. It seemed so long ago: the beautiful soapy girl for whom Clifford Lerner had lunged and bled, Hugh

Elliot's triple fellatio, Tom Gibbins poleaxed by a long-haired angel at the Club Tennessee. "It was good you didn't come."

"I thought so," she said. Griffin liked what came next, the knowing little grin, the playful and inquisitive question. "Was it any fun at all?"

"Yes and no. Sometimes. Maybe. Compared to what? I don't know. No doctors were called for. No police. No priests. It was just . . . what you saw. A bunch of writers. Travel writers, that is. It's a funny trade, like writing postcards for a living. The world never quite lives up to the billings you write for it. And you don't live up to the hopes you had for yourself. So every now and then you go out and roll around in your disappointment, defile yourself, and laugh at it all."

"Even though the joke's on you."

"*Especially* because the joke's on you . . . Uh-oh . . . we've been spotted." Griffin gestured at the musicians strolling in their direction. "Let's go."

Their driver pointed the car onto Roxas Boulevard. In front of the Cultural Center, workmen were assembling a seventy-foot Christmas tree, painstakingly nailing twig to branch to trunk. And, along the Boulevard, there were forests of white-painted trees for sale. Snow in Manila.

"Christmas," Griffin said. "They really bought the whole thing, didn't they?"

"The whole thing?"

"The American thing. Basketball. Movies. TV. Pop music. Fast food. Is there anything they've said no to?"

"Journalists learn fast."

"You've heard this before, I gather."

"Yes. That doesn't mean you're wrong."

"But you think I am."

"It's sad, that's all," Susan Hayes said, "and I hate to hear people talk that way. They imitate us and our response is to laugh at them."

"God, they must hate us."

"Why do you say that?"

"I would."

Susan Hayes turned away, looked out the window. They were well out of the center of town now, but Manila went on forever, a tide of corrugated metal, burning rubber, plastic buckets, dangling lightbulbs, half-dead neon, dripping pipes, wet splotchy concrete, hanging laundry. Air that was diesel, disco, and pork. Posters for karate movies, San Mig beer, baby formulas, Ricoh watches. And people everywhere. Squatting, spitting, shitting, cooking, whistling, washing. Traffic. Traffic as in business. Traffic as in people. Traffic as in traffic. Gridlock of appetites and ambitions.

"They've tried hating us," Susan Hayes said. "It wasn't any fun." She leaned forward and tapped the pane of plastic that separated driver from rider. "Excuse me."

The driver had been turning up the volume gradually, front and back: Engelbert Humperdinck singing "Please Release Me."

"Mum?"

"Could you turn it down please?"

"Yes, mum." The partition closed, the back speakers were switched off, so that the music seemed to have withdrawn to the front seat.

"What's he like? Your colonel?"

"I can't say."

"Can't say?" She laughed and turned toward Griffin, and he glimpsed a nice combination of well-turned, muscular legs and commodious thighs: rare combination. "At the embassy, when we say we can't say, it means we know but aren't permitted to talk. Is that what you mean?"

"In the morning, I walk from my hotel to his. He tries to be friendly. He makes sure I'm not hungry. There's coffee. But it's the kind of effort someone in a hospital makes to cheer up visitors."

"It sounds so . . . serious."

"To him it is."

"And to you?"

"I'm getting there." Now he swung around to face her, because what he was going to say was important to him and he wanted it to be important to her, but for a moment her face stopped him, and those green eyes. "He was a missionary's son. Was? *Is.* He doesn't have that faith. I don't know how he lost it. Maybe I'll find out. But he misses it. So—this is going to sound foolish—he comes to me . . ."

"Go ahead."

"He doesn't have religion. So he puts his trust in, well, me."
"That's a little out of your line, isn't it?"
"A *little*?"

"Tonight we have a round-table, open-house town meeting,"
Birdy Villanueva announced from a podium in a University of
the Philippines lecture hall. That was as specific as she got. The
others took it from there. A man who said he was an economist
evaluated a recent official claim that the nation's unemploy-
ment rate was a flabbergasting 4 percent. The artificially low
figure had been produced by defining employment as any paid
labor performed over a period of four months, watching a car,
say, or selling mangos. That amused the audience. So did Birdy
Villanueva's mock-breathless account of Imelda Marcos's upcoming film festival. Yes, she assured the audience, actor
George Hamilton would be coming and the nation could sleep
peacefully. Griffin was puzzled by the snickering until a fellow
panelist—a priest, at that—confided that Hamilton had fre-
quently been linked to the First Lady. Warming to his gossip,
the priest bandied other names from Van Cliburn to Mick Jag-
ger. He was tickled to have a chance to trot out old yarns. When
Griffin asked whether Marcos had been accused of any matching peccadilloes, the priest breathed deep, rolled his eyes, and
launched into a gorgeously detailed tale of trysts with an American B-movie actress in a famous cottage just off a Manila golf
course.
"They recorded him," he said.
"They what?"
"Put a tape recorder under the bed while they—you know—
rutted. You must hear it. Cries and whispers and then a snatch
of an Ilocano love song. The students used to play it on the UP
radio station. That was before martial law of course. Oh, you
must listen. It's a lulu!"
Not sure whether he was more surprised at Marcos's supposed
philandering or the priest's feverish recounting, Griffin turned
back to the main program. There was nothing funny about the
speaker now, a dark, granite-faced nun reciting a grim litany of
summary executions by army and police.

"What's a salvaging?" Griffin asked the priest.

"The army's way of salvaging a situation," the priest replied. "They shoot someone—while trying to escape, of course."

"And what's a 'lost command'?"

"Paramilitary groups—hit squads—operating on the fringe of things. Charley's Angels is one of them. Another was called the Kawasaki Boys. They rode around on motorcycles, murdering people down in Mindanao. There's a gang called 'the Fun Bunch.'"

". . . and Mr. Griffin, whom you may have read about in connection with the celebrated return of Colonel Harry Roberts Harding . . ."

Oh, my God! He was being introduced. Pipe in hand, genial, courtly Jun Villanueva was talking about him.

". . . about the role—if any—of tourism in the so-called Third World. The floor is open."

Griffin checked the room. He saw the genteel, well-dressed upper middle class whose power Marcos had usurped. Pity. And the students, skinny, earnest kids who stared at him, hard stares that stopped just short of insolence, a polite race, late in learning rudeness.

"I have a question." A nun arose, a Filipina, young, fervent.

"Yes, sister, go ahead."

"The government spent money bringing Mr. Griffin and other travel writers to the Philippines. Does Mr. Griffin believe the funds spent on his airfare and his meals and his hotels were well spent?"

"No," Griffin answered.

"No?" Jun Villanueva said. "Just no?"

"I think that says it all."

"Do you believe," the nun resumed, "that it is wise policy for such a nation to encourage tourism?"

"Probably not," Griffin answered. "Depending, I suppose, on what the money would have been spent on otherwise. On balance, I would say I'm harmless."

"Harmless?" Now the nun was challenging him. "What about the impact of tourism on local culture?"

"Local culture? Waiters? Bellhops? Taxi drivers? They get lonely . . ."

"There's more to local culture than that," the nun countered.

"All right, sister," Griffin answered. He was getting irritated. Sure, the questions were fair, the cause was probably worthy, but there was something whining and querulous about this group. He found himself missing the blaring jukeboxes, the "hey Joe" solicitations, the bar girls with names like Funny Face, Captain Marvel, Miss Sixty-niner. Who represented them? And what about the gangs of men you saw on every downtown sidewalk, clutching applications, bio-data sheets, photographs, queuing up outside labor recruiters who offered jobs for drivers in Kuwait, pipe fitters in Abu Dhabi, janitors and barbers in Riyadh?

"Forgive my flippancy," Griffin said. "But as far as a tourist is concerned, local culture is a meal they hope won't give them dysentery, some handicraft, a dance troupe, and—maybe—a few girls who aren't particular. If local culture is alive, tourism can't hurt it. If tourism hurts it, it was dying anyway. I don't worry too much about local culture. And I don't know many people who do."

"No regrets?" Jun Villanueva asked.

"I hope to redeem myself in other ways," Griffin replied, sounding pompous.

"Ah, yes!" Jun Villanueva had found his opening. "All of you know Mr. Griffin has been named to author the memoirs of MacArthur's Ghost, Colonel Harding. Not by chance, a movie is being made of these same adventures."

"Mr. Griffin!" It was one of the students, a heartbreakingly pretty Filipina who had to screw up her courage to speak. "What does Mr.—Colonel—Harding think of what has become of the country he fought for?"

"Fought *in*, not *for*," someone corrected. It was a male student, one of the hard starers. "He fought here, but not for this country. We should remember that."

"I thought it was a partnership," Griffin volunteered, more to help out the girl than anything. "An alliance."

"Then you were misinformed," the student countered.

"Is that so?"

"What Colonel Harding thinks, all his war stories . . ." The student's voice trailed off, then renewed. "There are other people here. They have memories also."

"I think he knows that," Griffin said. "It's why he came back."

"The story isn't over," the student said. "The fighting continues every day. Nothing is over."

"I think he knows that," Griffin repeated. "He's looking for the ending."

"There is no ending!"

"If there are no further questions," Jun Villanueva said, "I have one." He was sucking on his pipe, chuckling, the image of a sly, droll fellow. "Have you found Yamashita's treasure yet? At the end of the rainbow?"

"I haven't even found the rainbow," Griffin answered quietly.

17

"Birdy likes you," Susan Hayes announced later that night. They had just left the Villanuevas' postmeeting party at a seafood restaurant in Makati.

"Should I be flattered? Or rush to the airport?"

"I'd stay. She's hard to impress."

"Is it me or is it Harding?"

"Why worry? Anyway, the whole dinner revolved around you. All that historical talk."

Griffin had indicated he couldn't say much about the Harding book. It was a matter of "doctor-patient" privilege he claimed, and the other guests respected that. But the conversation was nonetheless historical. Jun Villanueva wondered aloud who were the heroes of the Philippines? Who were the men students should admire? That was when the merry-go-round began. They started with José Rizal, the physician-patriot whose monument stood near the Manila Hotel, guarded round-the-clock. "An American invention," someone sniffed, a dilettante liberal who went to his death believing Spain's feudal rule could be ameliorated. Then there was Emilio Aguinaldo, leader of the turn-of-the-century guerrilla campaign against American occupation. A feisty fighter—when he fought. But they said he'd sold out his country three times—to the Spanish; and then, after capture, to the Americans; finally to the conquering Japanese in 1941. What, then, of the commonwealth's great leader, Manuel Quezon? An upper-class oligarch. What of Roxas, Manuel Roxas, the postwar leader? A Japanese collaborator, personally retreaded by MacArthur. What of Ramon Magsaysay? A vigorous, well-meaning CIA stooge.

On and on it went, Mabini, Luna, Laurel, Aquino. Griffin
didn't know most of the names, but he was beginning to figure
out the game. In these islands, history was a series of compro-
mises and betrayals. All victories were tainted, all contests fixed,
all elections rigged. The border between heroes and villains was
permanently—deliciously—blurred. A merry-go-round. Heroes
were lowered and rogues were elevated and it was all a matter
of perspective, and why not, in a nation where people were
always changing sides? The longer you rode the merry-go-
round, the more you were accused of. And Marcos had ridden
the merry-go-round longer than anyone. The affable guerrilla
Griffin had seen on Corregidor, the choked-up old soldier, the
aging dictator—he was the uninvited guest tonight. He was
everywhere.

In the morning, the newspapers featured Marcos's photo,
greeting visitors, making speeches. He starred on television.
Harding and Griffin had spent a lazy morning watching Marcos
open a golf tournament at the Puerto Azul resort outside Manila. Wisecracking, joking with aides, he lofted golf balls out
over the course, onto the rough, into the jungle, spectacularly
errant shots, and an army of caddies raced after the balls, for
which they received a hundred pesos and a presidential handshake. Manila bristled with Marcos talk: guerrilla exploits, real
or imagined, elections true or false, trials fair or crooked. His
performances in office, in politics, in war and peace, were end-
lessly studied. His performance in bed, also, because if you
couldn't take your leadership personally, if you couldn't wonder
what—or who—the king was doing tonight, why bother? Bed?
Beds. Nuptial beds, extramarital couches, and finally, hospital
beds. Sexual speculation yielded to pathological gossip about
kidneys, heart, skin, lupus, cancer, shrapnel, allergies.

Maybe that was why Harry Roberts Harding had come back.
He could have done his memoirs anywhere, could have found
a better ghost-writer, a fatter deal. But he had come back here
and, in coming back, exposed himself to the same merry-go-
round that gilded and tarnished all the rest. No one was im-
mune, not even a hero. Especially not a hero.

"How about out at the university?" Griffin asked Susan Hayes.
"Was I okay there?"

"Sure."

"With Sister Mary Agony . . . and that fire-eating student?"

"Every year, that campus sends some students to the NPA. You attend these opposition meetings and they seem so pathetic. But people are getting killed. That's really pathetic."

"When Marcos goes, can you picture those kids marching out of the mountains?"

"There are alternatives. Jun Villanueva is one. Or some of the people in exile, like Aquino. And some of the cleaner army people. Nestor Contreras for one. American-trained."

The car stopped outside a walled compound in Pasay City. A security guard opened the gate. Security guards were at the beginning and end of every journey.

"A Chinese merchant had a big house," Susan Hayes said. "And built four identical houses for each of his children. Here's mine."

Griffin opened the door and stepped aside. "I'll walk you to the front."

"You don't have to."

"I know that." A dog was sleeping on the pavement. There were dozens of potted plants set out in tin cans. "I have a question."

"Oh." He could feel her tense. And he wondered why it was that, no matter how old you got, there was always this crunch when you walked a woman to her front door, that moment when she turned to face you under a porch light and you were back in high school.

"I was wondering," Griffin said. "The first time you saw me, with those travel writers, in the Champagne Room, I was wondering what you saw."

"Ah." She leaned against the door, then motioned him toward a wicker chair that sat out on the porch. She fished in her purse for a cigarette, lit it, sat across from him.

"I saw a potential problem. I'm trained to spot them. I saw someone who was smart. Reckless. Self-destructive. A problem."

"That bad."

"There's more. When I saw you, I said there's a man who has

read Somerset Maugham and Graham Greene and *Lord Jim.* There's a man who loves Sidney Greenstreet. There's a man who could be interested in a tropical-weight white suit and a wicker chair and a Manila cigar and an overhead fan. In short, *all that stuff."*

"Oh, my God . . ."

"A dreamer. I have a weakness for them."

"You do? How much of a weakness?"

"Dream on."

18

"Where have you been?" Harry Roberts Harding called out cheerfully. With half a dozen tourists and as many more security guards looking on, the legendary guerrilla was piling his luggage into the trunk of a yellow taxi. "I'm tired of listening to the sound of my own voice. Time we hit the road. We'll pick up your stuff on the way to the airport. We're going to Baguio first. And then . . ."

"You've got our campaign mapped out?"

"It's a guerrilla campaign," Harding said. "No itinerary. Targets of opportunity."

"I'm ready," Griffin said. Harding's energy was contagious.

"Not so fast," Harding said, speaking quietly. "There's a fellow in the lobby wants to talk to us before we go."

"A reporter?" Griffin guessed that Harding loved stirring things up, but he had hoped that phase was over. Watching reporters probe and test the colonel only reminded him of how little he knew. He wanted time alone with Harding to get ahead of the pack. But, no, the colonel told him, this wasn't another reporter. This fellow said he was from the U.S. embassy.

"I'm Phil Robinson," the man said. Thin, sandy-haired, thirtyish. Barong shirt, crisp blue slacks, loafers. Lively eyes.

"What can we do for you?" Harding asked, then adding for Griffin's benefit: "He wanted to see the two of us together."

"Yes, that's right," Robinson said. "How about some coffee and maybe a danish. I'm on strict orders to bring some back for the girls at the office."

"Well, I don't mind," Harding said. They followed Robinson out to the dining area at the edge of the swimming pool, which, like the Manila Hotel itself, was an amazing oasis of decorum and class in a city of disorder and decay. Clear blue water, spanking white lawn chairs, neatly clipped bermuda grass, two or three towel boys, cabana boys, barmen, and waiters for every Ludlum-reading tourist. Down beyond the sea wall at the edge of the hotel property was Manila Bay, a septic tide lapping in each morning's deposit of broken rubber sandals and soiled pampers.

"I won't keep you long," Phil Robinson said, offering a pack of business cards. "For openers, this is who I am and where I work and how I can be reached. Take a couple, please. It may mean nothing to you, but I'd feel better knowing you were carrying them around."

The cards showed his name, said he was in the political section of the U.S. embassy, and specified where he could be reached, day and night.

"I'd have looked you up anyway, even if I didn't have to," Robinson said. "I'm a history buff. I can't tell you the weekends I've spent over on Corregidor. I've crawled over that island by the inch. Colonel, when I heard you were coming back, it was the Dodgers moving back to Brooklyn. I can't wait to read your book."

"That's nice," Harding said.

"Now comes the hard part," Robinson continued. "This is where we advise you not to travel around the Philippines. This is all off-the-record. For now. This whole meeting's off-the-record. But the important thing is, you've been warned."

While Harding and Griffin traded glances, Robinson dipped his danish into his coffee. "Frankly, I'm glad that's over with."

"You mean that's it?" Harding asked.

"You're a ghost, Colonel," he said. "You really are. And people are scared of ghosts. It's that simple."

"I thought I was a harmless old man," Harding said.

"Like hell you did."

Harding smiled at that. He liked the sass. "Well, who's after me?"

"Who is it you're after, Colonel? Marcos? MacArthur? Contreras? The NPA? The opposition? Who? Is it the treasure? No, not the treasure. That's just bait. Who are you after, really?"

"All of 'em," Harding said. "None of 'em."

"Then they could all, or none, be after you," Robinson replied.

"Could be," Harding said. "Just tell me what you heard."

"Okay," Robinson agreed. "But what you hear depends on where you listen. You listen in other places, you might hear the same thing . . ."

"Where'd you listen?"

"We listen where we're worried. On the left. The NPA." He decided to include Griffin. "That stands for New Peoples Army."

"I heard it stands for Nice People Around," Griffin said, only wanting to show he'd been doing some homework on his own.

"That's an old joke," Robinson said, "and not a very funny one at that. The New Peoples Army is the military arm of the communist party of the Philippines. Ten or so thousand armed guerrillas, at least some of whom might be willing to deprive me of the book you fellows are working on. No joke."

"So that's what you hear?" Harding asked.

"Just a whisper. From a paid informant who's usually reliable. Usually, not always. I thought you'd want to know."

"That's nice," Harding said in exactly the same tone he'd received Robinson's enthusiasm for their book.

"It stands to reason, sort of," Robinson went on. "All the attention you've been getting. That picture of Marcos hugging you ran all over the place. And the movie. If they got you, it could embarrass the government."

"Well . . ." Harding finished his coffee, picked at the crumbs from his danish, brushed them into a pile, swept them into his hand, and deposited them in an ashtray. "I'm not surprised. You still game, Griffin?"

"Yes."

"All right."

Robinson signed the bill and accompanied them out to where their taxi waited. Harding paused before stepping inside.

"These people who whisper to you . . ."

"Yes?"

"Does it ever go two ways? You ever whisper back?"

"Yes."

"I thought you did. Whisper this. Whisper that my target— my only target—the only person I'm after out here is myself."

19

"Good-bye, Manila," Harding said as soon as they were on the plane to Baguio. "I think Elbert Hubbard Harding was right, heading for the mountains."

No argument from Griffin. Beyond them, Manila was a smudge, polluted air, littered land, poisoned sea, a triple-decker defilement. Where sky was smoke, rain was sweat, and the bay was a catch basin for all the world's infections. Now they were flying into a bowl of blue. There were rice fields and villages and a startling, solitary mountain rising out of the plains. That was Mount Arayat, Harding said.

"I never thought I'd see that mountain again," Harding reflected. "Damn. What was it Uncle Harrison said?"

"About what?"

"Come on," Harding urged. "You know, about places. When we were on that trail."

"Oh, yes," Griffin said, pleased that Harding would ask that kind of question, implying that once the story was told it was Griffin's property. "He said places don't acknowledge us. Neither do people. Unless we make them."

"Yes," said Harding, staring down at Mount Arayat. "That was it. Good line, huh?"

"Good line," Griffin answered. He studied Harding closely. Someday he might have to describe him. A tall man with narrow shoulders, tan skin, red hair, and blue eyes. Who could light a cigarette and let it burn all the way down to his fingers while he trailed a memory through the smoke. Who shuddered with pleasure at the first swallow of a San Miguel. Who stopped in mid-sentence when the memories came too quickly, immobile, like a pedestrian caught in some imaginary traffic that might carry him along or maybe flatten him, hit and run. A staring, brooding solitary man whom you thought your company might make less lonely, but it was as likely you'd catch what he had as cure it and that was a chance you were willing to take, because he was MacArthur's Ghost, who'd come back to get or set or put things right.

Suddenly the land below rose up and punched at the underside of the plane. Right below, there were wooded peaks, deep gorges, hairpin trails. The sun glinted on metal roofs and fast-moving rivers, and now they were in, and barely over, the mountains. The plane hardly had to descend to land: Baguio rose up to reach it.

"Slow down, Eddie," Harding said.

"I'm talking too fast for you, Colonel?"

"You're driving too fast."

"I got a convoy of press following me, sir."

"That's all right."

"Any particular place you want me to go?"

"Just meander," Harding said. He rolled down the window, sniffed the pine air. The well-paved road looped politely around estates, brushing hedges and fences, genuflecting at gateways and guardhouses. The older houses—the ones from the commonwealth period—displayed themselves proudly, mansions, no bones about it. The newer houses were more discreet: you could only guess what lay down those driveways.

"Goddamn," Eddie said, "I'm leading a motorcade. Where was I?"

"Cecilia Santos."

"I wish I knew what made that woman tick. I mean, what she really wants."

"Have you tried finding out?"

"I've seen some others test the waters. Macho guys. Money guys. They get nowhere. Miss Fire and Ice, they call her. Damned if I know what she does for fun."

"What's she been doing for work?"

"After the colonel spoke at the cemetery, she came up here and read the riot act to Hugh and Larry. Threatened to pull the plug on the whole project unless we started doing things her way, publicity-wise."

"What's that supposed to mean?"

"For openers, it meant I head you guys off at the airport. No arrival press conference. I take you straight to today's location and we have a press conference there, in a so-called controlled environment, the point being that the publicity we get should be to promote this movie in particular and movie making in the Philippines in general, rather than—you're going to like this—the 'promotion and self-promotion of a so-called book.' "

"Stop the car," Harding interrupted. Griffin doubted the colonel had heard a word of what Eddie was saying. He'd been looking out the window, watching Baguio pass by. Now he was staring up at a white three-story place that sat on a hilly lawn. He got out, slammed the door, and made his way across the lawn. Behind, on the road, the motorcade came to a puzzled halt. Doors slammed, people started getting out, talking to each other, like drivers stalled in freeway traffic, wondering what the holdup was. A couple of photographers followed Harding up toward the house.

"Author, author!" someone shouted. Clifford Lerner stuck his head through the window.

"Hello, Clifford," George said. "I thought you'd left town."

"And miss the greatest story since—since what, George?—the comet Kohoutek? The Ali-Inoki fight? Evel Knievel's Snake River jump? Why are we stopping here, George? Is this where Yamashita's treasure is buried? Should I follow him up there or wait down here? I loathe a parade . . ."

At the steps of the house, Harding chatted briefly with a servant, a liveried butler. Then he turned around and came back across the lawn, ignoring the photographers who scurried in front.

"Bit of an anticlimax, seems to me," Lerner said. "What was he doing, anyway? Asking directions?"

Harding crossed the road and came face to face with Clifford Lerner.

"Pardon me, sir," Lerner asked. "This treasure of yours. Is it animal, vegetable, or mineral?"

"Excuse me," Harding said, reaching for the car door, but Lerner gave ground slowly.

"Can it be found in your average kitchen? Living room? Bedroom?"

Griffin opened the door from inside and Harding got in.

"Is it bigger than a breadbox?" persisted Lerner, now putting on a show for some of the other press. Eddie Richter started the car, but Lerner shouted after them.

"And if I had it, sir, this Yamashita treasure, would I know what to do with it?"

They passed the Hyatt Hotel, a five-star high-rise planted among the pines, and they passed Camp John Hay, with WELCOME: MACARTHUR'S GHOST on a banner across the road.

"That was Uncle Harrison's house back there," Harding said. "It was the first place I recognized. I wanted to see who lived there now."

"Hey, Colonel, I could have saved you the walk," Eddie Richter said. "Place belongs to Larry Wingfield. His summer place."

"See?" Harding said to Griffin. "The old man had it right."

"Is Larry his son?"

"Nephew."

"No sons of his own?"

"No. I'm the closest he got to that."

20

It wasn't until they walked down to the location that Griffin realized the scene being filmed was the airport skirmish that Harding had described: "the last cavalry charge in the history of warfare." The press people were led to a roped-off area under a candy-striped tent, where bar and buffet awaited them. Griffin nodded to Cecilia Santos, who ignored him. Lerner came up to him, a plate full of lumpia in one hand, a whole pitcher of gin and tonics in the other.

"No popcorn," he said. "Tell me, Colonel, is this what it was like?"

"That was a war," Harding replied, his face set and grim. "This is a movie."

It was certainly that. The bitter melee Harding had recounted, the poignant beauty of the mountains defiled by a spasm of irrational violence that both sickened and exhilarated, was being transformed into a macho spectacle. Off to one side were the guerrillas, several dozen of them, Americans and Filipinos, including a few seductive partisans whom war had caught half dressed, barmaids come to battle, along with a kindly priest, a fiery Filipino nationalist, a genteel planter, and his Bible-reading wife. And the Japanese! They were all over the airstrip, spread out and dug in, foxholes, sandbags, gun emplacements and—no, it couldn't be!—a couple of planes painted to look like Zero fighters.

"Yes," Lerner said, "a movie it is. I love movies. What they lose in fidelity, they make up for in infidelity."

"Clifford, could you come over here a moment?" Griffin said. Harding was obviously crestfallen and Griffin wanted to save him Lerner's tiresome irony.

117

"Yes, George?"

"I don't get it, Clifford."

"What's that, my boy?"

"What are you working on? Who are you working for? What's up with you?"

"Do you think you're the only writer who ever had it up to here with pufferoos? That you alone are entitled to the dark night of the soul, the career crisis, the quo vadis? I'm joining you, George."

"Are you after the colonel?"

"The so-called colonel, George. Never take anything on face value. Lesson one. He got an honorary commission *after* the war. And it came from the Philippine army, not the U.S. And George?"

"Yes?"

"You could look it up. It's called reporting. My idea of a good time used to be an afternoon in some courthouse annex basement. Birth certificates, court transcripts, real estate deeds, licenses. People didn't like what I found. I got the message. I took up the travel beat. Nothing safer than writing up some frigging beach. But I can still report."

"You're staying on this?"

"Yes. And it's all your fault, my friend. When you look at me, Griffin, I see contempt on your face. Or is it pity?"

"Neither one," Griffin answered. He wondered whether to continue this. He decided he would, expecting to regret it. "It's fear. I'm afraid I'll turn out like you."

"Am I all that bad?"

"It's not how bad you are. It's how good you could have been."

Lerner nodded, as if he liked what he was hearing. "I'll show you how good I could have been," he said.

"You mean to follow us?"

"Good Lord no, I'm a reporter. Not a stenographer."

An explosion, a fusillade of shots, some screams: the cavalry charge had begun, a master shot that must have lasted a full minute, horsemen bounding out of the jungle, overwhelming sentries, dashing down the airstrip, leaping foxholes, racing toward the Zeros. Great stuff. As soon as cameras stopped, photographers had a photo opportunity before cast and crew broke for lunch. Then came Cecilia Santos's press conference.

A long table, white table cloth, a bank of microphones: it looked like the setting for a ritual. On the other side, rows of folding chairs, pretty aides with portable microphones, and a glossy press kit on every seat. And now the parish: hacks, stringers, fan-magazine writers. And the performers: Wingfield, Beaumont, and Pineda, the producers. Next, the director, Ernest Baum, a lively, prematurely balding chap who wore an L.A. Dodgers baseball hat.

"I missed his last film," Lerner said, riffling through the press kit. "Did you see it?"

"What was it called?"

"Amazing Mindanao."

"Who was in it?"

"Philippine Airlines."

Next to Baum sat Tom Selleck, still covered with dust and sweat from the carnage on the airstrip. To Selleck's left sat José Valerio, minister of culture, a white-suited smoothie who reminded Griffin of Ricardo Montalban on "Fantasy Island." There were two kinds of Filipinos: the vast majority who weren't going anywhere, and knew it, and the tiny minority for whom these islands were a launching pad. And next to José Valerio were the biggest surprises of all. Four old-timers, Harding and three others, four likeable old warriors, chockablock with yarns.

"We think it is appropriate that this film is an American-Filipino coproduction," Minister of Culture Valerio began, "which goes back to a time when our partnership was solemnly tested in the dark days following Corregidor and Bataan—"

"Tested and survived," Larry Wingfield interjected. "There's a lesson here. An important lesson about friendship and respect and love of country. Of more than one country, actually."

Then, like a baton in a relay race, the audience microphone was passed from one enthusiastic reporter to the other. Pattycake questions, until the microphone landed in the fist of a young Filipino who reminded Griffin of the radical student at the University of the Philippines. This could be his older brother, who had lost the angry substance but retained the adversarial style.

"There have been many sensational reports about this movie," he said, "and the story behind it. We have heard mysterious reports of secrets, mysteries, treasures. Is this your movie's theme?"

José Valerio said that he was glad that question had come up. Hugh Beaumont was glad too. So was Larry Wingfield. And Ernest Baum, the director, was happiest of all. There was a difference between a feature film and a documentary, he said, between fact and fiction, art and life.

"I thought it was Colonel Harding's story," the wised-up radical persisted.

"I'll speak to that," Hugh Beaumont said. "We're all proud and pleased to have obtained Colonel Harding's permission to tell elements of his story, and we were additionally delighted he agreed to come back and visit. But this is not the story of any one man. It's a composite adventure that draws on the experiences of many men, living and dead."

"It's a montage," Baum said. "A mosaic. There are so many stories. If we can only capture the spirit of that heroic time. Not the details of all campaigns, not even the details on any one campaign—but the essence!"

"Colonel Harding is one of a number of guerrilla leaders who are consultants to this project," Wingfield said. "I'd like to introduce them. Down at the end of the table is Colonel Harding himself."

Harding stared out at the meeting. "Hello," he said.

"Not so fast," someone interrupted, and Griffin's heart sank when he saw that it was Clifford Lerner. Not the genial, burnt-out hack, but a different Lerner, a tabloid bully, snide and sardonic. "These other men are fine and I can hardly wait to hear how the war turned out . . ."

The other reporters laughed and nodded at each other. A country with a neutered, self-censoring press nonetheless appreciated the adversarial style.

"I have a report I'd like Colonel Harding to confirm or deny," Lerner said. "Won't take a minute."

"What's that?" asked Harding.

"A report that your life has been threatened by the NPA. Any comment?"

"No."

"What I want to know is . . . is this a bona fide threat or is it something that you, sir, or your associates, have concocted to obtain publicity for your film? Or your book. Or yourself."

"I concocted nothing," Harding said.

"Is this nothing?" Lerner asked. He held up the front of a newspaper, a half-Tagalog, half-English ax-murder sheet with a banner headline: NPA PLANS BIG MAC ATTACK. He turned to show the headline left and right. He was more like a prosecutor than a journalist.

"What do you call this, Colonel? I call it free publicity."

"If we could move along . . ." Cecilia Santos pleaded.

"I *am* moving along," Lerner said. "I'm almost done." Now he gave Harding a look of sympathetic understanding. "An old man comes back, full of stories. Some he forgets. Some he remembers. Some he makes up, some he changes. No?"

Harding didn't deign to answer. He sat motionless, eyes forward.

"It was so long ago, after all, and who'll contradict you now? Forty years. With not much to show for them. Your postwar record. Your employment. Your income. On the spotty side . . ."

"That'll do," Larry Wingfield said. "We've got a press conference to hold. Not an inquest. Next to Colonel Harding is Captain David Freitag. Captain Freitag commanded a PT boat in Mindanao. After Corregidor, he went ashore, which is where he stayed till 1944. On Captain Freitag's left is Colonel Wilfredo Pintor. When the war broke out, Colonel Pintor was right here in Baguio, on the staff of the Philippines Military Academy. The academy had closed its doors and sent home its students a few months before. Well, Colonel Pintor made his way back to his home island of Panay—that trip is a movie in itself, believe me —contacted his former students, and led a postgraduate course in guerrilla warfare you wouldn't believe. Our fourth consultant we flew all the way from Connecticut, which shows what we think of him—Sergeant Jay Devlin, a defender of Corregidor and an escapee from the Bataan Death March . . ."

There was a round of applause when Beaumont stopped. Cecilia Santos then suggested that, while Colonel Harding had already been heard from and, indeed, had a "supposed" book in progress, the "less-publicized" veterans might share some of their experiences with the press. David Freitag, a dignified, bankerlike man, clearly accustomed to command, went on for an hour. Wilfredo Pintor was good for a second hour, a garrulous little popinjay. Then it was Jay Devlin's turn. Three hours of war stories, and, it was fair to add, war stories that were pretty well told. There were jokes, wisecracks, embarrassments. There was loss and pain. There were tears, and silences that indicated some stories never got told.

And no one gave a damn. You could watch it happen, little by little. That was the worst of it. Freitag described the beheading of an American prisoner, something he witnessed from hiding, trapped and powerless to prevent, and someone came for the director, who shrugged apologetically and slipped away. Pintor was recounting a moonlight rendezvous with a submarine off Leyte and someone tapped Tom Selleck on the shoulder. Off he went, trailing photographers. He was a movie star, the veterans were talking heads, old ones at that.

Jay Devlin was the worst-treated. He described the Bataan Death March—thirst, dysentery, shootings, beatings—and José Valerio glanced at his watch, displayed astonishment at how time passed, and interrupted Devlin to apologize. His services were in demand elsewhere in the republic, he told them, and that was when Griffin looked at Devlin, flushed, trembling, fighting tears, halfway through a story he'd never even told his wife, bayoneted comrades, an officer run over, and over, by a column of trucks, and José Valerio was saying that the bar would be open as long as anybody was thirsty and how he wished he could stay, and now only a dozen reporters were left, most of them wilted by humidity, logey with beer and lumpia, and it broke your heart, and Griffin found himself looking at Cecilia Santos, standing coolly at the back of the tent: her moment of victory. End this now, he pleaded silently, enough is enough. And to his surprise, she saw his look, nodded graciously, and headed toward the microphone.

"Wait a damn minute everybody!" It was a voice out of a cattle auction, a twanging, nasal voice that Cecilia Santos hardly

recognized as human. It ignored microphones, protocol, and her.

"Who are you, sir? And who do you represent?"

"My name's Bill Roach." The room was awake now, the booming voice even brought back some of the strays. Amazing. Now the director and star poked their heads in to see what all the fuss was about. It was about a tall, gangly, country-looking fellow with a narrow head, bulging eyes, a chin that disappeared and an Adam's apple that made up for the chin's absence. All this, a string tie and a beaded belt.

"And sir . . . who are you with?" said Santos.

"The *Daily Planet*, sweetheart. I've got a couple questions for Colonel Harding."

"I was about to close . . ." She was blushing, or flushing, and Griffin saw why. The stranger came forward and his T-shirt came into view: AS LONG AS I'VE GOT A FACE, HONEY, YOU'VE GOT A SEAT.

"This won't take a minute, darling. Colonel Harding, how you doin' sir?"

"Fine, thanks," Harding responded, much revived. "What can I do for you?"

"I want to talk about Yamashita's treasure, sir."

"The movie?"

"No, sir, the real thing. I hear you mentioned it the other day. I also hear you've saving the whole story for your book. But I drove five hours from Angeles City hoping you could tell me a little something."

"That's a long drive," Harding said. "I know."

"You've driven it?"

"And walked it too. And, sure, it was forty years ago. But it was as long then as it is now."

"Hey, Colonel, this may be out of line or something, but I just want to say I'm glad to see you. I really care about back then. And it plain tickles me, knowing that you've come back here."

"Ask anything you want. I'll try to oblige."

"Colonel, in the first place, was there really a treasure?"

"Yes."

"You saw it?"

"Yes." Harding snapped off his answers like a parade ground recruit, head forward, eyes shining.

"Gold? Art? Jewels? What was it?"

"I can't tell you that. Not now."

"Was it from Bangkok or Rangoon? Singapore? Malaya?"

"It was from here," Harding said. "It was home-grown."

"You fixing to get it?"

"I hadn't decided. The thing of it is . . ." Harding paused and Griffin couldn't decide whether he was honestly faltering or deliberately building tension. His voice was at the level of a whisper, which everyone, movie people, reporters, and all, leaned forward to catch. "This treasure hasn't been good for people. It hasn't made anyone rich or happy. It hasn't brought long life. On the contrary."

"Christ!" Bill Roach spun around, almost dancing, he was that excited. "I'm getting hard just thinking about this! You mean it's one of them jinx treasures, like the Hope Diamond or the Moonstone! The owner dies. It's a regular—what was that broad's name?—Pandora's box."

"You said it," Harding answered. "Pandora's box."

"This has gone a little far off course," Cecilia Santos said.

"Thanks a lot," Bill Roach shouted. "It was a real pleasure talking to you, sir, and I hope whatever it is you're looking for, you find it, and if you need any help digging it up, or spending it up, you can count on this boy."

"You're welcome," Harding said.

"Now," Cecilia Santos announced. "Out on the airstrip . . ."

Out on the airstrip, they were working on a scene that required a Japanese jeep and an American on horseback to charge each other at full speed and then, at the point of collision, the American horseman would jump in the air, leap over the jeep, toss a hand grenade into the driver's seat, then land safely on the other side. It was a great stunt and Cecilia Santos assured everybody that they wouldn't want to miss it. But it was too late. Harry Roberts Harding had the place buzzing with talk of Yamashita's treasure. He'd walked into a trap at the press conference. The trap was normality, repetition, boredom. And— with a crucial assist from Bill Roach—Harding had turned defeat into victory. Harding walked off, magic and mystery intact, while Cecilia Santos touted a horse-and-jeep act.

"I roughed him up." Clifford Lerner came over to Griffin. His sardonic press conference style was gone. He seemed chagrined. "I want to say I'm sorry. Will you tell him? I didn't realize this whole thing was a setup. It was clever of them, bringing in some other war heroes. As if they were saying there are *lots* of heroes, sung and unsung. If I'd realized what they were up to, I'd have saved my questions for another day. I'm sorry. Will you tell him?"

"Sure."

"I play by the rules. I didn't know the game was rigged."

"So what?" Griffin asked. "It was rigged. But in the end, he won it anyway. Didn't he?"

"I believe you're right," Lerner said, brightening. "He won it after all. He certainly did."

Part Four

★ ★ ★
★ ★

TO BATAAN

21

At night, after listening to the radio reports of fighting on Bataan, Charley Camper and Harry Roberts Harding started an
argument that was to last for forty years. It wasn't an argument,
really. It was just that they wondered, sometimes aloud, about
the same thing. They never solved it, and they carried their
wonderment throughout their lives, so that Charley Camper
would be feeding chickens in his farm overlooking the naval
base at Subic Bay, watching the fleet come in, and the whores
come down to meet the fleet, the whole thing a parody of attack
and counterattack, and he couldn't help musing what would
happen if this were, say, San Diego and those ships were foreign. What about those California girls? Would they be putting
their little bodies on the block?

And, half a world away, washed up on a Florida coast, Harry
Roberts Harding would find himself visualizing the conquest of
America. He tried guessing which current leader would take to
the hills, how long they'd last. He couldn't see a political campaign—Dole, Mondale, Kennedy, Tip O'Neill—and not wonder
about them. On his bad nights, he pictured all of them, the
generals, the candidates, the newscasters, all of them on trial,
war crimes trials, like General Yamashita's or the one at Nuremberg. He couldn't help himself. Would Alexander Haig mount
the gallows as stoically as Yamashita? Would he feign madness,
like Hess? How would Westmoreland conduct himself? Who
would bow, who would shrug, who would grovel? Would anybody find religion? Which of our Republicans would be a Goering, laughing and baiting, knowing he had a cyanide capsule
tucked away in his cell? Morbid thoughts for a Florida motel
keeper.

* * *

After the airport skirmish, Harding had led them to a place his father had marked, a rocky outcrop near the top of a wooded ridge west of Baguio. They could probably have sat out the war there. The place was inaccessible from below and reachable only by a narrow trail from above. The Mesa Verde cliff dwellings were a pushover, compared to this. They had good shelter, ample canned food. They had water, medicine, ammunition. They had a panoramic view of Baguio, the lost city. And that, finally, was what brought them down.

It started with what they called reconnaissance. They made records of convoys coming up Kennon Road from Manila. They noted plane landings and departures. They tallied armored columns pointing up into the mountain provinces. They crept near town at night, spying on Camp John Hay, purchasing beans and cauliflower, corn and strawberries from outlying farms. They took swims in the therapeutic waters at Asin Hot Springs. They weren't looking for trouble, they told themselves. But every trip brought them closer to it.

One night, Corregidor radio claimed that the Filipino and American forces had battled the Japanese to a virtual stalemate on Bataan, holding a line halfway down the peninsula, while the exhausted Japanese fell back to regroup. This made the isolation of the cave all the more disturbing. So did reports that a mile-long convoy was on its way from Hawaii, hundreds of planes, thousands of men. But it was an English-language broadcast from Baguio that really inflamed them. Singapore had fallen, the Japanese announced. The last bastion of imperialism was gone: 130,000 troops surrendered. To celebrate, there was to be a victory parade through the streets of Baguio the following day and the entire population was invited.

"You heard what they said," Meade remarked. "Y'all come."

"I like that," Sudul said.

"Like what?" asked Camper. It was too bad about Charley. He was the ideal sergeant, career army through and through, but he wasn't cut out for command. He missed the comforting presence of his superiors, of orders from above. He had no ideas of his own, no strategy, so he had fallen into this trap of letting the men propose expeditions, one more dangerous than the other.

"I like the idea of crashing the Japanese victory parade," Sudul said.

"That's dumb," Camper retorted.

"Was there something else you had planned for tomorrow?" Meade challenged him.

"You're pushing it," said Camper.

"I aim to push it," Meade replied, meeting him head on, a cocky country boy who spent most of his time figuring just how much he could get away with.

"Polshanski," Camper pleaded. "What do you think?"

"I think it's got to be," Polshanski said.

Harding was startled. He counted on Polshanski to know more than the others. Harding studied him closely: that thin immigrant face. Those luminous eyes that didn't miss a thing. Polshanski was the man who knew things. He knew what had to be.

They climbed into the cathedral bell tower and waited for the parade to begin. At dawn, the city was heartbreakingly like the place they remembered, the streets they'd come home on after all-night debauches, with only a few bombed out buildings to show that war had come. First light and roosters crowing from a hundred backyards, dogs sneaking around corners, thin plumes of smoke from cooking fires and women carrying laundry and firewood while it was still cool. Around the middle of the morning, they saw their first Japanese, an officer in a jeep, soon followed by a dozen soldiers and then several Filipinos. Together they decked the street with bunting, with Japanese flags, and with a banner that said FALL, SINGAPORE, FALL. But the street stayed quiet, almost deserted, and now it had the melancholy feeling of a failed carnival, a party that wasn't quite coming off.

Noon was the announced time for the parade, but the only spectators were some Japanese soldiers and a handful of Filipino police. A Japanese officer paced the speaker's dais, shouting at aides. At last, a car appeared and some Filipinos in civilian

clothes tumbled out. The officer stood on the platform, behind
a bank of microphones, haranguing the hapless Filipinos, an
oration aimed at an audience of two. When he finished, the
Filipinos went off, each of them in a jeep with a squad of Japanese, each carrying a megaphone. You could hear them moving
through the city. And now the Filipinos came, emptying out of
barrios, out of the marketplace, out of nipa shacks at the edge
of the countryside, till they lined Session Road by the thousands.
The Japanese officer had his audience now, yet his anger flared.
A look at the Filipinos told you why: their pathetic, hangdog
manners, their shuffling passivity, their draggedy obedience.
When they stood, they slouched, when they sat, they squatted.
Anyone who had ever served in an army, or gone to summer
camp or public school, could see what the Japanese saw, an
ordered-around group of people, just going through the motions, without enthusiasm or conviction.

"Pretty sad crowd out there," Charley Camper said.

"They should have stayed home," Meade said.

"They'd've been shot," Harding told him. "That's what the
announcement was."

"I'd've run for the hills then!" Meade said.

"Not everybody has that luxury," Polshanski said.

"You call it a luxury?"

"Afraid I do," Polshanski said. He glanced over at Harding, as
though he didn't quite have the heart to pass on some bad news
directly. "Afraid I do."

The parade began with a Japanese officer atop a horse that
Camper remembered from the polo stables. Next came a group
of Japanese soldiers, high-stepping it, and a military band that
entered to a snappy march, then paused in front of the speakers
platform and shifted into something semiclassical. The Filipino
cops circulated through the crowd with miniature Japanese
flags, pressing them on spectators. The whole occasion was so
forced, so awkward and uncomfortable, that before long Harding felt sorry for everybody, the prevailed-upon Filipinos, the
harassed Japanese, for everybody who ever attempted to fulfill
a plan, or keep a schedule, or meet a quota in the heat. But his
compassion ended when he saw what was left of the parade:
prisoners, hundreds of foreign internees, Americans and Euro-
peans, businessmen, commonwealth officials, doctors, priests,

nuns, retirees, infants, and invalids—a scared, bedraggled procession stumbling up Session Road while Japanese and Filipino cops exhorted the crowd to cheer, wave their flags, and shout, "Fall, Singapore, fall."

"Jesus Christ," Sudul said.

"What's this?" Camper wondered.

"It's a victory parade," remarked Polshanski. "With winners and losers."

"That's what you say," Meade responded.

"I never said I liked it," Polshanski said. "It's what it is, is all."

As the marchers came closer, Harding recognized some of them. A dentist who had drilled and filled his teeth. An umpire from softball games at Burnham Park. A Lutheran missionary and his pregnant wife. A schoolteacher who tutored him in plane geometry. Figures and faces from Easter egg hunts and Christmas parties, from dinner dances at the Pines Hotel, from Uncle Harrison's front porch.

You could feel the shock go through the crowd. No one was spared. It touched the marchers first, the humiliated ones. They weren't all good people. Some of them were clubby bores with nasty theories about how Filipinos could never stand independence; some were petulant, fussy women who complained about their servants. There were people who'd stayed too long, and some who should never have come at all. But this medieval ceremony absolved them: now they joined the ranks of victims. They'd never been closer to Filipinos, who were themselves shocked at the sight of a world turned upside down. Here again, you could watch it happen. The Japanese flags motionless in their hands. The chant of "Fall, Singapore, fall" melting away to nothing as one Filipino, then another, rushed out to offer water, fruit, bread. The guards stopped them, scolded them, cuffed them, and finally tossed some of the Filipinos among the prisoners, so that screams and crying broke out all along the route of march.

The Japanese were the most shocked of all that afternoon. It was hard to know what they had hoped for. Enthusiasm? Obedience? Respect? But the whole thing had gone terribly wrong, with one miscalculation piled on another, a victory parade turned into a barbaric spectacle. While Japanese officers shouted commands and the Filipino officials echoed them, the musicians discarded instruments and joined cops and soldiers in their struggle to separate the milling, weeping crowd from the marchers. After twenty minutes of shouts and shoves, shots fired into air, the Japanese cordoned off the prisoners. On a command from the platform, they were marched down an alley that turned off the main street, toward the very hill, and the same church, in which the Americans were hiding.

"Christ," said Charley Camper. "They're coming. They're coming this way."

"What for?" Polshanski wondered.

"What do they want with a church?" asked Meade.

Harding looked down at the procession that wound its way toward them. In front, a dozen men, Filipinos and Americans, prodded by bayonets. Behind them came the other internees, then hundreds who had watched the parade, all of them wailing and crying so that the whole thing was an echo of the countless religious processions that came this way on Catholic holy days, gold-plated madonnas, flowers, icons, priests, and choirboys.

"They don't want the church," said Harding. "They're going to the cemetery."

"The cemetery!"

"You heard me. They want to use the cemetery."

The Japanese and the prisoners they'd selected headed for a grassy patch right where the headstones began. Some of the soldiers guarded the prisoners. They weren't going anywhere. Many more soldiers faced out at the hundreds who filed in behind them. They fanned out all through the graveyard, filling gravel paths and flowered plots. Some sat on tombstones, some hunkered down on mausoleum roofs, and they kept coming. Soon they were sitting on the rock wall that ran around the cemetery while others, stragglers, packed the courtyard right below the church.

A couple of Japanese soldiers forced their way to the center of the crowd. They gave each of the dozen men a shovel or a spade. They began to dig.

"There's nothing we can do about this," Harding said to the others, especially to Meade. "You use your Springfield, there'll be ten times as many dead. There's nothing we can do about this today."

"Today?" Meade questioned. "Those people'll be dead tomorrow."

"I know. But *we* won't be dead."

"You got plans?"

"Yes."

"Promise?"

"Promise."

Digging one's own grave. A common enough expression, a useful metaphor, but only rarely is the deed itself performed. Do you take your time, knowing that each spadeful is a fraction of your remaining life, the equivalent of a month, a year, out of the span you'd hoped for? Do you work quickly, wanting the job to be over with? Do you dig a shallow, sloppy trench or make a proper excavation? Hard questions, and no time to decide. Some of the condemned men went at it furiously, like dogs rooting for buried bones, dirt flying over their shoulders, last one in is a rotten egg. Then they sat, tossing aside their shovels and waiting, like gravediggers, for the funeral to arrive. One of the Filipinos who finished fast saw that an American, a balding, elderly man, was faltering. He changed places with him and commenced to dig a second grave. It was an hour before everyone was done. A Japanese soldier moved in back of the group, arranging the Filipinos on one side of a semicircle, the Americans on the other. Some men sank willingly, even thankfully, to their knees. Others had to be forced down. In the crowd, people were saying the Lord's Prayer, in English, Tagalog, Spanish, some prayers starting while others were finishing, a broken chorus that the Americans in the bell tower picked up as a Japanese officer stepped behind the first Filipino, unholstered a pistol, and shot him in back of the head, an act he repeated five times, casual as a kid tapping a stick against the pickets of a fence. A soldier followed, pushing the spraddled leg, the extended hand, into the grave. That left the Americans still waiting to be shot. When that didn't happen, when the executioner stepped back and walked off, one of the Americans looked at the other, who shrugged, and a third, the bald one, turned around to see what was happening, what the holdup was, just in time to see the approach of a burly, oversize Japanese noncom with a long sword . . .

22

Three weeks later, Harding kept the promise he'd made in the bell tower. During that time, he had assumed command of MacArthur's Ghosts. It was nothing that was said or done, nothing acknowledged, but from the moment he'd promised he had a plan, he was in command. He kept the others at the hideout while he went into Baguio alone. He didn't confide. That was part of being a leader: setting himself off from the others. Biding his time.

"Tonight's the night," he said.

"You mean . . ."

"We get even tonight," Harding said. "Maybe we get ahead."

"I'm game," said Meade. "We've been waiting long enough."

He hefted his crotch as he spoke: as though Harding had offered him a woman. Maybe, for people like Meade, there was a connection between the act of killing and the act of love, all his energy converging on a weapon, pointing at a target, a duality that came out in the double meaning of the four-letter word Harding still couldn't bring himself to say.

The Pines Hotel was the grandest place in the islands, a sprawling white hotel that might have sat among the Rockies or the Adirondacks. It was a place for rich people and it was no accident that the place survived the Japanese bombing. Anyone who ruled the islands would come to esteem such gardens and golf courses, wrap-around porches with rockers and easy chairs, endless carpeted corridors and rooms with views.

The Americans waited in a grove of acacia at the edge of the golf course, just beyond a sand trap. They watched cars and jeeps pull up the curving driveway, deposit guests at the foyer. Sometimes people laughed as they took the driveway speed bumps a little too fast. Then the headlights jumped up and down over the trees in which MacArthur's Ghosts were hiding.

"Where's the loyalty?" Meade asked. "I don't understand those people."

"You expect the whole country to go into mourning because you got your butt kicked?" Polshanski asked.

"Those people, the Filipinos, what do they believe in? Do they believe in anything?"

"They believe in living."

"Well, I've got news. Those people are traitors. And the penalty for treason is death. Am I right?"

"Oh, shit," Polshanski sighed. "I give up."

"Am I right?"

"Like the clock that's broken, you're right."

"What's that mean?"

"Twice a day."

"That's good enough for me," Meade said.

Now even the fashionably late had arrived. The dance floor was crowded, and those who declined to dance emptied tray after tray of drinks. Along the serving table, a couple of roast pigs had been ravaged. Some of the chafing dishes were empty, with covering lids turned upside down.

"All right," Harding said. Meade and Camper trotted quietly toward the front of the hotel, the curving driveway, domain of doormen and chauffeurs, aides and orderlies, more people outside than in. That was something you noticed in the islands. Whenever someone was working or playing hard, he was bound to draw a crowd.

"Spread out," Harding said. Polshanski moved ten yards to one side, Sudul ten yards to the other. They rode across the grass, toward the back of the patio. The music reached out and invited them in. And the smell of food. Now they were a hundred yards away and still no one had seen them. Two dozen couples on the dance floor turning to music, twenty-four faces revolving before them, forty-eight eyes, yet none noticed three spectral figures, men on horseback, moving forward, raising their rifles.

"Ready?" Harding asked. Harding found a Japanese officer at the edge of the dance floor, cocktail in hand, aide or translator at his side, chatting convivially with a white-suited Filipino. The three men fired at once, and kept firing. Harding's officer spun around and toppled across a hedge at the side of the patio. The band dove for cover, dancers lay on the floor, hiding under tables. And now they could hear the commotion from out front, where Meade and Camper greeted the Japanese who rushed out to the parking lot. Then they heard a scream, not of pain, but of sheer exultation, and they knew it was Meade.

"Let's go around front," Harding said. At the entrance, Japanese sprawled in the foyer, lay across the front steps. Meade and Camper were still firing, but the Japanese reacted quickly, returning fire, so that the Americans had to pull back into the pines.

"That's it!" Harding shouted. Camper was ready enough to go, but Meade acted as if he hadn't heard.

"Meade! Come on!"

Some of the Japanese had gotten into jeeps and cars. Engines started, headlights switched on. They were coming toward them across the parking lot.

"Come on!"

"MacArthur's Ghosts!" Like a cowboy actor, Meade reared up on his horse, came down, and spurred the beast across the parking lot. He galloped to the side of the hotel, raked the verandah, shattering windows and chandeliers. He blew a drum off the bandstand, riddled some chafing dishes. Coming back, he rode down a Japanese who had wandered, dazed and wounded, out onto the grass. "MacArthur's Ghosts!"

That night, they knew what it was like to be hunted. By the time they got back to the ridge, the country behind them, every road and path, had lights moving on it, jeeps, trucks, flashlights, lanterns. And what surprised them, even Harding, was how good it felt. They were burning lights, they were staying up late in Baguio, they were breaking out weapons and organizing patrols, posting guards and poring over maps, all because of what MacArthur's Ghosts had done.

"We can't stay here," Harding said. "They're coming into the mountains. They'll follow us here."

"Where do we go?" asked Sudul.

"We'll have to leave the horses, take what we can carry . . ."

"Leave the horses?" There was real grievance in Meade's voice. He could have buried any one of them with less emotion.

"They can't help us where we're going," Harding said. "They'll leave a trail. They'll slow us down. They'll die."

"Where the hell are you taking us? I'm not so sure I like the sound of it."

"Farther up into the mountains. All the way across, almost, and then up north, to the Kalingas . . ."

"The what?"

"A tribe of mountain people my father used to visit. They'll let us stay as long as we want. It's safe there. If anybody's coming, they know it hours ahead . . ."

"To hell with that," Meade said.

"What's wrong?"

"I don't like the sound of it."

"You don't?"

"No."

"Then stay."

"What?"

"Simple. Stay. Keep the horses. Keep them all. I'm going. Ten minutes from now, I'm gone."

Harding had known there'd be a confrontation with Meade, sooner or later. Now that it had come, he was surprised at how well he'd managed. He went to the back of the cave, picking among the boxes they had stored against the wall, ammunition, first-aid kits, canned goods. Then he waited outside to give them time—not much time—to talk it over. Down below, a pool of light dispersed into the pine forest: every now and then you could see a glint among the trees. The hunt was on. This was what the others had wanted. Now it was up to them. He could be alone or he could be part of them. *I, we,* or *they:* it was up to them.

"Harry?" It was Polshanski, alone, the sad-eyed and knowing Polshanski.

"So?"

"It's this way. If these mountains of yours were an island and we got shipwrecked here, we'd say fine. Here we stay. We'll make out. Sooner or later, someone'll pick us up. Understand?"

"Sure."

"But this is different. Because there's thousands of men fighting a war down south. And the ground we're standing on is connected to the ground that they're standing on down there. The same island, see. And we want to stand—or fall—with them. Meade, in there? He's crying. He says he doesn't want to die in the woods like an animal. He doesn't want to crawl in a hole someplace. No one knowing whether he lived, where he died. The fact is, most of us feel that way. What we want to do is try and see if we can get through to where the others are . . ."

"You want to go—"

"Hold it. There's more. We want you to take us. Everybody agrees on that."

"You want me to take you—"

"To Bataan."

23

It was the noblest of enterprises and the most foolish. An epic
campaign or a dumb little foray, a long march or a wild goose
chase. It was a handful of men playing a joke on history and
history going them one better. They risked everything for nothing. They rushed to the scene of America's greatest defeat.

That, said Harding, was the short version and maybe the best.
But along the way there were things to remember, small things
along the road to nowhere in the wrong direction, but you
didn't forget them. How he had led them farther into the mountains, brushing Japanese patrols and Filipino police who were
working with the Japanese. How they'd thrown themselves
down at the edge of a trail and stared at the boots of the men
who hunted them. Or awakened in the night and seen lights
moving toward them, realizing that the enemy had been moving while they'd been resting. Or cowered inside a worked-out
mine shaft among rotten wood, mud and puddles, feeling they'd
already been buried a long time, that the sides of a coffin had
fallen away and the earth itself had swallowed them. The mine
—Baguio Number Seven—was choked with lumber, rusted
roofing, all left behind to deflect interest in the treasure Uncle
Harrison had stashed inside: boxes, crates, suitcases, dishes, and
furniture that waited forlornly for their owners to return.

"What'd you bring us back here for?" asked Sudul. He felt
uncomfortable in the storage cave: it was like desecrating a
grave. Chairs and sofas covered with sheets, dead people's
clothing hanging from pipes, toys and china and God knows
what along the wall.

"You walked right past it," Harding said. In a secondary tun-

141

nel off the main shaft, a dark bulky shape lay draped in canvas. "Come on. I need some help."

"That's someone's car in there," Meade said. "That car belongs to—"

"Harrison Wingfield. We're taking it to Bataan. We'll start at night. And every hour we make, every mile is a mile we don't have to walk. Or run. If we get one hour that's forty miles. Two days of walking. Two days we might get killed."

"The Japanese . . ."

"The Japanese are looking for us already. On trails. Around mills, mines, logging camps. But not on the south highway."

"I think I like it," Meade said. "I like it fine."

"You drive."

It took an hour to get the white Packard out of the tunnel, and almost as long again to replace enough debris so that the entrance was again blocked, but at the end came another one of those moments that stayed with you: the white roadster in a clearing in front of the mine shaft. Pine trees and brush around them and in front, the dirt road that led out of the mountains. Harding remembered what Polshanski had said, that they weren't on an island, shipwrecked, waiting for rescue from over the horizon. There was a war out there and this dirt road, this shiny white car, was going to take them there. The land they stood on was the land that was being fought on: it all connected. And this funny moment was a piece of forever.

"Well, gents . . ." Harding said. Meade was already behind the wheel, but the others waited for Harding to decide where he wanted to sit. He sat in back, directly behind Meade.

"All aboard," he said. And then, to Meade, "To Bataan. Better make it snappy."

South of Baguio they neared the main highway. It was night now, and they could see headlights coming up Kennon Road toward the summer capital. They were headed the other way, south toward Rosario, then west toward Lingayen, then south as far as they could get, along the coast of the South China Sea.

"How do you want me to do this?" asked Meade. "Fast? Slow?"

"Just normal to start with," Harding said. "But don't let anybody pass us from behind. A car comes toward us, give them high beams and the horn, like it's an emergency, we're on our way to the scene of an accident."

"Which we are," Polshanski said.

"Which we are," Harding repeated.

Even at night, they could tell when they'd come into the lowlands, the rice bowl provinces of central Luzon. They had the greenhouse heat to tell them, the smell of mud just off the road, an elemental heaviness in the air, shallow ponds of water that stretched off on both sides of the road so that rare farm-houses—nipa huts surrounded by bamboo thickets—were like so many islands in a dark sea. The villages they passed through were small, lost places, shuttered and deserted, that wanted to know nothing of what came along the road. In the first hour they passed a half dozen vehicles. They used high beams and horns to good effect. Sometimes they heard a squeal of brakes behind them, a belated horn, an inaudible curse. That was all the opposition they had. The first hour was fun, all the exhilaration of a college joy ride in a borrowed car. It felt as though they were getting away with something and that even if they were stopped at the next crossing, they would have this to remember, every mile a victory.

Around Lingayen there was trouble. Lingayen was where the Japanese had landed, coming in off the gulf, brushing aside Wainwright's opposition, sweeping on toward Manila. It had been over fast around Lingayen, and it had been over for weeks, but you could tell that the war had passed. There were barrios that had been fought over, concrete walls reduced to rubble, corrugated roofs crumpled like waste paper, burned-out tanks along the road, jeeps upended in the river, tires facing skyward like drowned animals' paws.

The trouble at Lingayen was the bridge. The main bridge had been blown by the retreating Americans, then partially re-paired by the Japanese: one lane only, one-way traffic, a sentry at either end, a sentry who was nothing more than a traffic cop. It was a meaningless post, far behind the lines, deep in the middle of the night. But those sentries meant that this river was a Rubicon.

They came forward slowly, up a ramp that fed onto the main span. There were three sentries, and the sentries saw the car coming, the improbable car, which turned them into gaping yokels. One sentry was peering into the high beams when Camper shot him in the face. Sudul caught another in the back as he dove for a field telephone. The third went running ahead across the bridge. Blinking headlights high and low, blaring horn, they went racketing across the wooden planking. The white roadster must have looked like an angry bull plunging out of a rodeo chute. Surprise was gone, but astonishment remained: it was hard for the Japanese to believe any of this. They fired indiscriminately at the car. One of them lowered a little candy-striped barrier: it snapped like a dry twig against the roadster's windshield.

A bullet or two must have found the muffler, for suddenly they were backfiring and belching as they roared through the empty streets of Lingayen, a plaza in the old Spanish quarter, then down toward the sea, the American zone, a blur of pillars and mansions, and finally the sea. Mud flats and nipa palms on one side, a long sandy beach on the other, and the Japanese behind them, no doubt about it now, three or four pursuing vehicles. For a while, the Americans thought they could lose them. Surely a Packard roadster could outspeed any military transport. But the road was an equalizer, all potholes and puddles, washboards and ravines, dust on high ground, troughs of mud in low spots. The road was made for jeeps. The angry cloud of dust and light behind them was catching up.

"Stop," Harding said. "Kill the headlights."

They were right at the edge of the sea. The beach was flat, gravelly, endless.

"From here on, we walk," Harding said.

"What about the car?" Meade asked. "I hate to leave it."

"You've got two minutes," Harding said.

Harding had expected Meade to riddle the Packard with bullets, or possibly burn it. But Meade jumped back behind the wheel, gunned the engine, lurched off the road down onto the beach. He floundered through the soft sand, but at the water's edge he found a hard-packed gravelly surface. He waved merrily, sped off down south, wheeled around, raced back toward them and, at the last minute, like a football player turning into a line of tackles, he took the Packard into the waves. He got

farther than you might think, a hundred feet or so, before everything stopped. Meade whooped, jumped out, dove off the hood,
swam, then waded back toward them. Behind them, the roadster looked like a landing craft, its dying headlights shining out
to sea.

"That was fun," Meade said.

They darted across the road into the nipa swamp. This was a
place they'd never been. Mud that sucked and slurped, tugged
and held and coated you. Branches that speared and slashed as
you passed. After the nipa palms they came into rice fields,
sliding on narrow dikes that were buttressed by thorns and
sharpened sticks, and the smells made you feel the world was
a puddle of piss in a field of shit. All the time, they worried they
were going too slowly. They slogged through rice paddies,
waded through fish ponds, punched through fields of sugarcane,
never knowing what the next thing would be, or when they'd
be through it, and once, from far behind them, they heard some
shots. Maybe the Japanese had shot at each other. That would
be easy enough. The only thing was to keep moving and see
what the world looked like in the morning.

"Harry! Wake up!"

It happened a hundred times, but Harding never got used to
it: coming into a place at night, feeling your way in, not quite
knowing where you were, or what it looked like, until you
awoke—or someone woke you—at dawn and you saw a face that
wanted something from you right away, and then you looked
around and saw where the night had brought you. This morning
it was Charley Camper begging him to awaken, and he saw the
thatched roof of a lean-to and some rotted burlap sacks beneath.
They had been his pillow. Outside, the sun was just coming over
the low brown Zambales mountains. In a minute it would be too
hot; the weak wind that rustled the bamboo would feel as if it
came from the inside of an oven. The others had heard Camper
wake him, heard the alarm in his voice. Reaching for their rifles,
they looked out to see what he saw: that they were on an island
in the middle of a rice paddy, a floor of mud covered by six
inches of water, bounded by dikes that gave the place the look

of a chessboard. With players. There were men on the dikes, all around them, some hunkered down in sitting position, others standing, all of them armed. Dark, wiry little men, dressed in shorts or trousers, half of them with bolos, half with rifles. Kinky-haired, black-toothed. Tattoos on arms and legs.

"We're surrounded," Camper said.

"We've been surrounded," Harding said.

"What do we do?"

"Wait." He glanced across the paddies. "For that."

They could see it coming from a mile away, across steaming paddies, through waves of shimmering heat, a mirage slowly turning into a parade. First came a couple of armed natives, others carried a chair in which someone was seated, and someone else held a black umbrella over the chair. It was the oddest thing in the world, a procession from out of a tiny kingdom, the umbrella like a reminder of death on a burning, cloudless, blue-sky day. The marchers followed the dikes across the paddies, picking their way, zigzagging, so that their approach was like a dance, left and right, forward and back, advance and retreat. At last the procession approached the island itself, and Harding could see who was in the chair, under the black umbrella. He was a tall, brown-skinned man, white-haired, white-bearded, with wire-rimmed glasses that gave him the look of a recording angel. The porters set down the chair and the old man rose to his feet, picked up a cane, and hobbled toward them. He stepped onto the island and passed in front of them as if they were on review. He took his time, staring at each of them, Harding last of all. Harding noticed a thin, scholarly head on top of a once-tall body that the years had warped and twisted. The man remained in front of Harding, studying him carefully, measuring, nodding.

"We . . . are . . . Americans," Harding intoned in the slow, careful English generations of American teachers, and masters, had afflicted on the islands.

"From . . . *America,*" Harding repeated, gesturing toward himself and the others. Then he made walking motions, scissoring his fingers. "We go Bataan." Then he raised his arms as if he were holding a rifle, pantomiming some shooting. "Fight Japan!"

The old man kept staring, but now a small smile played around the corners of his mouth.

"You didn't fight Japan much last night," the old man said, "when they chased you into the swamp. Seems that we did the killing. And you boys did the hiding."

"Who are you, mister?" Harding asked. The old man's English was startling. It was smooth, slow, ironic, with none of the dips and flourishes with which Filipinos celebrated their fluency. "*What* are you?"

"Around here, they call me Mr. Brown."

"Well, Mr. Brown, we need your help."

"I guess you do," the old man acknowledged. "You come along."

Now the procession resumed, the chair, the umbrella, the natives—Zambals, they were called—and the Americans, not sure if they were guests or prisoners. They marched across the paddies, through the cane fields, then along the reedy banks of a muddy river that meandered out toward the sea. For a while, they were in a sea of salt grass, walking on logs that traversed muddy flats, picking their way over rickety bamboo bridges, until they came to Mr. Brown's village, a collection of huts and boardwalks, ladders and landings, all on stilts. It was at the end and edge of everything, not quite land, not quite water, a brackish indeterminate place. Shells and shit smells, hags and babies, nets, boats, floats, coconut husks, cook pots, the beginning or the end of civilization.

Old man Brown saw to it that all the guests were taken care of, washed, and fed. But Harding was his special guest. Cane in hand, he led Harding to a nipa hut at the far end of the village, facing out of the reeds like the prow of a ship. The hut sat on a split-bamboo platform that was like a verandah, with chairs and benches looking out across the grass. Inside, the nipa hut was one room. There was no furniture, only some mats and a coverlet in one corner, a pile of books—school texts and an incomplete encyclopedia, and a dictionary that was as well thumbed as any Bible. That was unexpected, but the big surprise was against the wall, where clothing had been turned into ornament, art, even icon: the belts and boots, scabbard and hat, of a turn-of-the-century cavalryman.

"Take a good look," old man Brown said. "You won't find many like that."

Harding reached out and touched the old Sam Browne belt. The relics of another army, lovingly preserved, property of a cavalryman who had ridden across the seas and not gone home.

"That was a couple of wars ago," Mr. Brown said. "Another century, almost."

"What are you doing here?"

"Oh. That." The old man came forward. They were face to face. "I deserted. I killed an officer. I changed sides. I ran from the white people. Then I ran from the brown. This is where I came. Here's where I stopped running. So what do you think?"

The old man watched Harding to see how his confession had gone. But it wasn't what he'd done that got to Harding—desertion, murder, flight. It was the sheer passage of time. That he was here now. That he'd been here forever. A woman came with a pot of coffee, another with some fish and rice, sweet potatoes. A third rattled around inside the hut and emerged with some tin plates, knives, and forks, which they put on a small table and set in front of the two men. There was a quart-size beer bottle filled with a milky fluid Brown said was coconut wine. One of the women said a few words and went away laughing.

"She said her pillow was your pillow," Brown translated. "Have some wine."

He poured into a tin cup, which he passed over to Harding. When Harding was finished, he served himself and drank out of the same cup.

"You mind sharing?"

"Your cup is my cup," Harding answered.

"Your health, then," Brown said. "Now you've had a while to reflect, what do you think of me? A fancy-talking colored deserter living in a swamp. Queer, huh?"

"I suppose you had your reasons," Harding said.

"Everybody has reasons. Killers and victims. The people I chased and the people who chased me. The blacks and whites and in-betweens. The yellows too, I guess. There's no shortage of reasons."

Old man Brown glanced down. Through the slats in the floor

you could see the tide washing in across the mud. Land to sea, sea to land. Old man Brown had seen it change thousands of times, and through it all kept wondering. Everyone who knew his real name, who remembered what he'd done, everyone who'd looked for him, was gone. A new war was coming in with the tide.

"So you're going to Bataan," Brown said.

"Yes. And we need a boat."

24

The moments you remembered. They stood out like paintings on a wall, like dreams from sleep. Dancing with a long-haired woman in a musty officers club. The look on the Japanese orderly's face as the Americans rode out from between the trees and commenced to slaughter naked, swimming soldiers. The sudden appearance of a sword above a line of figures kneeling in the Baguio cemetery. Climbing into Uncle Harrison's white Packard: "To Bataan. Better make it snappy." Meade whooping with joy as he drove the car into the sea. Old man Brown being carried toward them across the rice paddies. And now: the departure. A tide that was high and a moon that was mostly full and a tired little pump boat that had been putt-putting up and down the China Sea, from Lingayen to Olangapo, since before old man Brown arrived. And old man Brown watching them pile on board, telling them to stay close to the coast, travel only by night, keep an eye out for patrol boats. He stood there watching them turn into the channel through the reeds. Seeing him there, Harding felt that he had seen his father again. Here was another one of those odd, wise, solitary men who landed in unexpected places, spent years traveling in universes of their own devising, wrestling with enormous questions and answers they never shared. Tall, lonely, nocturnal men, self-impaled. What he never imagined, Harding said, was that he would become such a man himself.

More pictures. Two nights along the coast and then a voyage across the wide mouth of Subic Bay, where a rainstorm protected them from patrols out of the captured U.S. naval base. When the rain lifted they were off the Bataan peninsula, a few hours before dawn. They could hear the muffled roar of artillery, distant thunder, an electric storm that had settled over the mountains.

First landing on Bataan, halfway down the peninsula: dark mountains, bulky foothills muscling down to an inhospitable coast, all cliffs and rocks and, in the distance, the roar, louder by the minute, that told you you were sailing toward the end of the world. They left Mr. Brown's boat among some rocks and moved inland. The war was well south of them—they could hear as much—but this ground had been contested. Up from the beach, on a grassy hill, was a blasted observation tower. Beyond, there were trenches and foxholes, shells and cartridges. Mess kits. Bandages. Mulch. They marched through burned-off cane fields and there were bodies in the charred stubble, fallen scarecrows, soldiers going back to earth. They had fallen, bloated, rotted, and now they were almost home, more earth than human, with helmets, dog tags, belt buckles left behind, personal effects of men taken into custody. Eyeglasses. Gold fillings.

"I can't believe that guy," Sudul said.

"I do," Polshanski answered.

Meade was in the cane field, on his knees, bayonet in hand, prising the gold fillings out of a dead man's teeth.

"It's okay," Meade said. "They're Japs. I can tell by the helmets."

"Come on, Meade," Harding said.

Meade waved away a cloud of blowflies and kept digging away with his bayonet, pointing with one hand, pounding with the other. Harding drew his Colt and held it against Meade's head.

"Let's go back to the boat, Meade. I can't stand the smell."

"You wouldn't . . ." Meade looked up and was surprised. "You would! Son of a bitch, missionary boy, I believe you would."

"I would."

Meade appealed to the others. "You guys . . ."

"I'd feel bad about it," Sudul said.

"Me too," Polshanski added. "For quite a while."

"Charley!"

"Do what the man says," Camper answered. "He got us this far."

Now Meade appealed to Harding. "Why?"

"Because I'm a missionary boy. All right?"

The next day, they came home. They rounded the tip of the Bataan peninsula. Ahead of them, a few miles offshore, lay Corregidor. On the left was the port of Mariveles. They sailed in through a soup of battered, ruptured vessels; it was like a dynamited fish pond, with a few stunned survivors swimming in a lake of broken bodies. Oil fires on the water, ammunition dumps exploding on land. Once ashore, they picked their way through crowds of wounded hoping for a boat to Corregidor; a field of stretchers, more coming in by the busload. The whole port area was a jumble of jeeps, buses, trucks, a junkyard in the making, resistance imploding into terminal collapse.

The newcomers wandered around, asking for headquarters. The response was shrugs, curses, a gesture here and there. Frustrated, Meade burst out that they were looking for General MacArthur's headquarters. That was the worst moment of the trip. A lieutenant pointed south. He was pale, rickety, filthy. Everyone was covered with bites and rashes, jaundiced and malarial. The whole world had diarrhea. How far south, Meade asked, for where the lieutenant had pointed was nothing but the sea. The answer was: Australia. Seeing them dumbfounded, the lieutenant asked where they came from. They told him. They had to report to someone, they insisted. The lieutenant wondered why. It was April 8, 1942, and in a few hours, Bataan was going to surrender.

The Americans and Filipinos were beaten, chopped down as surely and steadily as cancer fells an athlete: it didn't matter how big you were, or how good, at the start. Tomorrow they'd all be prisoners, saints and slackers, heroes and cowards. Who would ever sort it out? Harding remembered something a French general had once said, ordering wholesale execution of prisoners: "Shoot them all. God will sort it out." When he'd first heard that line, he thought it was the epitome of cynicism. But here on Bataan, it sounded like a declaration of faith: God would sort it out. It was a faith Harding didn't share. He pulled his men together and led them to the harbor, just in time for another defeat: the sight of their boat making for Corregidor, virtual flagship in an armada of rowboats, rafts, bancas, floats, and barges that were less like vessels than like the wreckage of a larger ship, Bataan itself, that had already sunk.

"Hey, sonofabitch, come back here!" Meade bellowed, rushing down to water's edge, shaking his fist.

"Give it up, Meade," Camper said.

"You can't blame them," Polshanski said.

"Red damn sails in the sunset," Sudul added. Red sails indeed. A postcard sunset bent on illustrating the end of an era. "I hope they make it."

"Me too," Meade said. "I hope they make it." That amazing remark, that moment of sudden charity, stopped them all, and they probably never felt closer than they did in the silence that followed, watching their boat sail away and darkness fall.

The Japanese artillery, coming into range, sounded like a monster lumbering across the ocean, landing randomly, then closing, bracketing, slaughtering. Light returned to the dark straits, the light of burning boats and fuel-oil bonfires, the sounds of screams and explosions coming into shore, boats sinking, men burning or drowning or both. The artillery heightened, pounding, pounding, a pointless stupid exercise, like sledgehammering boulders into rocks, rock into pebbles, pebbles into dust—only these were boats and rafts blown into boards and splinters, men blasted into chum and bait. Which the sharks did not decline.

Part Five

★ ★ ★
★ ★

BEER AND MEMORIES

25

"Do you know what day it is?" asked Harding.

"Our third day on the road. That would make it . . ."

"Christmas Eve."

"Damn! You could have fooled me." Could have fooled almost anybody, Griffin thought. They were on the terrace of a rundown beach hotel outside Olangapo. It was another melancholy little corner in a country that seemed to have more than its share of them, a country where a resort hotel could go from splashy five-star pretense to shabby desuetude in a single season, without witnesses. Here, Tahitian-style huts sat alongside a stagnant man-made lagoon where backed-up sewage and paper festered. A broken catamaran was pulled up on the sand. A styrofoam float, iceberg-shaped, sat in an algae-green swimming pool.

"Christmas," Griffin reflected.

"I wanted you to have this," Harding said, handing over an envelope. "Merry Christmas."

Out of the envelope came the photograph Griffin had seen in Harding's hotel room, Harding and his guerrillas before something called the second Battle of San Leandro: young faces staring out from yesterday and one of them—the old man beside him—staring back.

"I wanted you to have it," Harding said. "Time we get done, it'll mean something to you."

"It already does."

"We're getting there," Harding said. They were comfortable now, alone together, drinking San Miguels and waiting for sunset.

Out on the beach—the same beach where a soldier named

157

Meade had driven a white Packard roadster into the waves—a
half dozen sailors out of the naval base at Subic were emptying
a case of San Miguel. They sat in a circle on the sand, a satchel-
size tape player at the center, where a campfire might have
been. Diana Ross and Lionel Richie, singing about endless love.
Griffin and Harding could hear it from where they sat. So, probably could the organist they shared the lonely terrace with;
nonetheless he belabored "We've Only Just Begun." Sometimes
the songs conflicted, sometimes they blended. No objections
either way. Griffin wondered if Harding saw anything of himself
in the sailors on the beach. Was there any connection between
the missionary boy who'd led MacArthur's Ghosts down this
coast forty years ago and the brawny rock 'n' rollers who had
ridden Hondas up from Subic, on the prowl for steak and cunt?

"You've been patient with me," Harding remarked.

"They're paying me."

"Is that it? I don't think that's it."

"No . . ." Griffin felt a little off-balance. "I was in bad shape
before you came along, Colonel."

"So was I," Harding responded. He hadn't lost his shyness. His
gestures at friendship were as tentative as a teenager's. Griffin
had normal social instincts and was used to gamely filling awkward pauses. This time he decided to wait.

"It's not easy for you, I know," Harding said. "My story. My
rules. Telling the story in order, moving through time, not giving you a peek at the ending. That must frustrate you."

"Sometimes," Griffin admitted. He could hear Clifford
Lerner suggesting he was a stenographer, not a reporter.

"It's the only way I can do this," Harding said. "It's not like
I had a choice. It's the only way. You'll see why. There's something else . . ."

"Yes?"

"Remember that business about the *I* and the *we* and the
they? It's in the story."

"Sure. Your father's question."

"All my life that question's been coming back at me. Sometimes I ducked it. Sometimes I came up with the wrong answer,
probably. But I think of us . . . as a *we*. This is something we're
in together. I just wanted you to know that."

You never knew about Harding, Griffin thought. He'd seen it

on Corregidor, he'd seen it at the press conference in Baguio, and he felt it now, when Harding looked at him the way a father —his own father, possibly—looked at a son, waiting for his words to sink in. It was his special combination of awkwardness and inspiration, tongue-tied fumbling and savvy calculation, elements—conflicting elements—so deeply mixed they complemented each other. And captured you.

"I'm with you," Griffin said. "In for the duration."

"I want you to finish this job. I want you to promise. I don't care what kind of mess you made of your life before this. And whatever you do after, that's up to you. But you're in this with me."

"Okay," Griffin said.

"Colonel Harding? Colonel Harding, please. Colonel Harding." A voice sounded out over the public address system. The two Americans looked at each other and laughed: you'd have thought that the place was jammed with conventioneers.

"What the hell's that?" Harding wondered.

"Maybe they never used it before," Griffin suggested. The organist had stopped, halfway into "By the Time I Get to Phoenix." The waiters consulted. Even the sailors down on the beach looked up at the terrace, as though the next announcement might be a call to quarters.

"Over here," said Harding, waving at the waiters. After another consultation—one talking to another, who checked in with a third—a waiter scooted off toward the lobby. The organist resumed. And two Americans threaded their way among the empty tables, over to where Griffin and Harding were sitting.

"I remember you!" Harding exclaimed, and for a moment Griffin thought that some shadowy comrades from years before had tracked him down. "You were at the press conference!"

"You bet I was." It was the cowboy with the scarecrow body, square dance clothes, and passion for treasure.

"I forget your name."

"Roach," the man replied. "Like in cockroach."

"Is Cock your first name?"

"No, sir. Around here they call me Cadillac Bill. The reason for that is parked outside. And this is my partner, Sammy Macias."

Macias couldn't have been past thirty, but life had cast him

as a sidekick, a clown, a bit player, and part of that role had been
to get as comically fat as he could, so now he wore an obsequious
grin, a puffy stomach, and a T-shirt that proclaimed him a "Sex
Machine."

"We'd like to have a talk," Roach said. "Okay if we sit down?"

Harding nodded. In just a few weeks, Griffin had come to
admire Harding's politeness with people who approached him.
But these two were something else.

"We followed you all the way from Baguio. You crossed us up
though. We thought you'd be heading for the mountains. You
know, right in the direction of Kiangen . . ."

Roach paused, let the name Kiangen hang in the air, waiting
for a reaction that didn't come.

"Okay, play it your way, Colonel. You headed down this way,
meandering all around. We said, he's a shrewd one, throwing
folks off like that, stopping in every little shithole barrio . . ."

"What do you want?"

"Same thing as you do, Colonel. The treasure. Yamashita's
treasure."

"Oh," Harding said. "Yamashita's treasure. Is that all?"

"Sammy and me have been researching that yarn for years."

"Why?"

"*Why?* Gee, Colonel, I'm glad you asked."

It was a hobby at the start, Cadillac Bill said, but hobbies had
a way of sneaking up on you; the farther you got into them, the
farther they got into you. Guns, stamps, license plates, hubcaps,
it didn't matter. Go at it long enough, hard enough, and a dab-
bler became a killer. By now he'd read most everything that had
appeared. The first stories suggested that when Yamashita retreated into the mountains he took along trunks of gold bullion
from Singapore and Rangoon. During the fifties, the treasure
mutated into jewelry, statues, paintings. After that came the
most fanciful report of all: three gold Buddhas, sitting deep in
the mountains.

"There's been guys come looking over the years," Cadillac
Bill went on, "and some guys looking still. There were a lot of
false sightings."

"What's that mean?" Harding asked.

"It means mistakes. There were dozens of gold mines around

Baguio. I don't have to tell you that, do I, sir, tight as you were with Harrison Wingfield?"

That was a jolt. It was as though a character had escaped from their still-incomplete pages. Someone else had a line on Uncle Harrison and there was no telling how many other confidences and secrets would turn out to be in the public domain.

"Well, there was gold in some of those mines and some bozos claimed they'd found the treasure. Some other mines, there was like—household goods—stashed away. And folks shouted, 'Eureka.' And that was also bullshit, Colonel, as you well know. You of all people . . ."

Harding sat back, listening carefully, and it seemed he was almost enjoying himself. The beer and the sunset and the talk of treasure: he was feeling alive again.

"That's the pattern. Folks show up, they look around, they make a little noise, and then they leave. The mistake they all make is looking for the treasure. I believe in looking for the man who had the treasure."

"Not Yamashita."

"No, sir. You. I've known your name for years, Colonel Harding. You were the man who knew the mountains. You were close to the man who ran the Baguio mines. You were the head of MacArthur's Ghosts. You went into the mountains after Yamashita. You brought him out. You visited him in his cell the night before they hanged him! Goddamn, I'm pleased to meet you, Colonel!"

"All right," Harding conceded, "I'm your man."

"Damn!" Exuberant, Cadillac Bill signaled for a round of drinks and a platter of "horsey-derveys." And he slipped two fifty-peso notes to the waiter.

"That first one's for you," he said, "and the other is for the Hammond organist."

"What was it you wanted to hear, sir?"

"The sound of silence," Cadillac Bill said.

He watched as the waiter walked across, dropped the fifty in a glass goblet that sat on top of the organ. The waiter and the organist whispered and the organist launched into "The Sound of Silence."

"Shit!" Cadillac Bill shouted, slapping the table. "I love this country. Here, Sammy, take another fifty pesos and tell the guy to take a break."

He turned to face Harding, star-struck as any movie fan. "Seeing you makes me feel like celebrating! I've got about a thousand questions, Colonel. You gonna make me ask them? What it is. Where it is. And why you waited so long. That's the one that really gets me."

"Gets me, too," Harding acknowledged.

"You could've died. Had a heart attack, got hit by a car, slipped in a bathtub. Then where'd we all be?"

"I lived," Harding said. "Just my luck."

"I'm not begging for answers. I'm not pushing it. But if you're telling the truth, you got problems, which maybe you don't know about. Moving the stuff, shipping it, cashing it in. I figure the treasure's up in the mountains, where the war ended. The Yamashita Pocket, the last Jap redoubt. Kiangen. *Your* mountains. But there's other folks in the mountains now. It's not just missionaries and tribes anymore. There's the NPA, there's the army, hit squads, lost commands, bandits, vigilantes, outfits like the Fun Bunch. There's local politicians who run mini-empires. There's multinationals, lumbering and mining and building dams. They all play hardball. Hell, I wouldn't even trust the nuns up there."

"And I can trust you, Cadillac Bill?"

"Yeah, I believe you can. I want you to keep us in mind."

"I'll do that," Harding said. Then he explained what he and George were up to, retracing the events of the war, more or less in order, getting back in touch with the land, telling the story along the way.

"And the treasure," Cadillac Bill said. "That's the big ending, right?"

"Something like that," Harding said. "I'm not there yet. But if I need you when I get there—when we get there, I should say —you'll hear."

"Fair enough," said Cadillac Bill. He insisted on making an evening of it. He sent Sammy into the kitchen. "See what they have to cook and watch 'em while they cook it."

While they waited for their food, Cadillac Bill talked about himself. "What you see," he said, "is what you get." From his

Coors belt buckle to his Old Spice aftershave, he was American through and through, born in West Virginia, raised in California, shipped to Vietnam. He had taken time returning from Vietnam, taken so long it now felt he might never make it all the way home. The Philippines was his place now, and the more you listened to him talk about it, the more sense it made. It was impossible to think of the likes of Cadillac Bill confronting a major culture, China or Japan, or surviving in a highly competitive city like Singapore or Hong Kong. The Philippines was just his speed: it was low-down and small-time, it was violent and talkative and fun. It was the sort of place that Cadillac Bill could learn and even master. By now he was an expert, and as if to show off his knowledge he talked about the history of the place, a chain of mayhem and betrayal that went on forever. He talked about assassinations, hits, "salvagings." Killings in nightclubs, at cockpits, on airplanes, in hotel lobbies. Killings by bolos, gunshots, car bomb, garrote. He relished the famous assassination of a hoodlum who had fallen out of favor with Malacanang Palace; the bullets were spaced a few inches apart, up and down his legs, up and down his arms, one at a time, till finally he was shot in the mouth and dumped in the lobby of the five-star Makati Hotel.

"Hell of a place," Cadillac Bill concluded. By then they were drinking Irish coffees. He reached into his pocket and handed over a card, which listed a half dozen businesses in Olongapo, outside Subic Naval Base, and Angeles City, next to Clark Field. "Was it always like this, Colonel?"

Harding shrugged. "Yes, but I didn't always know it."

"Well, damn it all, how could you stand to leave?" He asked it rhetorically; it came off as a joke. But he was a shrewd joker. His second question showed that. "And how could you stand to come back?"

Three times, Griffin placed the call to Manila. The third time, she answered.

"Susan Hayes . . ."

"Hello. It's Backyard Faraway. Merry Christmas."

"George Griffin! Where are you?"

"Closing in on Bataan. It's early 1942 and the Japanese are looking strong. The Battle of Midway's coming up in a month or so, but we don't know that. No telling how long the war will last. How are you?"

"I'm fine. But it sounds like you're in a time warp."

"I am. Where have you been? I've been calling every half hour. That way I knew I wouldn't wake you up."

"Embassy Christmas party. We sang Christmas carols. We had a grab bag. I got a coffee cup. One of those things that's just half a cup and says so on the outside. Some luck, huh?"

"Are you alone?"

"Yes."

"I wish you weren't."

"I wouldn't mind."

"Not that I know you."

"No," she said. "That's true. You don't know me."

"It used to be simple to get to know people. When you're young, what is there to know? You sort of like the looks of someone, the style, whatever, and that's it. Simple. You get older, you collect a history, and everything gets complicated. I've been thinking about you . . ."

"I see."

"And I've been drinking . . ."

"Me, too! Wassail punch. I can feel it."

"Irish coffees on this end. I wish you were here. It's easy to say, over the phone. If you *were* here, what would I say then?"

"You'd think of something."

"You know what I was wondering?"

"Yes."

"You do? Let's hear it."

"All right. You were wondering if you stood a chance with me. You're lonely and a little drunk and . . ."

She laughed that low conspiratorial laugh that Griffin had heard from her just once before, when she'd asked about his night out with the boys. It was a laugh that said that, in addition to all her other selves, diplomat and God knows what else, there was a congenial carnal spirit tucked away in there. She laughed again.

". . . frankly, you sound horny. You must be the only man in the Philippines who is."

"Is this a secure line?"

"We've both been drinking. It's my only vice."

"Only?"

"Well, there are some virtues I haven't disclosed as yet."

"What are you doing New Year's Eve?"

"You won't be with the colonel?"

"He'll be with Charley Camper, an old buddy of his who lives in Olangapo. I thought I'd slip back into Manila."

"I see," she said. She paused. There was an odd, embarrassing, electric silence on the line. He wondered what she looked like while she considered. Griffin remembered Harding's account of the pornographic postcard he'd found in the Baguio mansion, the expression on the woman's face, not whorish or leering, but knowing and experienced. It was an expression that signaled to the missionary boy that the woman was ahead of him on a road someplace, a wise and willing traveler, waiting for him to catch up, and that was the expression he pictured on the face of Susan Hayes just now.

"I'm not making any promises," she said. "You don't know me. Remember that."

"I was only asking for a date."

"A date you've got," she said, "Mr. Backyard Faraway."

26

"Sometimes," Harry Roberts Harding remarked the next day, "the past is so real and near, it's like I can reach out and touch it. Other times, I have to ask myself who cares? What happened, happened. So what?"

Memories were rough. When they came to you unbidden, in dreams or nightmares, they screamed for attention: drop everything and follow me. But when you went after them, they turned whimsical and dodgy, they stranded you high and dry in a place like Mariveles. The port on the tip of Bataan was a sad place, potholed roads winding through a shanty barrio, a scuffed-up fishing fleet pulled up onto an unkempt red sand beach. Women did their laundry on the grass next to the tablet that marked kilometer one of the Death March. You couldn't blame Harding for asking himself: so what?

The drive north did nothing to lift their spirits. They passed through something called the Bataan Export Processing Zone, a realm of empty factories, shuttered offices, weed-filled parking lots. The sooner they got to Charley Camper's place in Olangapo the better, Griffin thought.

"Stop here," Harding ordered abruptly. They were on a stretch of Death March highway that curved close to the sea. On one side, rice fields leading toward Mount Samat, with its towering memorial cross. On the other side was a row of huts where people vulcanized tires and sold hot lunches and warm beers to truck drivers. "Meade died here."

"Meade died." It was eerie. It happened forty years ago, but what with Harding's way of telling a story, it was news to Griffin. He was sorry to hear it.

"He'd be tickled they put up that cross on the mountain, worried as he was about dying in a hole someplace, like a sick

animal that crawls away," Harding said. "Too bad he couldn't
know. But we never do, do we? Those are the rules of the game.
Shoot them all. God will sort it out."

"Well, we're here. Sorting things out."

"Let me ask you. I'm just checking. Tell me—based on what
I've told you—what you think of Meade. Or what you think I
thought of him."

"Fair enough," Griffin said. It was more than fair, he thought.
It was moving. Here they were, weighing the character of a
soldier who'd been dead for forty years. Where else did Meade
live now, but in their talk of him? His parents were dead. His
friends had forgotten him. Every woman he'd ever slept with
was a guaranteed crone. All the things that kept a name alive,
love and blood and property, had failed poor Meade. Except the
missionary boy, who wanted to give him a fair epitaph. The
missionary boy wasn't counting on God to sort things out. He
was hoping that he and George Griffin could get things straight.

"I think there was a lot about him that must have shocked
you," Griffin began. "The way he kept shooting at that Japanese
soldier who was wounded in the water. The time he went for
the fillings in a dead man's teeth. The way he was with women.
A cruel streak."

" 'Mean' Meade . . ."

"But there was more."

"There was more. I was hoping I got some of it across."

"The way he played the piano that night at the officers club.
And cried, when he thought he might have to spend the war in
the mountains, maybe dying in them. He seems like a bully who
was afraid of the dark. Some of that must have touched you.
Because, in the end, of all your men, he needed you the most."

"Yes."

In April, 1942, the surrendered peninsula was in chaos, prisoners, stragglers, skirmishes, surrenders, random butchery. The
place was like a frying pan, and Americans were bacon. The
burner was off, but the meat kept writhing in the skillet, curling,
crisping, burning, spattering. The missionary boy kept them
moving into the damn mountains. What bothered Meade was
that the mountains weren't real mountains like, say, the Rock-

ies, that raised themselves up above the timberline, above the clouds even. These mountains were frauds. They were more of the mud, the jungle, the heat that plagued them down below. More of the same.

The missionary boy brought them to a village near the top of Mount Mariveles. It was as bad a place as Meade had ever seen: a cluster of thatch huts in a muddy clearing that the sun never reached even when it was shining, which wasn't often because the mountains caught whatever rain was within a thousand miles of the place. It was like the clouds said, hey, Meade's here, why waste our water on the ocean when we can run over to Bataan and piss on Meade? Hell, they lined up in holding patterns, the clouds did, like the convoy that had never come. Why was it, he wondered, the rain could reach through the trees overhead, but not the sunlight? Some shitty umbrella. Funny, though, no one else complained. Eating goats, lizards, monkeys, picking worms out of cornmeal, they were pleased as punch with their mountain hideaway. Hell, they even collected a couple of new recruits who came out of the woods, a Texan named Vernon Waters and a Virginia gent named Owen Edwards. Some piece of work, that Edwards, the upper-crust kind of guy who walks through the movies saying, "Tennis, anyone?" The first thing he did after he came in was trim his beard. He'd been on Corregidor near the end, right in the tunnel. Then he rafted over to Bataan, decided to take his chances in the boondocks. When they asked him how it went on the Rock, he said, "Oh, it was some brouhaha."

They were waiting for things to settle down, the missionary boy said, and then, by God, he'd take them to a place that was even safer. More mountains, farther north, where they'd begun. That was a trip Meade wasn't planning to make. He was looking for another kind of ending. And toward the end of the third week, he found it. With their move north approaching, Harding wanted to feel his way out a little, see how things were. He asked Meade if he wanted to join him on a scout.

Down from the mountain, they came into a battlefield that was way past ripe. Shells, ration cans, burnt-out jeeps and trucks. An officer who'd been tied to a tree and bayoneted, like a hunk of suet left out for birds. A field hospital, with shredded tents flapping in the wind, rain-soaked piles of used bandages composting in a corner. Some things rotted, some things rusted: nothing survived.

"Amazing how quickly nature takes things back," Harding said, as if it were good news, spring coming on, blue skies after rain. Meade didn't respond.

They wanted to see what kind of traffic was on the coast road. Edwards had told them the Japs had marched forty thousand sick and starving prisoners north along the road, shooting or bayoneting anyone who lagged behind. But now the road was almost empty. They paralleled it for an hour and only a half dozen vehicles passed, trucks piled high with surrendered rifles, canteens, tires: personal effects of an army that died. Then Meade spotted something down the road, a parade, a ceremony, an accident, he couldn't say. Coming closer, they still couldn't tell what was going on. From the edge of the jungle, on a slope a couple of hundred yards above the road, they saw several hundred American soldiers and a handful of Japanese. The Japanese were armed, all right. But so were the Americans!

"Christ almighty!" Meade exulted. "Could it be?"

"I'm not so sure."

"What it looks like to me. It's the landing, the convoy!"

"I hope you're right," said Harding.

"Hope? I don't get you, missionary boy. Sounds like you don't hardly want the fleet to come. I don't get you. Not from the day I saw you. That night we had girls over the officers club, paid for and delivered, you walked away. There's a war on, you walk away again. You're always wanting to walk away. Anybody wants to come with you, that's okay, but if they don't, that's okay too. I don't get you."

"Do me a favor, Meade. Just wait a minute."

A minute was all it took for the scene to sort itself out. For it was a scene, a scene straight out of a movie, a Japanese movie, newsreel footage reconstructing the conquest of Bataan. The Americans filed past the back of a truck, where they were handed rifles. Helmets and canteens came out of other trucks. But what used to be weapons and uniforms were props and costumes now. A camera truck came into view, a Jap director shouting orders through a megaphone as the camera panned over the dispirited Americans. The Americans surrendered again, a second time, a third, from a distance and close up, in twos and threes and by the hundreds. They surrendered on request. They were at it an hour or so, and they were still surrendering.

"Don't try and stop me," Meade said suddenly. He'd gotten up and started backing away from Harding toward the jungle.

"Where are you going, Meade?"

"Stick around and see," he said. "Don't stop me, don't even try. You can't stop me."

"What are you going to do?" Harding asked, but in his heart he knew. And he wouldn't try to stop him. Meade was doing something that Harding had always insisted on his own right to do. He was walking away.

The film crew had almost finished. The Americans had surrendered a dozen times and the Japanese accepted, sternly, nobly, firmly. That was how history got recorded, if you left it to the winners. Which you always did. Now they were setting up for the finale. Three Japs clambered on top of a burned-out tank, set to wave flags, hats, rifles, and lead a victory chant: "Banzai, Banzai!" First they shot it from a distance, the prisoners standing while the victors whooped it up. Then the prisoners sat down while the camera moved in for a closeup: Banzai, Banzai! The prisoners were extras now, the trio of Japanese on top of the tank were stars. Banzai! Banzai! It was the last sound they ever made. Three shots tore into them, blowing two of them backward, off the top of the tank, spinning the third around and pitching him into the captive audience below.

It happened so suddenly, so stunningly, there followed a moment of silence, a tiny wondering vacuum before all hell broke loose and in that while you could hear a shout. Mean Meade, right at the water's edge, shouting, "MacArthur's Ghosts! MacArthur's Ghosts!" He was knee deep, wading forward, firing and shouting. Meade had transformed himself. He'd become what he'd hoped for, the rescue, the mile-long convoy, the promised return. Already wounded, he stood on the beach, waving to the scared, dumbfounded prisoners, waving merrily, come on in, the water's fine. As the shots came back at him, he went down slowly, to his knees, then up again. He fell backward, floating in the shallows, only moving with the waves, as needless bullets splashed around him.

27

"Pigs, pigs, pigs!" Forty miles from where Meade had died, forty years later, Charley Camper leaned against a pen fenced by slabs of corrugated metal roofing and called his livestock. Griffin and Harding had arrived in the late afternoon. While Harding was napping, Charley offered Griffin a tour. "Pigs, pigs, pigs!" Right out of the Ozarks, the call came from deep in his chest, part grunt, part squeal, part serenade.

"See how red their backs are?" Camper asked. "Suckers get sunburned. I got to rub my darlings down with coconut oil. They love me. Bet you didn't know that."

"Daddy!" One of Charley's daughters ran up with a handful of corn husks. Griffin didn't have the arithmetic of Charley's family down yet—hadn't even seen his wife—but this girl was younger than the teenagers he had seen at the Manila Hotel. She squealed with delight as she tossed the husks to the pigs. "Peeks, peeks, peeks!"

"I got chickens, too," Charley said. "Free-ranging chickens, as you can probably tell from the bottoms of your shoes. You ever taste a chicken that hasn't been caged, force-fed, doped up, and kept awake all its life, which is maybe three weeks?"

"I can't say that I have."

"Well, you will tonight. I been marinating a bunch since yesterday, got 'em floating in soy sauce, lemon juice, hot chili peppers. You'll see. Come on, I got something else to show you."

Charley Camper's farm was a collection of trucks, huts, kids, appliances, toys, and sheds perched on a bluff overlooking Subic Bay. Camper and his brood lived in a pair of World War II vintage Quonset huts, dumpy functional half shells of sheet metal that sat on concrete slabs. There'd been thousands of

them right after the war. Now they were an endangered spe-
cies, Camper said.

"Here we are," Charley said when they came to the edge of
his property. "This is my spot." A pair of hammocks, a couple
of automobile seats, an oil-cloth-covered card table with some
folding chairs, a horseshoe pit, a barbecue. A series of extension
cords feeding an overhead light bulb, a prewar cathedral-style
radio, and a refrigerator that was covered with *Playboy* center-
folds Griffin remembered from college days.

"Check out the view," Camper said. He was down on his
knees, pouring a bushel of coconut-shell charcoal into a barbecue that consisted of a sheet of the ubiquitous corrugated metal
straddling a couple of cement blocks. Griffin could see the broad
sweep of the harbor that Harding and his men had once crept
past in the rain. He saw the American naval base barracks and
lawns, houses and offices and baseball fields, a kempt and orderly world. Next to it, the lights, cranes, wharves, and drydocks
of the ship repair facility. And pressing against the base, the
bright lights of Olangapo.

"Three hundred nightclubs, eight thousand licensed prostitutes," Camper said, coming up with a couple of San Miguel
beers. "This here's Sodom. Angeles City—that's near Clark
Field—is Gomorrah."

"Get into town much?"

"Not like I used to." He pointed Griffin toward one hammock,
parked himself in another. The whole scene was a cartoon, the
life of Riley. Beer in the refrigerator, chicken about to land on
the grill. And down below . . .

"More women than . . ."

"What's that?" Camper asked.

"I was just thinking . . ."

"More women than you can shake a stick at? That what you
were thinking? Well, you can say that again. I shook my stick at
quite a few."

"Did you always pay for it?"

"You always pay for it, one way or another." Charley turned
in the hammock to face Harding. He had the kind of body that
big hammocks told stories to little hammocks about when they
wanted to frighten them. His stomach pressed against each

space in the rope, like a prisoner peeking through jail bars. "I guess I sound like some red-neck ignoramus, but the way I see it, the trouble is when you don't pay. Too many people running around trying to get stuff for free."

"What about your wife?"

"She's the exception," Camper said, "that proves the rule. I met her down there, in one of the honky-tonks. We been together for twenty years. We got family here. Lot less than before. They ship out to California. 'Make business in the U.S.A.' A dozen already, riding on my tickets and my passport. My wife's over there. Damn near lives there now."

"What made her different from all the other girls? Your wife?"

Charley laughed. "You asked the wrong question. You got it back assward."

"How's that?"

"My wife's beautiful. Was. Is. Always will be. She has it all. Take my word for it. Well, look at me. What you see is what she got. You think that I was ever handsome?"

He raised himself out of the hammock, broke wind, and walked toward the refrigerator for another pair of beers.

"I believe I see the colonel coming out," he said when he came back. He stood over Griffin, scratching his belly. "What I'm saying is, that night we met, her and me, she wasn't the one who got lucky. It was me. So you shouldn't be asking me what was different about her. You should be asking her what was different about me."

"I'd like to meet her," Griffin said.

"Well, that's a problem. She loves California. She just got a real estate license, can you believe it . . ."

The big man stood there, still running his hand over his gut, as though he'd eaten something that was bothering him.

"Twentieth Century Fox she works for. Servicing the Filipino fat cats who are taking money out of this country by the planeload. Putting it in condos."

"Twentieth Century is a movie company."

"Wait a minute . . . Century Twenty-one. She wears a yellow blazer. When we got together, I figured we'd stay forever. Me and my local girl. I thought she was the end of my traveling, but

I was just the beginning of hers. Sometimes it feels like we were headed in separate directions all along, only I didn't know it."

"What about your daughters?"

"California girls," Charley answered.

That night, after they'd feasted on Charley's chickens, a whole bird each, and killed the first case of San Miguel beers, Charley rang a cowbell and one of his daughters came out with a pot of coffee and a bottle of Irish whiskey. Another ring produced a box of Manila cigars. They talked the sort of talk that passes between men who like each other enormously, who sense more than they actually know about each other and feel more than they can say. Inadequate talk, by some standards. Politics, sports, travel, food. And memories. They traded in memories, which blew around them like cigar smoke, lingered in the mouth like coffee and whiskey, shone and guttered like the neon in Olongapo, and stretched out, dark and endless, like the South China Sea.

"Charley," Harding said. "I have a favor to ask."

"Anything you say, Colonel. You know that."

"I want you to tell a story. Not *a* story . . . *the* story. Just a piece of it."

"What piece would that be?"

"Moving out of Bataan, after Meade died. Start there."

Camper cast a vast, sad sigh. His arms folded in back of his neck, his stomach heaved, and he stared up at the stars. "I got to wonder how much of this matters. I really do."

"It matters to me."

"Well . . ." Charley heaved himself out of the hammock, stood, stretched, paced. He rubbed his stomach as thoughtfully as a scholar ever stroked his beard. He belched as though to clear his throat. At the last moment, he grabbed a beer, tilted it back over his throat the way a mechanic feeds a can of oil into an engine that's starting to smoke. Then he began . . .

"MacArthur's Ghosts. The Japs talked about us on the radio. Sometimes they laughed about us. They liked the idea that all we were was ghosts. Then they took us serious and started hunting. Some villages we came into, they were scared to death of us. Others, things were queer and slow and just didn't feel right. Even though there's smiles all around and food cooking, it's not right. More than once, we just looked at each other and ran. We were real skittish. There was one place we got a warm welcome, a house for each of us, and we could hear them murdering a pig in our honor, and some women made us take off our clothes, which they proceeded to slap to death in a nearby stream and Polshanski—him of all people, down to his underwear—starts getting fidgety. Something was wrong, something he couldn't put his finger on, but he didn't like it and pretty soon none of us likes it and then we see a bunch of men coming down a lane, not Japanese, but Filipinos, at least ten of them, cops we thought. Well, we couldn't count on cops to be on our side. We ran out of the houses, guns and underwear was all we had, we splashed out into the rice fields, right past the women who were washing our clothes. What a bunch we were, like kids caught swimming in a posted lake. Finally Sudul looks around, tells us to stop, because that bunch of cops we worried about were at the edge of the village, waving to us, and when their waves don't bring us back, they break out their instruments and start playing music—'Oh, Shenandoah' I think it was. They were a village band, coming to serenade us in our hour of defeat. And now we waded back in, trying to act dignified, like maybe this was a drill or something.

"We were sneaking through Pampangas, the rice country, low and wet and flat. We moved at night, walked, swam, waded. Days we hid out in the fields, unless we'd found a good village. We were in bad shape now. Insects, leeches, rashes, burns, infections. I was rotting from the inside out and outside in, and I figured that when what bothered me on the outside, molds and sores and all, met up with what was hurting me on the inside, diarrhea and fever, well, that would be like two armies shaking hands over a mutual foe. Me. I'd be dead. No great loss. . . . Well, we had this Filipino boy with us, he'd been a cadet at Baguio and he'd fought down on Bataan. His name. Let me think. I'm real bad at names . . ."

"We called him Connie," Harding prompted.

"That's right!" Camper said, snapping his fingers as though he'd just remembered. "Connie it was. A bright boy, a real go-getter. He was the one we counted on to sniff out the situation in the villages. And we started talking about the villages like they were women. It started simple. If a village looked good, Connie would say, the girl is willing. If Japs were there, he'd say, the woman is married. If it was shaky, one way or another, he'd say the woman is married and her husband is away on business. But then, it got more and more elaborate. We made a game out of it. Instead of a village being a good woman, she'd be a ripe young virgin, and a bad village would be an old hag having her last period, and an iffy village would be a horny, insatiable slut, anxious to meet us after dark. Jokes were all we had. And then, deep in Pampangas, the joke was on us."

Charley walked as he talked, pacing back and forth inside a cage of memories. Now he wanted Harding to let him out.

"That's it," he said.

"No, it's not."

"You want me to keep going?"

"Yes."

"Do I have to?"

"I can't make you do anything, Charley," Harding granted. "But yes . . ."

"We were actually getting someplace, moving across them watery plains. Up north we could see Mount Arayat setting there all by itself, heaving up out of the rice fields and swamps and fish ponds, it was almost like an island. What's more, Connie heard there were guerrillas on that mountain, real hard boys, organized and fighting, so we had reason to believe that if we got to that mountain, it wouldn't disappoint us. And every day, it got a little closer, a mirage that turned into a silhouette and then into a real green peak, with cane fields on its lower slopes, and rain forests higher up, and clouds stuck round the top. Mount Arayat. Sudul turned it into Ararat, where Moses landed in his ark after forty days and nights of rain . . ."

"It was Noah," Harding said.

"What?"

"Noah and the ark," Harding said. "It was Noah."

"Said I was bad on names," Camper responded. "Anyway, we came into a nice little village, and I'll never know whether they betrayed us on purpose or whether that's just where our luck ran out. I could find the place today, I could find it easy, because I remember the church where we hid out. I remember the cool

of the cement floor and the way the wood smelled, just like the
top of your desk when you took a nap in kindy-garden, and the
plate glass window, all bright colors. I got it memorized, that
church, so I guess I could go back and ask, ask the old people,
whether they meant that we should die. I could ask. Trouble is,
I don't know what I want to hear—that it happened on purpose
or that it happened by accident. Because either one would
break my heart.

"A nice little village. Or, as Connie put it, young virgin, four-
teen and ripe. A neat little schoolhouse, and nipa huts, and a
white-painted Catholic church. Flowers everywhere, and dogs
and kids and chickens and wash draped over the tops of bushes.
We came in at dusk when the men came in from the fields, as
if we'd all been working out there together and now we were
home. That evening we sat out on the square, the way folk do
in small towns, and we talked. I liked that feeling. Kerosene
lights coming on in houses and wood fires and cooking smells.
Music from an old hand-cranked Victrola. And us just sitting
there, like we really belonged. They knew about the Japs, they'd
seen them moving on the main roads. But no one had come into
the village yet. It was like prewar. Polshanski said maybe that
was the best way to get through a war, to be an unimportant
person in an unimportant place. Anyway we felt good. There
was only one road that led to the village, and a bridge on that
road was washed out and the villagers were in no rush to repair
it.

"We were sleeping in the church, stretched out on mats
they'd given us. Some of us were in the open area, the foyer,
near the front door. Others had tucked themselves in between
the pews. About a dozen of us, I'd say. I was the only one awake
when it happened. I'd just stepped out to pee and I caught that
first little hint that dawn was coming on, which isn't sunrise,
isn't even false dawn. It's like the darkness gets diluted, it thins
out some, and there's a little breeze starts stirring round the
square, and a ripple out on the rice fields, and in the swamps you
can hear the reeds rustling. Dogs get up and stretch and flop
back down, and it's that time when old men like myself wake
up and lie in bed with their eyes open, knowing they've gotten
all the sleep they're going to get, and young men—young the

way I used to be—wake up hard and try to score that last piece
of ass, before the night turns into morning. Maybe that's what
our friend Connie was doing, somewhere in the village. All I
know is I was back inside the church, looking up at the colored
glass windows, wondering if I could put my finger right on the
second when the first light hit the glass, the first little glow, and
suddenly Connie slams the doors open, rushes in, and shouts
that there's a patrol of Japs coming into the village, and there's
no doubt about it this time, I can see them through the door,
running down the road, breaking into two groups as they hit the
village square. Ten already and more coming. This is no damn
patrol. It's an attack.

"I grabbed my rifle, ducked behind the door, and started
firing into the square. Some of the others followed me. They're
all awake now. How could they not be? The Japs are firing at the
church, the doors, the windows. That same window I was studying, a shepherd and his flock, shattered on the floor. A piece
caught Polshanski in the cheek. 'Had to be,' he says, 'had to be.'
With him, everything had to be, but just this once, I asked why.
'It was so nice here,' he says. Like that explained it.

"It was odd, what happened next. The firing stopped. And
for a little while, it looked like a normal day in a small village.
It got light and bright, like every morning. It got hot. A dog
trotted across the square, sniffed at one of the dead Japanese,
just sniffed and went about his regular morning business.
Now . . ."

Charley Camper took a deep breath, glanced at Harding,
walked to the edge of the terrace. Down below, the neon lights
of Olongapo pulsed and glimmered. Fog was coming off the bay
now, so the lights glittered and guttered according to the winds.
From in back, out of the Quonset where Charley's daughters
lived—"the girls' dorm," he called it—came the sound of the
Eagles singing "One of These Nights." Sometimes it felt that all
of this was meant to show how long ago it all was, how old
Harding and Charley had gotten. A couple of old soldiers sitting
on a hill, with party lights spread out below. And then you saw
the look on Charley Camper's face when he came back to his
story and you knew you were wrong. It was only yesterday.

". . . in the middle of the morning, we hear a commotion out
in the square. We crack the church doors and see about thirty

villagers, men, women, and children marching toward the church, shielding the Japanese, who are walking right behind them, and the people were saying, 'Don't shoot, Joe, don't shoot.' They were begging, praying, crying, crossing themselves, it looks like a religious procession, a baptism maybe. Baptism to fire. And one of our men, Edwards it was, says he saw this before on the Agno River and Harding asks what they did and Edwards says they opened fire, that it wasn't pretty, but at least he lived to tell us about it. 'That's great,' Sudul says, 'just great, thanks a lot and glad you made it.' The Filipinos are fifty feet in front of the church now, with the Japs right behind them. One of the Filipinos—a nice old man we'd sat out with the night before—shouts we should surrender, that way no one gets killed, not them, not us. Edwards says we don't have a choice and then the missionary boy gets a look on his face. 'Shoot them all and God will sort it out, that it?' Poor Edwards doesn't know what to say. The missionary boy says, 'Shit.' He sends the whole bunch of us to the other end of the church, back of the altar. Only two of us are by the front door, down on the floor, rifles pointed out at the local parish. Jesus, it felt like I was on a firing squad. Him and me.

"When the men in back are ready to run for it, Polshanski gives us the signal. The sign of the cross. Can you believe it? Like he was forgiving us for what we were about to do. Then he and the rest go rushing out into the rice fields, like some marines rushing down the ramp of an LST. As they go out, the colonel and me open up on the Japs and Filipinos who were standing outside the church. That's what the hell we did."

Camper stopped and watched Griffin's reaction to the confession. What did he expect? It was one of those moments. If you were taping you'd switch off the machine. If you were taking notes you'd stop writing. But you wouldn't need your notes or tape. You'd remember anyway.

"We aimed low, at the ground in front of them, and as soon as we fired there was panic. They threw themselves on the ground or screamed and ducked for cover, Japs and Filipinos both. Then we scooted out the back door and followed the others out into the fields."

Griffin was relieved. "Jesus, you really had me there, you two. You had me going. I need a beer."

"Go have your beer," Charley Camper said. "But we ain't through yet . . ."

"It ought to be the ending. Another getaway in the nick of time. Only we didn't get away. We ran through the rice fields, going as fast as we could. They were firing at us from the church. Know something? You get a queer feeling in your back, when you know that someone behind you is aiming at it. You feel an urge to turn around and face them. You want to see it coming, whatever it is. It's like the animal in you wants to run as hard as it can, putting space between you and the barrel of the gun. But the human wants to turn around and look. Well, at the start the animal's the boss. I ran and, let me tell you, running through a rice field that time of year was like trying to hop through fresh cement, but you tell yourself every inch is an inch more that a bullet has to travel, an inch harder shot for the Japs to make, you tell yourself that as long as you can. Then someone inside says, oh, the hell with it, I want to *see* what's going on. I turned and I saw the Japanese standing right behind the church, Japs and Filipinos together, not shooting, not chasing, just standing like spectators at some kind of a sporting event, maybe a turkey shoot, and I saw three or four men who'd been shot the way I was afraid I'd be shot, shot while they were running. Now they were stretched out in mud and muddy water, not floating, not sinking, not moving. I stood right next to Owen Edwards, him with the fancy manners and the ten-dollar words. We must have run out of breath at the same time. It was about all we had in common, that and the fact we were puzzled the Japs weren't after us.

" 'I don't get it,' I said. Just then there's a shot, not from in back, but in front, where the rice gave way to sugarcane, and the shot gets Edwards in the stomach. He spins around, a full circle, looks at me and he says, 'I got it.' His hand is against his stomach, blood coming through his fingers. He holds his hand there and folds forward, so it looks like he's taking a bow. Then he sits down in the mud. 'Don't let me keep you,' he says. He died then.

"No wonder the Japanese hadn't chased us. No wonder they

stood and watched us run. They'd flushed us like a flock of ducks. More Japs were waiting for us, hidden at the edge of the cane field, like hunters in a blind, and when we got close they cut us down.

"I lifted my head and tried to make out what was left of us. It wasn't easy because we were all down in the mud, lying flat. At a glance, you couldn't tell the living from the dead. Then I see something slithering toward me, a human mud worm, and it's Connie, the Filipino boy I told you about. He tells me the idea is not to move, not to move at all, but be ready to fire when the Japs come out of the cane field, which they were going to have to do because if I couldn't tell the living from the dead, neither could they. Sooner or later, they'd come out to finish the job. They'd wait, but sooner or later they'd come.

"I remember. I remember watching that cane field. One minute it was a green hedge, waving in the wind, next minute out pops a Japanese soldier, scared as shit. He was expendable and he sure as hell expected to be expended. He's crouching down real low, the way a baseball player crouches when he wants to cut down the strike zone. Nothing happens, out comes another, then another, a dozen of 'em in all, and the last of them, an officer, steps a couple feet out into the rice field and sights around. What he sees is a bunch of muddy bodies ready for burial, some half buried already. I can see he's suspicious. Maybe his men were good. Maybe they were better than good, maybe they were lucky. But how good and lucky would they have to be for them to have gotten all of us, each and every one? No one firing, no one running, no one moaning, it was queer. He drew a sword and he ordered his men to fix bayonets. It was harvest time all right, and these were the grim reapers. The officer moved toward the nearest body. He nudged it with his boot, tried to turn it over, but dead weight in mud don't flip over easy. I saw him draw a pistol and shoot into the body. Nothing happened. He stepped over to the next body, same time as he waved the other Japs into the field. He holstered his pistol, raised up his sword, and I remember thinking, maybe he's right, maybe we *are* all dead, and I saw the sword go up in the air, and stay there, glinting in the sun, and stay and hesitate, and wave crazylike, side to side, because the dead body had sprung up out of the mud and jammed a knife in the officer's stomach. It was our missionary boy, come back to life, the same time a half dozen others of us open up, me last of all, but I had time to pick off a Jap who tried running back into the sugarcane. Oh, that was something, that was really something, it was the kind of comeback we'd been wanting since Bataan, getting up off our stomachs and making them run. 'Mean' Meade would have loved it.

"It was over in a minute. Eight of us get to our feet. As many others didn't. Some were slower than others getting up. It was like somebody had divided us into two groups, the living and the dead, and now we were seeing which pile of mud and bones and meat wound up on which side. Harding was up. I saw Polshanski lift himself up, surprised he was alive. I found myself looking at Sudul, I knew it was him, and I said let's go, it's time, but he'd gotten picked out for the other side, the dead ones. And that was that."

"We're almost done," Harding said.

It was late, past two, and the neon boil down in Olongapo was simmering down. The ones who were destined to get drunk, get laid, get in fights, had accomplished this. They were tucked away, and now the night belonged to men who couldn't sleep. The wee hours, the cool of the evening, when memories spanned the years the way radio transmissions bounced around the globe, odd songs from faraway places. Charley Camper returned from pissing. He brought more beer.

"I was thinking," he said. "Right after the war, when folks want to know what you did, what you saw, you don't want to talk about it. Years later, you're ready to talk things over, no one wants to hear it. Am I right?"

"Yes," Harding said.

"Then you come along," Charley said. "And here we sit."

"Yes."

"Well, I'm glad you made it," Charley said. "You too, Griffin."

"But you're not done yet," Harding cautioned.

"I know. But I will be in a minute. And then I can get back to worrying about my wife, the California condo woman, Ms.

Century Twenty-one. And my California girls. Other night, one of them told me she thought she was 'ready to go all the way.' You believe it?"

"The older one?"

"Uh-uh. The younger." Camper glanced from Harding to Griffin. He shrugged. He laughed. "A world of problems. You know something? I think it's nice we talk about the dead. Like we were saving them from being forgotten. For a little while, anyway. It's like a visit. Seeing 'Mean' Meade again. Sudul. Yeah . . ."

"And Polshanski," Harding said. It sounded like a reminder. That's how Camper took it.

"Yeah," he said. "And Polshanski.

"Where the rice fields ended, the swamps began. I mean swamps. Ponds and bogs and reeds and rivers and islands. A wonderful place, what with leeches below your waist and mosquitoes up above. No way of knowing how long the swamps went on. All we could do was point toward the one place we knew that wasn't swamp. That mountain. Arayat.

"We spent the night in the swamp. That was the worst night I ever had. The mosquitoes! They were everywhere, not just on your face and hands, but around your ears, like aircraft in a holding pattern, dozens of 'em standing by while one or two came in strafing. I tried waving 'em away. Then I waited for them to land, so I could swat 'em. Then I waited for them to bite so I squashed them in my own blood. I was crying, I was so hurt and frustrated. Christ, with the Japs on our tails, you'd think we could meet them on solid ground at least, in uniforms that weren't covered with mud. You'd think we could meet them without being bit and cut and feverish, on feet that weren't swollen, with toenails falling out. Your life on the line and you smell like shit!

"At dawn we joined the navy. There was an old raft pulled up into the reeds, a dozen poles lashed together is all it was, enough for four men, and it only took an hour before we had made another just like it. We used belts and clothing to hold the contraption together. Then we set off in our armada. Where the water was shallow we pushed along with poles. In deeper water, going was tough. We didn't have no proper oars, so we had to try paddling with our arms and legs, which I guess looked comical, except we were running for our lives. Oh, it was Huck Finn time for a while, weaving down those channels, high reeds on either side of us, birds spraying into the sky as we came near, fish jumping, we felt like explorers, like in the Everglades maybe, or the Sargasso Sea someplace. At the end we came upon an honest-to-God lake, a half mile across maybe, and on the other side was proper land, high and dry, with a couple of nipa huts around some fish ponds and, behind them, hills, all covered with trees and vines and creepers, and those hills were the bottom of the mountain we'd been aiming for, and it felt so close now we could kneel down and kiss its feet!

"All right. This is how the story ends. We saw the shoreline. We whooped it up and waved and then we by God raced across the lake, poling until the water got too deep, poling and then paddling with our arms and legs, crying and splashing like kids at a swimming hole, but we didn't have kids' energy, not anymore. About halfway across we pulled up, gasping. I remember I lay back, panting for air, and there was water on my back, and overhead a range of blue sky and, right in front, that gorgeous hunk of mountain, with clouds covering the top. I heard my own breathing, the slap of water against the edge of the raft, right up against my ears, tickling, the screech of a bird that dive-bombed overhead, a white bird that wasn't a plane, it was just a bird after a fish, a bird that maybe flew down from our mountain. And then: the sound of an engine, an engine in the water, a boat that was headed toward us, a boatload of Japs, and on the shoreline, out of the nipa huts, a bunch of white-uniformed Filipino cops. One if by land, two if by sea: either way they had us.

"I never felt worse in the whole war. You could take a beating. You could be proud of the beatings you took. You could stand losing a fight. Any fight that's worth fighting is worth losing. What really hurt was looking foolish, small, silly. And sitting on that pile of wood, paddling with my damn hands, I never felt more ashamed unless it was the time my mom caught me playing with myself in the bathtub.

"Harding tells us to swim for the reeds. He said it was our only chance, losing ourselves in there. When I'm in the water, I look and Polshanski's still on the raft, lying down.

" 'Come on, Polshanski,' I say, and suddenly he's got a shit-eating grin on his face, as though he'd put one over on us all, now he had the raft all to himself.

" 'Can't swim,' he says. And he's raising his Springfield toward the Japs. And what I see next . . ."

Charley Camper broke off and turned away, his fist in his eyes. He'd been talking fast, but the tears just ambushed him, came out of nowhere right in the middle of a sentence. Harding hadn't even seen it happen. He leaned back in his chair, eyes closed, watching in his mind's eye the story that Charley was telling.

". . . what I see is Polshanski, down on the raft, firing at the boat. The Jap with the megaphone is gone. The window in the wheelhouse is smashed and bloody, like after a car accident. The soldiers are crouching down behind the gunwales, firing and ducking, but a skinny man on a skinny raft isn't the easiest target in the world, especially when he's firing back. And Polshanski keeps firing. And the thing of it is, he takes time between his shots. Oh, how he takes time! You could light a stubborn pipe in the time he took. Those soldiers who are popping up to fire at him, he's actually trying to time them! He's watching for them, trying to guess, and while I'm looking on, he by God guesses right and drops a Japanese soldier over the railing. I must have shouted, because he looked over at me and he smiles, does Polshanski, a sneaky smile that says, see, I showed you something after all. I guess I was the last thing he saw on earth, because this time he waited too long. He got shot two or three times by soldiers on the boat. That was it for him. I think he died right off, even though the men on the boat kept shooting and the boat kept coming, bearing right down on him, like a destroyer ramming a submarine, running right over him. And that was the last I ever did see . . ."

Another of these moments, Griffin thought, a moment that you wished was over and you wouldn't have missed. You weren't with them. What you pictured, vivid as it was, wasn't exactly what Charley Camper saw as he talked. But it was close enough. You watched him cry. You saw him yank the bottom of his T-shirt up toward his eyes and wipe them. Then he dabbed at his nose with the same piece of shirt.

". . . the last I ever did see of my friend Polshanski. So."

A deep breath, a sigh of relief. The hardest part was over. Now he was only talking about himself.

"We were in a clump of reeds, not much of a place, more roots and water than dry ground, and we fired at that boat. Then one of us got hit—Vernon Waters, it was—and the incoming fire was so much we couldn't move, and they tossed in a grenade, and pretty soon it was going to be all over. This time we have no choice. We step out of the reeds, hands over our heads, and the boat's about fifty feet away. The Japs make a motion like they want us to swim over to the boat. As we approached, though, it pulled away and the Jap soldiers—laughing, now—motioned that we should keep swimming. And we had no choice. The joke was on us all right. So was the movie camera. That was the gimmick. They were getting footage of the ending of MacArthur's Ghosts.

"The boat reached shore, tied up at some dinky pier. We're still paddling away. They set up their camera on land and signal for us to come on in, come out of the water with our hands up and walk real slowly to the camera.

"I remember I looked at Harding, and I confess, I kind of blamed him for all this. This wasn't supposed to happen. This was his fault. Where were his brains, his magic? Why'd we have to run out of luck now? And he looks at me and he says that I shouldn't worry, everything was going to work out. He looks at me in a way that gives me the willies. 'I promise,' he says.

"How about it, Colonel?" Camper asked. Interrupting his story, he walked over to Harding, kneeled in front of him, like a player consulting with his coach. "Gonna tell me now?"

"Not yet," Harding said.

"Ever? 'Fore I die?"

"Maybe."

"What you got to understand," Camper said to Griffin, "is now we're talking legend. Not legend that you hear about. Legend you see. I was there. I saw it. And the trouble is, I still don't know. I don't know whether this man was just trying to buck me up and make me feel better about surrendering or whether he knew what was going to happen. I don't know. I told the story a dozen times. It made the papers in the States, later on. And

I still don't know the truth of it. How about it, Colonel? Give an old buddy a break?"

Harding put his hands on Charley's shoulders, patted them, drew him forward, into an awkward hug.

"Charley . . ."

"All right." Camper lurched away abruptly. "Look at him, Griffin. Look at him good."

Blue eyes, narrowing somewhat when he knew they were watching. Hands steadying Charley, holding him close. The trace of a smile.

"There," Charley said. "Now you got it. He hasn't changed a bit. That's just the way he looked back then.

"Well, there was a kind of double line, a gamut of Japs and cops, jeering, prodding, snapping pictures, and we had no choice but to walk that walk when I hear shooting, lots of it. At first I thought somebody was celebrating, but it kept up, and someone screamed. Then I see the line in front of us come all apart, there's people down on the ground, cops and soldiers all tangled together, on their backs, on their knees, rushing past us, bumping us out of the way. Suddenly we don't matter a bit, and I still don't know what the hell goes on.

"Then it's over. There was still some firing now and then, here and there, but it's the difference—you can hear it, I swear you can—between a battle, with both sides going like hell, and the end of a battle, which is a series of suicides and executions. The way it always ends. Mopping up, they call it.

"When it's quiet, we stand up and watch these soldiers come out of the village toward us. I saw they were Filipinos, dressed like peasants for the most part, though some had bits and pieces of different uniforms. Some had guns, some had bolos. But they all had one thing in common. You could see it in their walk. A certain something I've seen in barrooms and football fields and boxing rings: they were tired, but they'd won. They'd kicked ass. They'd taken some shots, but they'd given better than they'd gotten and in the end they'd won. You could see it in their walk.

"They stand off and look at us, talking among themselves. Some go to the shore and slap water on themselves. Others are showing weapons they must just have captured, guns, packs, clothing. They must have stripped the losers clean. At last, one of them fellows separates himself from the rest and walks toward us. No uniform or rank or nothing, he looks like all the rest. He takes us in, the sorry-looking bunch we are, and then he goes straight for me, like he knows me, and maybe I should know him. He looks familiar, but I can't place him.

"'Hey, Joe,' he says, smiling but a little sarcastic. 'Hey, Joe, you have a name?'

"'My name is Charley Camper,' I say. 'Sergeant Charley Camper.'

"And he says, 'My name is Flash.' Can you beat it? The same guy I bossed around Baguio turns out he's running a peasant army—the Hukbalahaps, they were called. Huks for short. And he saved my life! Talk about a world turned upside down. Or maybe, right side up . . ."

"That's it, Charley."

"A bunch of dirt-poor pissant peasants saved my hide," Charley cried out, "and I haven't forgotten that. Nothing I can do about it now but—"

"That's it, Charley," Harding repeated, louder, and this time the big man heeded him.

"That's it, huh? I'm finished?"

"You're finished."

"But you're not, are you, Colonel?"

"No, Charley."

28

The next morning, Griffin was up early, light-headed from the beers and the Irish coffees. Ready to leave for Manila, he walked down to where he'd sat till just a few hours ago, Charley Camper's hammock roost, barroom, barbecue pit. The big man was there, a mug of coffee in his hands, staring out at the bay.

"Howdy," he said.

"Good morning," Griffin answered. "Colonel Harding still in bed?"

"I guess."

"You're the one who should be tired."

"Somebody has to feed the pigs."

"Some view," said Griffin. The neon was gone, the city had receded. Now he noticed the curve of the mountains, the sweep of bay. There was something sensual about a harbor. Sailors talked about harbors the way men talked of women, flanks and thighs and coves. Secret places.

"A piece of ass," Camper said. "I know what you're thinking."

"I was?"

"The country, I mean. Territory, nation, colony, commonwealth, whatever. I read about all these places that get their independence. They spit on the old flag, rename their streets and cities. It's like a bad divorce. But this is different. They're still our piece of ass. And we're their John. The talk changes, the price goes up, but they're still putting out and we're still putting up."

"I've got to go," Griffin said. "Take good care of the colonel. Maybe I'll see you after New Year's."

"I'll be here," Charley answered stoically. Then he warmed and added, "Come on back. I'd like that."

"So long, Charley."

Charley kneeled in front of his refrigerator, in front of a pile of empty beer bottles. He lifted one up, poured out a last few sour drops, deposited it in a wooden beer case for return to San Miguel.

"See?" Charley said, gesturing to the bottles. "Dead soldiers."

Part Six

★ ★ ★
★ ★

A FURLOUGH FROM THE PAST

29

MacArthur's Ghost is heroic, solitary, melancholy. He is old and doomed. He is mysterious and historical, weighed down with feelings that torture him and with memories he dispenses to me a spoonful at a time. He enlists—somehow—the loyalty of everyone he meets. An aging flack like Eddie Richter. A beery pig farmer like Charley Camper. And me. I would follow him anywhere. I've enlisted. I'm in for the duration. Duration of what? Of a paper chase, a treasure hunt, a forced march down memory lane. He exhausts me. Does he ever get drunk? Did he ever fall in love? Does he have opinions about politics? Is he a Republican? A Yankee fan? Has he seen *Apocalypse Now*? When was the last time he hit someone? Or cried? He carries me along into the past. And when, as now, I tug toward the present, to a life I call my own, I still feel him behind me, in the dark hills over Subic Bay, waiting for my return.

Outskirts of Manila. Rice fields yielding to a zone of factories and warehouses. Blocks of apartments, a ring of neon around the ground-floor shops, like the residue of an electronic tide: SAN MIGUEL BEER, GOODYEAR TIRES, BRUCE LEE LIVES. Plants, laundry, kids on every floor of high rises that look more like refugee ships than residences: which way to America? New construction, cranes atop towers, like great birds of prey. Clustered around building sites, like smaller birds picking crumbs, the huts and sheds the workers live in, campfires and cooking pots all pressing against the unfinished structure, as if the people who built things had claim to live in them.

Now, Manila itself. Traffic. Horns. Music. Pall of smoke and diesel. Kids playing basketball on a raggedy asphalt court, five-foot-five-inchers scuffling and elbowing. First signs of America: franchise food places with familiar names. Pizza Hut and Shakey's. Dunkin' Donut. They're like the mission stations the Spaniards built in California, fortress, church, and business all combined. Happy, sad little places, making promises that won't be kept.

I left my heart in a city by the bay, all right. Alleys of noise and fumes, hives of tin and tar paper, habitat of beggars, lawyers, whores, and pistoleros. City where all things are possible, anything goes. City where Americans strayed and stayed, a prodigal city for prodigal sons, westward outpost of American history, here where manifest destiny hits its dead man's curve.

30

Griffin walked into a fenced enclosure that appeared to be an open-air market, filled with stalls catering to tourists: herds of carved water buffalo and flocks of screaming wooden eagles; hammocks and tablecloths and T-shirts, ten-foot salad forks, wicker and rattan chairs and chests and cradles and bird cages, a maze of handicrafts through which he wandered, working his way toward a sound at the center of it all, heart of darkness herself, Donna Summer, singing how she wanted to be made love to, again and again, every which way.

At the center of the bazaar stood a rickety nightclub, thatch-roofed, concrete-floored, with lean-tos and outbuildings converging on a stage where the Donna Summer clone was matching the original, beat for writhing beat, shimmy for shimmy, and from Donna Summer she went into what was clearly her finale, "Jungle Fever," an equatorial lied that consisted mostly of moans, grunts, and adroitly simulated orgasms.

"Too bad you missed Christmas," Clifford Lerner said as he came up to greet Griffin. "You should see her do the Hallelujah Chorus. How are you?"

"Tired. You?"

"Never better," Lerner said. "I've been running all over town, diddling your movie company, poking into people's war records, the First Lady's film festival. Know what I've learned?"

"No."

"Of course you don't. Well, the first is that this is a great town to be a journalist, a foreign journalist, I mean. It's a dictatorship, but it's a small, corrupt dictatorship, hot, tired, and worried, George, worried as a barmaid past midnight and on the wrong side of twenty-one. That's the first thing."

"That's plenty," Griffin said. A midget fire-eater was onstage and a hefty German tourist was summoned to dance with her. The dance consisted of the little woman—Little Lucy, she was called—scooting between the Teuton's legs.

"The other thing is—is what really grabs me, George, makes me feel like a tiger. What I've found here is that everything connects. I don't know why it is. The size of the place, or that it's an island, the climate or the history. But here, nothing exists alone. Understand? You start poking around any subject, doesn't matter how isolated, and before you know it, you're talking politics, you're doing history, you're trading in names, and the names are always the same. I'll give you an example. Take this movie that's paying you . . ."

There was a commotion onstage, a blare of horns and roll of drums. Lerner leaned forward excitedly. "I want you to see this," he said.

A woman in tights had dragged five customers onstage, each from different sections of the audience—an Australian, Arab, Japanese, German, and American. Across the stage stood a short, muscular Filipino with baggy pants and a pirate's mustache. He was holding a cement block off the ground with a hook that passed through his tongue. When he turned his back to the audience, you could see his back had been made a target, with concentric circles of what looked like shoe polish. Bull's-eye was right between the shoulder blades.

"What is this?" Griffin asked.

"The spirit made flesh," Lerner replied.

The hostess presented each of the men with a dart, steel-tipped, feather-tailed. Around the room, the emcee moved from table to table, revving up the action, as if this were an international competition, an Olympic demonstration sport.

First up was the German, Dieter so-and-so from Dusseldorf, a precision tool manufacturer. The crowd applauded. Dusseldorf Dieter sighted carefully, the distance, the dart, the wind and the variables, and let fly a shot that hit the target at the right shoulder blade, where flesh was thin. As soon as the man flexed his muscles, the dart fell to the floor. The crowd hooted, the emcee made a joke about darts that fell out without achieving penetration, and Griffin wondered if you could do anything in

Manila, clip a toenail, boil an egg, without the performance assuming sexual overtones. The Japanese, a Mr. Hirota on a special "Eros Tour" of Manila, was next. His dart landed feathers first and tumbled to the floor, and now the emcee talked about how all Japanese performances were sanitary and over quickly.

"So much for the Axis powers," Lerner whispered.

Next was a man from Kuwait, a tall bearded Omar Sharif type in a white suit, "Mr. Ahmed, a regular visitor to Manila."

"I'll bet he is," Lerner said. "They have a couple hundred thousand Filipinos working for them. They go to the desert to work and he comes to the islands to play . . ."

Mr. Ahmed hit the target all right, a hard stabbing shot that landed in the left buttock, a location that convulsed the audience. "Nice shot, Mr. Ahmed," the emcee congratulated him.

The Australian, a lumber industry executive, was a jovial pub-crawling sort, thoroughly pissed. He glanced back at his mates for encouragement and then sent a dart that implanted itself in the band that circled the target's innermost ring. It was there to stay too: a single drop of blood attested Australia's firm intentions. The dart girl hugged the Australian. Even the Filipino turned around and gave what was probably a grin, though the cement block suspended by a hook through his tongue made it hard to tell.

"What a place," Lerner sighed. "Decadence or decay, who knows? Anyway, I love it. Know what I'm going to call my article on your film? 'Rouge on a Corpse.'"

"Who's publishing?"

"Would you believe it? I haven't even thought about that yet."

"I thought you were cash-and-carry. You've really changed."

"Virtue is its own reward, my boy. Look out, here come the Yanks."

America's hopes rested with a brawny, crew-cut serviceman from Clark or Subic. "Win one for the Gipper," someone shouted, and everyone laughed. The American was an awkward, boyish chap, ill at ease onstage but by God determined to go for it. He raised the dart and aimed.

"Oooh, what a hunk," a voice from somewhere crooned. Concentration broken, the serviceman dropped his arm, laughed, mopped his brow, then took aim again. Part Eagle Scout, part Lieutenant Calley: it all depended where you put him. Griffin knew that the American would win. He closed his eyes and heard the cheering. When he opened them again, the dart girl was plucking the missile out of the target's back, the man had removed the hook from his tongue and was beaming, the band struck up the "Halls of Montezuma," and Lerner was ordering another round of drinks.

"You were going to give me an example," Griffin said, "of how everything connects. From the movie . . ."

"Well, here we have a film that hearkens back to the glory days of Filipino-American cooperation. A film that celebrates the guerrilla period in a country led by a former guerrilla chieftain, Ferdinand Marcos. And a film that is a primary ornament of Mrs. Marcos's pet project, the ruinously expensive Manila Film Festival. So I checked into who owns this film. The local connection. Humor me a little, George. Guess."

"Marcos, or a front for Marcos?"

"No."

"His wife?"

"Our Lady of Cinematography? She's an insomniac, so they say. She has a screening room in Malacanang Palace, watches film cassettes all night long, while Pops is sleeping down the hall. Good guess. But no."

"One of the American producers, then. Wingfield, Larry Wingfield. His uncle was out here. Or Beaumont . . ."

"No again. All of those people have a piece of the film, sure. The whole film is a bit of a wank. Spend a little money here, claim to have spent a lot, accrue your profits overseas where the film is shown. But do you know who's the initial sponsor? Aurora Santos Villanueva . . . a.k.a. Birdy . . . a.k.a. First Lady of the opposition. So tell me, George. What do you think of that?"

"I don't know. It doesn't make a lot of sense. Birdy Villanueva loathes Imelda Marcos. You should hear her carry on. What she says . . ."

"What she says doesn't matter," Lerner interrupted. "Oh, I know the line. Imelda's the First Lady and Birdy's the wife of the opposition standard bearer. But from where I sit, they're two of a kind. How much would change if Birdy and her crew took over? You think you could tell the difference on del Pilar Street? In Tondo? In the provinces? Birdy and her pipe-smoking spouse might get to move into Malacanang someday. Call it a victory if you like. A victory for good manners or professional bookkeeping or sound business principles. Just don't call it a revolution."

The nightclub was emptying, although you had the feeling someone would bring them drinks as long as they could pay for them. Manila was a city that never slept; it just rested between customers. Lerner and Griffin wandered out through the deserted handicrafts bazaar. Velvet paintings, lacquered coconut crabs reposed in silence. Woven hammocks and wicker bird cages hung still, screaming eagles called it a night and came to roost.

"I've got something else for you," Lerner said. "Your friend, Colonel Harry Roberts Harding. I wondered about him. A small matter, something missing, a gap, a hiatus, a lacuna, a stretch of time unaccounted for . . ."

"Such as . . ."

"Such as about forty fucking years!" Lerner burst out laughing. "That's a little longer than a lost weekend. I don't suppose you've wondered . . ."

"He was running a motel in Florida, I heard," Griffin volunteered, knowing that it sounded lame.

"Sure. For five years. But what about before that? And what did he do for money? Remember, all that colonel stuff is local, honorary. He didn't even qualify for veteran's benefits."

"Was there money in the family?"

"There was money all right. He got it in 1949, in a will. Before that he was working construction. The money came from here, about half a million dollars of it. From the estate of a Baguio millionaire whose nephew just happens to be one of the film's producers . . ."

"Uncle Harrison?"

"A name you know?"

"Harrison Wingfield."

"See, George. Everything connects. . . . Are you free tomorrow afternoon? Around one?"

"Sure. What's up?"

"A little travel. A little history. A little mystery. Who knows?" Lerner had stopped in front of his favorite place, the G-spot. A door opened and the place breathed out at them: beer, cigarettes, perfume, and Tina Turner's version of Proud Mary. "I have an appointment with my fellatrix. Care to join me? It might do you good."

"Good night, Clifford."

"Good night, partner."

31

Dawn in Manila. In the park outside the Manila Hotel, elderly Chinese finger and punch the morning air. Tai chi. Waiters at the Aristocrat play chess. Nurses wheel baby carriages into the children's playground behind the Quirino grandstand. Harry Roberts Harding says that sometimes you shrug off the present and sometimes the present shrugs you off. Sometimes, like this morning, it more than shrugs. It giggles, farts, makes babies. It sings, cries, whistles, beeps horns, pisses everywhere, mops sweat, hawks phlegm, and goes about its daily and unhaunted business. Ignorance and bliss. Sure, those who don't learn from history are condemned to repeat it. But if they don't know their history in the first place, how can they be aware of the repetition? Think about it, Colonel Harding.

The U.S. embassy to the erstwhile territory, commonwealth, and now republic of the Philippines sits on a grassy expanse that juts from Roxas Boulevard out into Manila Bay. Its seaside posture, the surrounding fence, the guards—understandable, of course—give what would otherwise be a pleasant campuslike complex the feeling of a beachhead, hard-pressed. A show of passport gets me past the Filipino security guards who are the first line of defense. Inside, I sign in and wait while a clerk calls Susan Hayes, the woman of my recent dreams. Immigration. Visas. Veterans affairs. Social Security. On the walls are pictures of Monument Valley, Crater Lake, the Shenandoah Valley: another planet.

Whoa! Hold it! A woman is looking at me, a long-haired fox is giving me a sidelong glance that is recogni-

tion and conspiracy combined, like when you see a kid
hiding from his playmates behind a tree and the kid
pleads with you not to betray his hiding place: please,
it's just a game we're playing, don't give me away.
Where do I know her from? She sits across the hall with
a six-footer, all crew cut and muscles, who must be a
serviceman. He is puzzled by a sheaf of papers. She is
not. She leads him through one question after another,
pen in hand, brushing aside her hair when it gets in the
way, hair that is cascade, veil, and entourage. The same
hair—now I have it!—which entranced travel writer
Thomas Gibbins a few weeks ago. He's probably back
home, impaled by guilt, while she of the raven tresses
sits in the U.S. consulate, helping her latest candidate
fill out papers that declare their intention to marry and
live happily on the mainland.

Susan Hayes is unavailable, "tied up in meetings."
Escorting me out, her Filipina secretary gives me a tour
of the consular section. (She also gives me a handwritten
note, confirming New Year's Eve.) Like toll booth col-
lectors outside a tunnel—an eight-thousand-mile trans-
Pacific tunnel, in this case—the Department of State's
document inspectors sit facing a room full of Filipino
visa applicants. Immigration is handled elsewhere, with
waiting lists that stretch for years. Immigration is a slow,
slow game. Gourmet cooking. Visas are fast food. The
document inspectors have a few minutes, not more
than five, to scan letters, plane tickets, promises of employment, tax returns, lists of relatives, references,
sponsors, all in order to determine whether the appli-
cant can be depended upon to return to the Philippines.
They look for reasons that would make Filipinos return:
family, job, money, property. All these can be fab-
ricated. Documents can be purchased across the street,
suits rented, and prosperous-looking Rolex watches.
People can also be rented: there are visa impostors,
white-haired grandmothers, saintly and harmless in
Manila, who are nineteen-year-old taxi dancers when
the plane touches down at Oakland.

The revolution is not for today. Or for tomorrow . . .

32

"All right," Clifford Lerner said. They were standing outside the Manila Hotel. "You remember that day out on Corregidor? Marcos hugged your colonel. 'Welcome home' and all that. You remember?"

"Sure."

"And did you have the feeling, during and after your colonel's speech, exemplary and extemporary as it was, that something had gone slightly awry? A false note, an indiscreet reference of some kind, something not quite . . . in the script?"

"Yes," Griffin answered. There was that consultation inside the hospitality tent, right after the abrupt departure of the Marcos party. Hugh Beaumont had worried aloud about a loose cannon on deck. Cecilia Santos propounded the Philippine government's right not to be embarrassed. Larry Wingfield wanted Harding shipped back to Florida.

"And being, sort of, a reporter, did you ever find out what was causing the fuss?"

"Well, in general, there was some concern that—" George stopped in mid-sentence. He sounded like a unit publicist. "No, I don't know what it was."

"I checked the text of Harding's speech that ran in the papers the next day," Lerner said. "They're real good at running out the text of speeches. And then I found a radio chap who'd preserved the whole history-making moment on tape. I was looking to see what, if anything, they'd left out. And guess what? It was the part where he mentions people he fought with back in the glory days. A list of names just like in the detective novels. The first was—"

"Mr. Clifford Lerner?" Their driver, a slight, polite young man, led them to a jeepney that had been decommissioned.

Gone were the chrome statues, the phosphorescent paint, tape
decks, mirrors. Gone, for that matter, was the dashboard Jesus.
All there was was a sign that said: HIBERNIAN FATHERS MISSION.
And, below, TONDO.

"The first was Walter Cushing," Lerner continued when
they'd climbed in back. "He was a mining engineer in northern
Luzon, same general area your fellow author comes from. He
organized resistance activities, had a merry old time until the
Japs cornered him. He saved the last bullet for himself. The Japs
were so impressed they gave him a proper funeral."

"No harm mentioning him, then," Griffin surmised. "A dead
hero."

"No harm," Lerner agreed. "Another name was touchy,
though. Felipa Cualala."

"A woman?"

"Sort of. A big mannish woman, must have been on the rough
side. She led what most folks agree was the first battle of the
war, the guerrilla war that is. A running battle out in the Candaba Swamps north of here, against a combined force of Japanese soldiers and Philippine police. She was a left-winger, all
right, part of the early Huk movement. You've heard about the
Huks."

"Not from you."

"Hukbalahap guerrillas. They started before the war. Peasants organizing against landlords. Private armies. Nasty. During
the war they fought the Japs. And after the war, they fought the
Philippine government—and its U.S. advisers. It went on for
years and there are some people who would tell you it never
stopped. But in the fifties, under Ramon Magsaysay, the government got its act together. Combination of glove and fist. Free
land to surrendering rebels. Bribes, amnesties, military pressure. You know . . ."

"And this woman . . ."

"She was long gone by then. She turned bad, they say. Became a bandit. Court-martialed and executed by her own side,
the Huks. Went in front of the firing squad saying anybody
who passed up a chance to make money had shit for brains.
Anyway, she made Harding's list. Understandable. She had her
day . . ."

"Who else?"

"An aviator, Jesus Villamor. He's even on postage stamps. A provincial governor—Ablan, Roque Ablan—who took to the hills and refused to collaborate. Another okay choice. Christ, will you look at that! We're in Tondo!"

If someone, a perverse movie director, say, had asked a set designer to throw up an image of poverty, a squatters' community, money no object, and if the result were Tondo, you would accuse everyone involved of having gone too far. Tondo was excess, wretched excess. Its alleys were too narrow and went on too long, its wooden shacks crowded too close together, its roads were too potholed, too filthy to be believed. The canals that cut through Tondo, open sewers that they were, did they have to be so foul that they bubbled and festered on their way to sea? Did every dog have to be scabrous and sag-titted? Did every wide-eyed rickety kid have to be a beggar, every baby have to squall, each open lot have to be a plain of garbage? It was too much. Too many clouded eyes, too many running sores, bad teeth, curved spines. Too much misery in the crowd of hey-joe kids who swarmed their jeepney when it paused in traffic. Hey, Joe. Hey, Joe. Echoes of MacArthur's victory forty years before, chocolate bars and kisses and I have returned. Hey, Joe.

Passing by an empty lot, traffic at a crawl, they saw some kids crowded around a tethered dog they were taunting and torturing. Two or three older kids took turns clubbing, while half a dozen giggling youngsters looked on. Bloody-mouthed, broken toothed, half blinded, the dog didn't know what to do or where to turn, whether to grovel, snap, growl, bark, or whine.

"They're killing the dog," Lerner said. "To eat. They say the slow killing makes the meat more tender. Think there could be anything to it?"

"I don't know." Griffin prayed for a break in traffic. He looked away from the dog, only to have his gaze land on a pile of culverts, round pipes stacked on top of each other, with people peeking out of the openings: a return to the caves.

"They massage beef in Japan," Lerner reflected. "I did a piece on it. George, you can cut that stuff with your fork, no kidding. Kobe beef, beer-fed. Incredible stuff."

"Come on, Clifford," Griffin pleaded. "Back to the names."

"All right. Names. Names of dead warriors so far. And some not so dead. Nestor Contreras is very much alive. A three-star general. Quite a record. Teenage guerrilla during the war, then a can-do junior officer all through the Huk rebellion. Magsaysay found him, promoted him. 'Living proof that a poor boy can rise to the top of a democratic army.' That sort of thing. He's been shipped off to the U.S. two or three times. There's a photo of him with Jack Kennedy. The thing of it is, despite working under Marcos, Contreras has stayed pretty clean, kept his distance, made himself a name. 'Dedicated, competent, personally honest.' Some people think he's just the ticket after Marcos goes. So when Harding came back and mentioned him on Corregidor, people noticed."

"And we're going to see him?"

"I'm working on that. He's in the field somewhere, they say. No, we're going to see one of the others Harding mentioned. A real war-horse. Fought the landlords, fought the Japs, kept fighting. A Huk. Felipe Olmos."

"I know you," the priest exclaimed. "George Griffin, isn't it?"

"Yes. But this is Mr. Lerner. He's the fellow who called you. I just came along."

"Of course you did," the priest said. Murphy was his name, and Griffin couldn't place him. He was a hearty, jovial Irishman, a brogue on his tongue, a cement mixer in his front yard, a conspirator's twinkle in his eyes.

"You say we've met before?"

"In Quezon City. At one of Birdy Villanueva's get-togethers. I sat next to you."

"Now I remember." The priest who relished *National Enquirer*–caliber rumors about Malacanang Palace. Affairs, babies, hit squads, salvagings.

"Well, I won't detain you. I've got work to do. The rules are, I should see everyone who asks to see Felipe Olmos. Not a very onerous duty. He's upstairs."

"Father," Clifford Lerner asked. "Just wondering—an old lefty like him—what's he doing here?"

"He's a believer, Mr. Lerner. So am I."

"Surely not a believer in the same thing."

"I'd like to think he is, yes. Social justice. Fair government. Equitable distribution of wealth—all that."

"And religion?"

"Good Lord," Murphy said, snapping his fingers. "Religion. I almost forgot. I must ask him sometime what he thinks about religion. After you're done."

Griffin nodded and followed Lerner out of the room, toward a flight of steps.

"Gentlemen?" Father Murphy came out behind them. "Don't think me frivolous. He's a believer. I am. If we believe in the same thing, fine. If it turns out our faiths are different— well, that just doubles the chance that someone around here is right."

Felipe Olmos stood waiting at the top of the stairs, an alert, wiry little man in plain khaki trousers and a blue short-sleeved shirt. He greeted Lerner politely but perked up when Griffin was introduced.

"MacArthur's Ghost's ghost! That's a lot of ghosts, I think."

He laughed at his own joke, a distracted giggle, as if someone were tickling him.

"You want to put me in the movie?" he asked. "You want me to play a part? I can be the good guy. I can be the bad guy. I've played many parts."

"No, sir," Lerner said. "We had more serious things in mind."

The interview was all downhill from there. Maybe it was too long ago. Maybe he'd shared too many platforms with "I led three lives" FBI men and ministers who'd escaped from behind the iron curtain. It seemed it was easier for him to remember the things he said than the things he'd done. He offered memorization, not memories. A paragraph about his love of American democracy, from Thomas Paine to Martin Luther King. A sad, sweet little riff about old socialist times in Luzon, the twenties and thirties, when he and a handful of others corresponded with Eugene Debs and Leon Blum. Textbook dissertations about revolution and counterrevolution, ancient intramural spats between populists, socialists, agrarian reformers, Marxist theoreticians, all the feuds and schisms of a long-lost cause. According to Lerner, Juan and Felipe Olmos had risen high in the rank of the Huks. "Felipe was the talker, the theoretician, the philosopher. Juan did the fighting. A one-man land-reform program, Juan was: six feet of ground for the oligarchs, two hectares for the peasants." Felipe Olmos had been caught or surrendered—that was unclear—in 1950 and served fifteen years in prison. Marcos had released and adopted him, used him as a kind of traveling exhibit: see how the New Society reconciles and absorbs its former enemies. For years he'd been traveling the lecture circuit, detailing his disillusionment with communism, his discovery of Jesus. It was sad, about the revolution he led. Not for today, not for tomorrow. Also: not for yesterday.

Griffin shifted in his chair so he could see out of a back window, out onto the shoreline. A colony of squatters lived out there, right behind the mission. At first glance it looked like a fishing village, with nets drying in the breeze. Then you saw the nets were plastic garbage bags, retrieved from dumps, emptied, cleaned and hung out to dry. Now he turned back to Olmos: bright eyes, wrinkled face, dark crew cut, and not a pound over his fighting weight. More lives than a cat, more skins than a snake. What do you have in common with the man you used to be? Would you recognize the youth who helped Charley Camper empty out a Baguio mansion? Was that a rehearsal for times to come, a revolutionary drill? Do you remember the day that Harding came out of the swamp? How about it? I come to you from Harry Roberts Harding, from out of the realm of memories and regrets. What about you? Have you left that land forever?

"George?"

"Sorry," he said. "I drifted off."

"Perhaps we all have," Lerner said, a hint that was impossible for either Griffin or Olmos to ignore. Lerner breathed deeply, turned back to Olmos, ready for one last try. "Since the Huk rebellion sputtered out thirty years or so ago . . ."

"Sputtered out?"

"Well, you were captured. So were many others. Lots of men were killed. After the mid-fifties, things got quiet. So I would say it sputtered out. Yes."

"You don't understand. You like your history neat, with beginnings and ends. World War Two? It began on a single, certain day, with a shocking attack on an innocent fleet at Pearl Harbor. No? And it ended with—what do you call it—'V-J day.' Atomic bombs. You have it all down, date of birth, date of death. You think you do. But history isn't like that. Your colonel knows . . . things die down. They don't die out."

"Ah, so you're suggesting there's a kind of symbolic link between the Huk movement and today's NPA?"

"Yes."

"Only symbolic?"

George sensed it at the same time Olmos did. Lerner had been going out of his way to be argumentative, cocky, and a little dense. And it was, all of it, an act.

"What do you mean?"

"I mean your brother, sir, I mean Juan Olmos. Another name that Colonel Harding mentioned on Corregidor." Now he turned to George, to fill him in. "It's interesting. They announced his death five times from 1946 to 1954. They say he surrendered, brought in a whole army, all on the condition he be sent overseas with a fortune. They say he had plastic surgery, ran for office, changed his name. They say he wound up in Cuba, or that he runs a gold mine in Apayo-Kalinga or a last command in Mindanao or he smuggles drugs and guns between Borneo and Zamboanga. And some people say he's still out there fighting. That's the wildest rumor of all."

Felipe Olmos listened to all of it with a smile. "People ask me all the time."

"I'll bet they do," Lerner said. "It's the Hollywood touch. Juan Olmos, Scarlet Pimpernel of the People's Revolution, Red Robin Hood, guerrilla ghost, the missing link between the Huks and the NPA, the light that failed and the fire to come. I love this stuff! What became of your brother, Mr. Olmos? Not that you'd tell us . . ."

"The movement I led"—the old man walked toward them, holding an imaginary something over his head—"was like a chalice . . ."

Let's get out of here quickly, Lerner's look told Griffin. This guy's daffy.

". . . which, when history dashed it, broke into a thousand

pieces. Some pieces fell to the left. Some to the right. Some moved. Others lay still."

"Yeah, well, great," Lerner said. "What about Yamashita and his treasure?"

"Yamashita. He and I have something in common. Guess what?"

"Really . . . I don't know. George, do you?"

"No."

"We were both war criminals!" Olmos shouted.

"War criminals?" Griffin asked.

"We lost." Olmos laughed at that, laughed alone, and it occurred to Griffin that maybe there was something to be said for death in action, when you compared it to years of sitting on the sidelines while new wars were fought, new leaders took sides, and changed them.

"They hanged Yamashita." That was Lerner's rather heavy-handed observation. "You lived."

"Yes," Olmos said. "So I hear."

"And the treasure? Colonel Harding says it exists."

"Colonel Harding may be right. I heard about this Yamashita treasure. I heard about it from my brother. From some of the other Huk fighters as well."

"When?"

"Toward the end of the war."

"What did they say about it?"

"I'm not sure. They said they had it. Or would have it. And that it would save us all, protect us from our enemies."

"It didn't. Did it?" That was Lerner's parting shot. He got up and thanked the old man for his time. It was nothing, Olmos said. Lerner didn't dispute the point.

"Mr. Griffin," Olmos said. "Do you think you could stay behind just a moment?"

"Clifford? Okay?"

"Sure. I'll be downstairs. Thanks again."

When Lerner had gone, Olmos gestured for Griffin to take a seat. Griffin obeyed and waited. The old man went over to the window Griffin had stared out of at the squatters' hovels, the poisoned beach, the plastic garbage bags rustling in the wind.

"Out there," Olmos said, without turning around, "they bury babies in cardboard coffins."

Downstairs, someone had turned on a radio, and there were kids playing in the churchyard. Father Murphy had the cement mixer going; he could hear it turning. And now a song on the radio. "The Tracks of My Tears." You couldn't miss with music in a place like this: if it didn't complement, it contradicted; what it couldn't illustrate, it mocked. Olmos stayed by the window till the song was done.

"So," he said, finally turning around. "How is my old friend?"

"Fine. Traveling around. Working with me on this book. I guess you know."

"Has he mentioned me?"

"Yes." To forestall further questions, and longer answers, he explained Harding's strategy of telling the story in order and visiting places where things had happened.

"He's not really telling the story," Olmos said. "He's reliving it."

"Yes, you could say that."

"He wants it to come out differently this time. Poor man."

"Any messages?"

"He knows about what happened to me. The war. The war after the war. The prison after that. This . . ." Olmos took a breath, then resumed. "I'm a Communist. I'm a Marcos puppet. I'm a Christian. I'm a turncoat. What does he think of me?"

"I don't know. He remembers you the way you were, when he knew you."

"Yes."

"And . . ." He was way out of line now and he might regret it. "I think that he's hoping that you remember him the same way."

"He was something, Mr. Griffin. He was something." From the way his voice drifted off, no formulas, no paragraphs, no protests, Griffin knew that this time Olmos had gone back to the past, broken through to the place he shared with Harding. He closed his eyes and lingered there a while. "He was something."

Clifford Lerner was outside, in the shade, watching Father Murphy shovel sand into a cement mixer.

"Get what you wanted?" asked the priest, without breaking the rhythm of his shoveling.

"Oh, sure," Lerner said.

"They almost won, back then."

"No they didn't," Lerner said. "They never had a chance."

"Oh, I see," the priest conceded cheerfully. "If you say so."

"You haven't seen Juan Olmos, have you?"

"Looks like Felipe, only taller? No, I haven't seen him. I haven't seen Santa Claus either. Or God." He mopped his brow. Red hair, freckled skin that the sun was feasting on. "But that doesn't stop me from believing. Happy New Year, gentlemen."

33

For blocks around, the streets surrounding Jun and Birdy Villanueva's place were lined with cars. The driver offered to take Susan Hayes and George Griffin right to the front, but they decided a walk would go well, so they got out where he parked, four blocks away. Other couples walked ahead and behind, while chauffeurs lounged beside cars, bantering with security guards.

"Birdy asked for you," Susan said. "She asked if *we* were coming."

"I like that," Griffin said. He liked being thought of in connection with Susan. He liked walking toward bright lights and music with her on his arm. What he liked even more was the way she'd come out of her home, tossing what had to be an overnight bag onto the front seat, a little white leather bag that had sent Griffin's heart soaring.

"This party is an annual event," Susan explained. "The A-list of the opposition."

" 'Next year in Malacanang.' Is that the slogan?"

"I suppose so."

"In the meantime, this isn't so bad." The Villanuevas' compound was outside Makati, in a section of lawns, walls, and mansions. If you removed a few local touches—armed guards, checkpoints, shards of glass embedded on top of walls—you could have been walking in Beverly Hills. They were a long way from Tondo, Griffin thought, and you had to wonder whether this world would make it up to Tondo before Tondo came out here to settle accounts.

"What are you thinking?" Susan asked.

"About Tondo. I was there this afternoon. They were beating a dog to death. Tenderizing the meat."

"You went by yourself?"

"No, I was with Clifford Lerner."

"Why do I know that name?"

"He's another travel writer. He's like me. He decided to stay around and look into things. He's interested in Harding too."

"Competition?"

"Not really. I've got Harding to myself. Lerner's looking into the people Harding mentioned when he spoke on Corregidor. Who they are, or were, and what's become of them."

"Is he any good?"

"When he wants to be. Right now he wants to be. He's still at the G-spot every night for a cold beer or two and a warm body or two. But when he's on duty he's formidable. Today it was Felipe Olmos in Tondo. Contreras is next. Harding mentioned him in his speech."

"General Contreras?"

"Yes. Why?"

"Well, let's just say he's saving the toughest name for last."

Close up, the Villanueva compound looked like the site of an old-fashioned Hollywood movie premiere, with guards, gawkers, chauffeurs, glittering entrances. Susan took a deep breath, as if to steel herself for some hectic socializing.

"Here we go," she said. "Let's not stay long."

"Why stay at all?" Griffin said. Touching her elbow, he turned her toward him. "Why not go where we want to go and . . . so forth?"

"What an elegant suggestion!"

"You know what I've been wondering about? Those green eyes of yours."

"How I got them?"

"How you use them. You've got a certain green-eyed look . . ."

"All my looks are green-eyed."

". . . that stops me cold."

"I wouldn't want to do that." She looked in toward the party. She was weakening, no doubt about it. He thought of kissing; she thought of it too. Then she looked one way, he the other. And the moment was ruined: suddenly they were four and someone was hugging her. Not Griffin.

"Sepia bombshell!" It was Phil Robinson, embassy political officer, World War II buff, New Year's celebrant. "What say you and I go mud wrestling?"

"Phil!" Susan took his wild-and-crazy-guy act good-naturedly, winking at Robinson's wife, a petite and probably long-suffering Chinese woman.

"Wild women! Dream lover! Were you waiting for me?"

"Of course not," Susan said. "Phil, do you know George Griffin?"

"We've met. Hi, Griffin. Colonel Harding back in town with you?"

"No. He's in Olongapo."

"Everything all right so far? Safe and sound?"

"Yes."

"Well, God bless. Shall we see what Birdy's up to? Honey . . ." He turned to his wife. "Did you bring the orgy butter?"

A couple of hundred people circulated around the Villaneuvas' swimming pool. There were two open bars and there were half a dozen food stations, with lumpia and sushi, satay shrimp and beef, roast pig, cheese and fruits, salads, tarts and petits fours. A band filled the air with movie theme music, so it was easy to feel this night was special. Great scenes to be played.

"Mr. Griffin, back from the wars, with Miss Susan Hayes for company!" Jun Villanueva was glad to see them. "At last I can relax. Birdy will be delighted."

"Delighted to be here," Griffin said.

"And how is your book?"

"Coming along nicely. I'm learning something every day."

"I'm sure we will all learn something," Villanueva suggested. That could have been a compliment or a barb or nothing at all, Griffin thought.

"I doubt it," he said. "You've all been here so much longer. What's new to me is old to you . . ."

"Mr. Griffin!" Birdy Villanueva swooped down in white silk trousers and blouse that Griffin thought of, vaguely, as lounging wear, a daring stroke of informality at a party where everyone else was formally dressed.

"Happy New Year," Griffin said. "Any resolutions?"

"Yes." Birdy stood next to Susan like a sports car, light and jaunty, parking next to a capacious and luxuriant Cadillac. Two such different vehicles hardly belonged on the same lot. "One resolution is to break dear Susan's monopoly of you. May I?"

"Promise to return him?"

"Of course."

"Intact?"

"Of course not!"

Birdy took him by the arm and ushered him around the party. There were ambassadors, college professors, businessmen. There were lots of people who used to be journalists. Everywhere she introduced him as "the writer." No one asked what he was writing. That was left for Birdy.

"How is your work?" she asked when they were at the edge of the party, with only two poodles for company.

"It goes well," he answered cautiously. He was puzzled by this flattering intimacy with Birdy Villanueva. Suddenly, a beautiful and powerful woman was his dear friend.

"I can't wait to read your book," Birdy said, and Griffin resisted a subversive impulse to ask what else she was reading in the meantime.

"I can't wait to see *your* movie," he said. Subversive impulse after all. That perked her up.

"What did you hear, my friend?"

"That you and Imelda Marcos are partners in *MacArthur's Ghost.*"

"We could say that art makes strange bedfellows."

"We could. We could also say that bedfellows make strange art."

"I think you know my reasons."

Griffin leaned forward, waiting for her to continue. What a pair of conspirators they must look like, whispering together. It was embarrassing; he felt conspicuous. Anyone would think they were having an affair. But maybe not. Birdy transcended sex. She performed it and moved on.

"You're going to make me say it, Mr. Griffin? Very well then. Two words. Or three, title included. General Nestor Contreras. But of course you know that."

Griffin knew nothing of the sort. "Ah. Contreras." While Birdy waited for more, Jun Villanueva returned with Susan Hayes on his arm.

"There you are," Jun said. "I have a joke."

"Jun!" Birdy protested. She was not happy that he'd come along just then.

"No, really. Why are men like snowflakes?"

There was a silence that affable Jun thought was the time they took pondering their answers. Birdy's eyes said otherwise. She went off without waiting for the punchline.

"Because you never know when they'll come, you never know how many inches you'll get, and they melt before you know it."

Griffin forced a laugh and Susan Hayes managed an "Oh, Jun," before taking her leave. "Ten minutes," she whispered.

Ten minutes with Jun Villanueva. A few more jokes, then some war recollections. Jun had spent the war in America as a very minor, very junior aide to exiled President Manuel Quezon. He was with Quezon when he died at Saranac Lake in 1944. After the war he was attached to Carlos Romulos's U.N. mission. Eventually he served as ambassador to Egypt, France, and Norway. When Marcos replaced him with a crony, he came home to head the opposition, "to watch and wait."

"That's your strategy?"

"What is the expression you have in Las Vegas? 'Lay it as it plays'?"

"Actually, play it as it lays."

"No? Really?" Jun Villanueva took correction well. "I like my way better!"

Susan was across the pool, talking to a striking woman who, though her back was turned, looked familiar. That long black hair! Surely not Gibbins's girl from Club Tennessee? No, but the effect was comparable. It was one of those figures that made you dread the moment when she turned around, because either she'd be a monstrous disappointment, or she'd change your life. The conversation must have been lively; it took ten seconds of solid staring before Susan felt his eyes upon her and looked up at him. They exchanged time-to-go nods. Then she motioned him toward her.

"I think you know Cecilia Santos," Susan said.

"Yes, we've met," Cecilia said. The front of her was no disappointment: a dress that was black below, gold on top, and money all over. "I thought you were in Olongapo, Mr. Griffin."

"I'm not," Griffin said. "I came in for the New Year. Happy New Year, Miss Santos. Let old acquaintance be forgot, and never brought to mind . . ."

"The colonel came with you, I assume."

"No, he's still there."

"I thought the arrangement was that you were to accompany Colonel Harding at all times."

"I missed the part about being a bodyguard," Griffin said. He took Susan by the arm and started leading her away. "Nice seeing you."

He felt Santos's eyes on his back as he walked out toward the street.

"That wasn't so bad, was it?" Susan asked.

"I don't get it. What on earth was Cecilia Santos doing there?"

"Why? Did it surprise you?"

"She works for Marcos, doesn't she? And she shows up—does she ever show up!—at a party given by the leader of the legal opposition, the man all lovers of democracy and military bases hope will succeed Ferdinand. I don't get it . . ."

"Look at me," said Susan. "Are my eyes a little greener than usual?"

"I've done it, haven't I?"

"Cecilia Santos is Birdy Villanueva's younger sister."

"What?"

"Welcome to Manila."

34

Riding through the night, sharing the back seat of a car with a desired woman. Tingling combination of intimacy and strangeness. Shine of headlights down the highway, low gleam of instruments along the dashboard, rolled-down windows open to the wet, summery air.

"That's it, isn't it, for the parties?"

"Not quite," she said. She was curled up, studying him.

"You're giving me a green-eyed look," he said.

She reached forward and pulled a curtain that separated the driver's seat from the back of the car. "Come over here."

He'd wanted her ever since they met at the Manila Hotel. Now he found the feeling was mutual. She was in his mouth, in his hands, surging closer, no equivocation or hesitation about this last New Year's Eve party. No stopping, either. Until she stopped.

"Since it's very clear we're going to fuck . . ." She said it so briskly, like a diplomat delivering a communiqué, Griffin had to laugh.

"I'm glad to hear that."

"So am I. You'll see. But now there are some things I have to tell you." She lit a cigarette, and from the way she inhaled, he guessed she enjoyed the few that she allowed herself. She seemed like a person who rationed pleasures. "I was born and raised in Atlanta, Georgia. I played tennis, I rode horses. I loathed gospel music. I was a scholarship student, a superachiever. First black this, first female that, first black female something else. At the time, it seemed important. A lot of people were watching me. I got married the June I graduated from

college, from Spelman. My husband was an all-American from
Morehouse. Academic all-American . . ."

She inhaled again and Griffin admired the way she told the
story so far, so evenly that he couldn't decide whether the
academic all-American husband she'd just mentioned had been
wrenched away in a tragic plane crash or dumped off in divorce
court. He was interested in finding out.

"When a marriage ends, it ends in one of two ways," she
continued, still so perfectly reasonable she might have been
talking about tourist visas. "One way is that somebody fails to
keep the terms of the original deal. That's sad. What's sadder is
the second way. When somebody decides to change the deal,
wants something else, something more. That was me. It wasn't
about money or kids or sex. I didn't know *what* it was about.
Maybe it was that I wasn't going to be the first female this or first
black that anymore. I was going to be the next or the latest of
just another . . ."

"So you saw an ad for the Foreign Service."

"When I studied for the examination it was . . . something to
do. The way people study for law school, just to see if they have
what it takes to get in. I did."

"I'll bet you did."

"At first I was playing. But I'm not playing now. I'm serious
now. I want you to know that. I can see you getting hooked on
Manila. The mystery and the intrigue. I don't blame you. I felt
the same way too. But then I realized I had a choice to make
and I had to make it before it was too late. So do you. You have
to decide whether you want to be a part of the history of this
place or whether you want this place to be a part of the history
of you. Do you understand?"

"A marriage or a fling."

"Put it that way if you like. Whether this is where you stay or
whether it's an episode on the way to someplace else. Well I've
made that decision. I'm here to do my job well so I'm in line for
advancement. That means the same job in a better place or a
better job in a place like this."

"I see," Griffin said. "You have work to do, places to go, people to see."

"You make it sound silly. Maybe it is. Anyway, I'm here now.

Next year I'm gone. So no promises, Mr. Backyard Faraway. That's all."

She sat back when she was done, relaxing as if the delivery of that speech had been the last item on a long list of things she had to do before leaving work. Griffin wondered if he ought to reciprocate, if this were part of what it was all about when you got into your thirties. You exchanged credentials. Maybe it was his turn to clear his throat and offer up his childhood in New Jersey, newspaper work, lure of New York City, travel writing as a ticket round the world. He turned to begin—it seemed only fair—but the car moved onto a rough road, headlights probing a driveway flanked by orderly ranks of coconut palms.

"We're here," she said. "Hallelujah!"

"Where are we?" Griffin asked, chagrined that he'd missed the chance to respond to her preconjugal speech. Maybe she knew all she had to know. Or all that was worth knowing. Maybe she didn't care.

The car pulled in front of a main house, plantation style, verandah and all, with one light on in an office at one side. The driver drove off, leaving Griffin standing outside while Susan entered, stepped behind a registration desk, and found some keys that had been left out for her. Outside, Griffin's eyes adjusted to the darkness. He saw a dozen cottages scattered among the palms, like illustrations in a children's book, a peaceful village in a happy land.

"Hidden Valley," she said. "It's my getaway spot. A little resort."

"Is it a plantation?"

"You'll see. And George . . ."

"Yes?"

"Let's forget all the other stuff for a while. Your career, my career . . ."

"Let's."

Inside their cottage, she slipped into the bathroom, and came out in a white terry-cloth bathrobe. She told him to take off his clothes and wrap a towel around himself.

"Come on," she said. "We've got ten minutes. It's New Year's Eve, remember?"

She was smiling her green-eyed smile, the wise and knowing smile he'd noticed before, the smile that Harry Harding had seen on a postcard once and never forgotten. The waiting-for-you-down-the-road look. Had Harding ever caught up with such a smile?

She led him past the main house, past a thatched shelter that looked like a dining area, with tables, bar, and the inevitable bandstand. They passed through the palms, into a wooded area, a jungle that had been tamed and trimmed into a botanical garden. They crossed a stream, passed one pool, then another, then a stream again. The sound of running water was on all sides.

"Bathing pools," Susan said. "The man who owned this place wanted an old-world spa like Carlsbad or Baden-Baden. Each pool tastes and feels a little different. Some are warm, some are icy cold. . . . Hurry up!"

She took his hand, tugging him along. The path hairpinned up the side of a hill, squeezing around rock faces, skipping over roots, brushing through rustling thickets of bamboo. The sound of water grew louder.

"It's a cascade," she said, almost running. "My favorite place."

At last they were there, at the place she'd chosen for the stroke of twelve. A pool fed by a waterfall above, feeding into a waterfall below, lined with moss-covered rocks and fern-covered banks. A rock garden with hanging vines and creepers, overarching trees. Above it all, a cleft of night sky and a fleet of stars.

"I've always wanted to be here with someone I liked. . . . I haven't managed that." She stood next to him, drew close. "I have to be careful," she whispered. Her lips were at his ears, her hands circled around him, meeting at his chest. "You understand. A single woman. A black woman. I have to be discreet." Her hands retreated; she was tugging at her bathrobe. "A woman in a foreign country, a diplomat besides . . ." She drew against him again, this time without her bathrobe. "But every now and then," she said, putting her hands on his shoulders, guiding him into a turn so that he would come face to face with her, "especially when you're in a perfectly nice place," and he felt her legs against him, and her breasts, and her arms wrapped around, and his hands moved down her shoulders, down and down, but he kept his eyes on hers, because he wanted to see what they looked like the moment he caught up with her, "with a perfectly nice man," and her lips moved across his, across his cheek to his right ear, "on New Year's Eve, twelve midnight," and to his other ear, "I say fuck discretion."

Griffin awoke at sunrise—a habit he'd acquired during his travels with Harding—got quietly out of the bed he'd shared with Susan, slid open the screen door that gave out onto the cottage verandah, and stepped out into the morning. It was the best part of the day, the old man always told him, first and best and now, not even a tumultuous night, making love from pool to pool, a night so close to erotic fantasy it was almost frightening, not even Susan could deprive him of it. "Top of the morning," the old man always said. Though it lasted only twenty minutes, you could always count on the top of the morning. He could picture Harding sitting on a front step somewhere with a cup of coffee and a cigarette, or leaning against the hood of their car, using the first light to look over his father's maps, which he must have memorized by now, yet carried like a Holy Book. Count on the morning. Count on *him* in the morning: he was there. Hovering. Why else was it when he opened his eyes and found Susan beside him, when he was all full of pleasure and pride and wonder, he felt a small twinge of guilt? The same sort of guilt he'd felt when Lerner took him out to Tondo to face Felipe Olmos. It was as though, in giving himself to someone else, he'd gotten off the track. Oh, had he ever!

He looked down at Susan, spying on her. He saw tousled hair, shrewd face, luxuriant breasts, full thighs, a body so ripe, so manifestly sexual, he had to marvel at the force of will that had kept her out of maternity wards and landed her in an embassy across the world. She'd made herself a diplomat, but that wasn't the direction nature had pointed her in. She was something so gorgeously out of fashion the words for her were 1950s words, dated and sexist words like bombshell, knockout, piece of ass. For her, last night was a relapse, no doubt about it, an attack of something she'd seen coming. That explained that odd cautionary speech in the car: what you get tonight, Mr. Backyard Faraway, isn't what you get tomorrow, or the next day. No promises.

Now, out on the verandah, he watched the first light infiltrate among the palms and sparkle on the morning grass. The dew was so heavy, you'd guess that it had rained. Now there was sunlight on the hedge of croton, turning waxy yellow leaves to gold, lighting up the red and purple bougainvillea blossoms, white flowering ginger. You could smell the ginger. And another scent. Oh, God! The smell of coffee and frying bacon from the kitchen across the lawn!

"Why are you laughing?" She came out and sat beside him, wrapped in the terry-cloth bathrobe from the night before.

"Because it's perfect. It's unreal."

"You're right," she said, settling down beside him. For a while, they were content to sit together and watch the place come to life. A dog trotting by and a boy leading a mud-caked carabao out to pasture, and someone in the kitchen deciding that, it being all of 6:00 A.M., it wasn't too early to start blasting a Wayne Newton tape.

"We have all sorts of options. Breakfast, of course. A morning swim before breakfast, though. And before the swim, I'd like us to . . ."

"Yes?" He knew what was coming, but he wanted to see what she'd say. A question of syntax. Would she say "make love"? Or did she have a coarser verb in mind?

". . . make love," she said.

The sign on the door said DO NOT DISTURB. They were sprawled on the bed, exhausted, contemplating each other: the sort of regard that gently segues from gratitude for past pleasures to a lust for new performances. But there was a knock on the door.

"Miss Hayes?"

"Yes?" she called.

"A phone call, mum. A Mr. Robinson."

"All right." Already she was changing: brisk, competent, back on duty, while Griffin was still resenting that Robinson knew her plans so well. "I have to be reachable," she said over her shoulder. She went out the door to take the phone call in the office. When she came back, she said they'd have to leave. Colonel Harding had disappeared.

35

It was New Year's day and the embassy air conditioners were off duty. Griffin felt his shirt stick and come unstuck every time he shifted on the couch outside Phil Robinson's office. Amazing how things could go downhill. At sunrise, everything was perfect. But there was something in the world that could come out of the end of the phone or the inside of a letter, or off the tip of your tongue, a force stronger than gravity that hated happiness.

"Hey, so how's the budding author?" Eddie Richter sauntered into the office. "Looks like it's really hit the fan."

"What do you know?"

"I hear he slipped the leash, ran into the boondocks. The newspapers are on it. I got some calls."

"You mean you made some calls."

"All right already. They were gonna hear anyway. Better they should hear it from me. It's happening fast."

"Can't hurt the movie, can it, Eddie?"

"No, my boy. I won't lie to you. You noticed. Another thing it can't hurt is your book. In case you didn't notice that . . ."

"Gentlemen . . ." Phil Robinson opened the door to his office and stood aside to admit them. This was Phil Robinson on overtime, sleeves rolled up, cigar in hand, crisis-managing. "Come on in. . . . I think you know almost everybody."

He knew Susan, though Eddie didn't. Robinson introduced them. They both knew Cecilia Santos, in her bruncheon finest, and they both knew Charley Camper, in dungarees and T-shirt.

"Phil, I haven't had the pleasure." The speaker, off to one side, was a bright, good-looking young man in the uniform of the Philippine army.

"Sure. Eddie Richter, George Griffin, this is Major Prospero Herrera of General Contreras's staff. Now, just let me recap. Colonel Harding is missing, since the day before yesterday, early in the morning. In the course of—what should I call it?— a sentimental journey through the Philippines, with his memoir writer in tow, he visits Charley Camper, wartime associate, now residing in Subic Bay. After one night, Mr. Griffin leaves Colonel Harding and goes to Manila. Whose idea was that, by the way?"

"It was mutual," Griffin said.

"Mutual? You both thought of it?"

"Yes."

"At the same time?"

"I can't say. We'd covered a lot of ground together. A lot of emotions. I wanted to get back to Manila for a while . . ."

"What about those emotions you mentioned?"

"His or mine?"

"His, of course. Anything that suggested he might do something?"

"Something . . . like what?"

"Come on, Griffin. Like what he did!"

"I'm not sure what he's done," Griffin countered. "He's visiting Charley Camper. And he decides to leave. So?"

"Okay," Robinson acknowledged. "Mr. Camper, why don't you tell Mr. Griffin what you told me."

"George?"

It hurt to see a big man scared, to watch him shift uncomfortably in his chair, lean back, rock forward. "I thought I'd take him out fishing. I got the use of this boat. I thought he'd like that. Or maybe we'd go into town and shoot pool, or watch a movie at the base. Lots of guys around who wanted to meet him. You know that."

"Sure."

"He's not the easiest man to be with, one on one, with nothing to do . . ."

"I know that, Charley."

"He stayed inside, the day you left. I only saw him to eat. He stayed up late that night. The light was on in his room. Toward dawn, he comes into my room. He says he figured he'd be leaving. I ask where. He shrugs his shoulders. Like he was saying 'out there.' I tell him I'm coming with him. He says no. What's he looking for, I ask him. Old friends, he says. That's what I am, I say. There's more out there, he says. I say, they're dead, the ones I know about. Maybe, he says. Maybe not. 'Who you looking for, Colonel?' I ask. 'Who you really looking for?' He says, 'Juan Olmos.' "

"Christ!" Robinson burst out. "Yamashita's damn treasure wasn't enough. One crock of shit wouldn't do. He had to have Juan Olmos too."

"The treasure was all right," Eddie Richter said. "We had plans for treasure. We could maybe tie it to the movie. Could've had a contest, could've had maps and clues in the newspapers, and the first person figures out where we put the treasure gets a trip from Manila to Hollywood, like they used to do with—what was it—Canadian Club whiskey . . ."

"A suggestion that was canceled," Cecilia Santos interjected with a withering stare at Eddie Richter, "because of its flabbergastingly bad taste."

"And its danger," Eddie fired back. "Seems like it's touch and go up in those mountains. Things out of control. One revolution or another, I forget."

"Mr. Richter," Major Herrera intervened. "You know Colonel Harding. Any notion of what he has in mind? Friendship? Revenge? Or—forgive me—publicity?"

"Sorry," Eddie said. "I don't know him that well."

"Mr. Griffin?"

"I can't say."

"But there is something you can say," Herrera continued. "You can say why you and Mr. Lerner went to Tondo yesterday afternoon to visit Juan Olmos's brother."

Very nicely done, Griffin thought. A trap well sprung. Not a fatal trap, a small snare, but very well done all the same.

"That was an interview Mr. Lerner initiated. I just tagged along. I suggest you talk to Mr. Lerner."

"Mr. Lerner left the Philippines this morning. Luckily we were able to chat before he left. Mr. Lerner insisted it was a background interview. Harmless and historical. But we gather you stayed for a private session with Mr. Olmos."

"That was at Olmos's request," Griffin said. "Not mine."

"And?"

"He sent a message to Colonel Harding. I haven't had a chance to deliver it. Maybe I never will."

"What was that message?"

"Something about how it was better to remember the way things—things and people—used to be."

"That was all?"

"Yes."

"You are working on this book," Cecilia Santos said. It was all she could manage not to call it "this so-called book." "What is the . . . form of this book now? Do you have a typed manuscript? Handwritten notes? Have you used a tape recorder?"

Christ, she despises me, Griffin thought. She looks at me, it's as if she were checking symptoms: rash, chancres, discharges, pain in urinating. I'll treat you, but I won't touch you.

"Notes," Griffin answered. "Tapes too."

"That could be helpful to us," she said. She glanced at Robinson for support.

"There might be things he told you that could help us find him," Robinson said. "Clues to his intentions, state of mind. Names of wartime associates. Even place-names. Things that mean nothing to you might mean a lot to someone else."

"I don't think I can go for that," Griffin said. "I can review the material myself. Tell me what you want, I'll look for it. But I won't show it to you and I won't give it to you."

"Mr. Griffin?" It was Susan. His Susan! Remember me? Last night we fucked. This morning we made love. You paid for the room. I paid for the car.

"Yes, Miss Hayes?"

"We understand you have a relationship of trust and friendship with Colonel Harding . . ."

"I'm glad you do," he snapped.

". . . and if he were in danger, you would try to help him, wouldn't you?"

"Yes. If he were in danger, which I'm not convinced of," Griffin said. "And if I found myself among others who wanted to help him. Which I'm also not convinced of . . ."

"Phil? Miss Hayes?" Major Herrera handled himself well, Griffin thought. "We're all on the same team, are we not? So I think we ought to play fair with Mr. Griffin. Put him in the picture."

Phil Robinson frowned. But Herrera ran right over him. "The picture," he repeated.

Robinson sighed, picked a manila envelope off his desk, and handed it to Griffin.

"That's an early copy," Robinson said. "Tomorrow it'll be in the newspapers, courtesy of the NPA."

It looked like another, much older photograph: two ranks of Filipinos, one kneeling, one standing, with guns and bolos. The same skinny fighters, the same staring faces that were in the forty-year-old picture Harding had given him for Christmas, and there, in much the same position he'd taken in the earlier photograph, there stood Colonel Harry Roberts Harding.

"The NPA's got him," Robinson said. "The New Peoples Army."

"Holy shit," Eddie Richter exclaimed, shaking his head back and forth, so it was impossible to say whether he was measuring deep personal loss or counting free publicity for the movie. Griffin, meanwhile, kept staring at the picture. There were differences between the one he saw and the one he remembered. The guerrillas in the old picture wore peasant clothes, cotton shirts and trousers. The NPA wore jeans and running shoes and T-shirts that advertised NIKE, San Miguel, Dairy Queen. Another difference was in Harding himself. In the old photo, he was blank-faced, a stranger to the camera. Here—the more Griffin looked the surer he was—the old man might actually be smiling. Damn! Griffin exulted. He wanted a reunion. He wanted to break back into the past. That's what it was all about. And it looks like he made it. You son of a bitch, you magician, you old fart. MacArthur's Ghost indeed! I wish you'd taken me along! He caught himself, controlled his emotions, and turned to Robinson.

"At least he's not alone. That's good."

"Beg pardon?"

"I was worried about him. Slogging around in the mountains in the rain. He's not the healthiest man in the world. There's a medicine cabinet full of pills in his bathroom."

"Hey, Griffin," Robinson burst out. "That's not Outward Bound. That's the New Peoples Army."

"I still say it's better he's not alone."

"Now that you understand the situation," Major Herrera said, "would you reconsider your position on your notes?"

"All right," Griffin said. "I give in. I'll bring them over."

After that they left Griffin alone. They wondered about what Harding was up to; everything from murder to suicide, from sentimental journey to senile breakdown. They talked about how to manage the search and how to manage the press. And Griffin found himself remembering what Harding had told him. Something Harrison Wingfield had said forty years before. That the land doesn't remember you. Neither do the people. Unless you make them.

"That was brutal," Charley Camper said as they stepped out on Roxas Boulevard.

"You want a drink at the hotel, Charley? For that matter, you could stay the night. I've got his room . . ."

"No. I'm going home. Come with me to my truck, will you?"

They walked slowly along the sea wall. It was dusk now. A weak wind came in off the bay, fresh air's small, doomed counterattack. There were people living among the rocks against the sea wall, as if the tide had dumped them there.

"I'm going to look for him," Griffin said. "I have a few ideas. He's an orderly man. I figure—"

"Stop right there." Charley put a firm, friendly hand on his shoulder. "I don't want to hear about it. The less I know, the better."

"I was thinking you'd go with me."

"Can't do it."

"Charley, it's the colonel."

"Can't do it!" Charley cried. "I can't afford no more problems. That embassy colored woman cleaned my plow!"

"What did she do? Tell me!" Griffin's anger flared. It wasn't right for Susan to call Charley in and break him.

"It wasn't her fault. It's my wife."

"Your wife?"

"You still don't get it, do you? Carmen Pedroza Camper. A one-woman airlift. Of maids, go-go bands, chefs, chauffeurs. The IRS is on her case, and Customs and Immigration and Departments of Labor, State, and I don't know what else. My little local girl, spreading her wings. I tried to tell you. I'm pussywhipped, George. I'm beat."

Charley pulled out a burlap sack and started loading it with bananas, tomatoes, avocados, and a soft green fruit he said was soursop.

"Hey, that's enough," Griffin protested. "I'll never eat it all."

"Take it," Camper said. "There's something special at the bottom. I said I'd get it to you. Now I kept my promise. And I'm out of it. So long, Griffin. I won't be seeing you again."

"So long, Charley."

Driving out of the Aristocrat parking lot, waiting to turn onto Roxas Boulevard, Charley set off his wolf-whistle one last time. It was the saddest, loneliest sound in the world, Griffin thought.

"Is this George Griffin?" The phone rang as he entered the room. It was long distance, fuzzy-voiced.

"Yes."

"Hold the line, sir."

"George, it's me. Lerner."

"Where are you?"

"Guam."

"Guam! What on earth are you doing on Guam?"

"They got me, George. They got me where I live. I was trying to set up an interview with General Contreras. I went to army headquarters for a preliminary screening. They showed me some photographs they took. . . ."

"Of us? In Tondo?"

"No, George. Of me. Me and a couple of girls at the G-spot. Doing the nasty . . ."

"Blackmail?"

"Yes. They asked how I thought my . . ."

There was a silence on the line, the waves and winds that blow around the world. The sounds of distance.

". . . how I thought my wife would like to see them."

"They would send the pictures if you didn't leave? Is that it?"

"No. They said they'd already sent them. They said it was a race between me and the postal system. They laughed. Male-man versus mailman. Clever. Major Herrera."

"I don't know what to say. I'll miss you."

"You know, when I was a kid, I used to read reporters' books. Stuff by Quentin Reynolds, William Shirer, Lowell Thomas. Anything with a trenchcoat in it. It always bothered me, I never lived up to that. Till Manila. Then they nailed me. Watch it, George, they'll nail you too."

"Don't worry."

"But I do. They got me. I'm smart. Smart as you are, George, though you don't like to admit it. And I've been smart longer. Trouble with you is, you got cynical before you got experienced. You're not tough enough. You react to things sensitively—like a writer and all that—but you don't act on your own."

"I admit I'll miss you, Clifford."

"You bet you will. Watch out for yourself."

The tape recorder was inside the produce bag Charley had given him. It was his spare tape recorder. Harding had asked to borrow it, just in case he thought of things while Griffin was away. Griffin turned on the machine and heard the silence he expected, blank reproachful tape, symbol of a job not done. Then he heard Harding's voice: "It's like in Florida . . ." He listened for half an hour. Then he made a decision Clifford Lerner would have liked. He acted. He acted on his own. He ran.

Part Seven

★ ★ ★
★ ★

HARDING'S TAPE

36

"It's like in Florida. I'm sitting up in the middle of the night, when the rest of the world is sleeping. I used to just sit up, wondering if I would die sometime, pretty soon, and never get to come back here. I'd wonder if that was how it would be, letting life move me away from the heart of things till at the end I was so far away, and so far gone, I could only dream of going back.

"By the time you listen to this, there'll be a commotion going on. I suppose you'll be feeling betrayed. Well, I want you to know that I meant what I said about how you and I make up a 'we.' And even though I'm going where you can't come, I'm leaving this behind to give you more of the story, so that if I don't make it out of the mountains and meet you where the war ended, you'll still be able to keep your promise to finish, no matter what. In for the duration: remember?

"In my life, there have been three men who mattered. Elbert Hubbard Harding was one. Harrison Wingfield was another. And the third was the man I saw in May 1942, squatting at the edge of the Candaba swamps, taking apart a captured Japanese machine gun. He was tall for a Filipino, five feet ten, and thin. He had thin arms and legs, a narrow face, and long bony fingers —I can see them now sliding across that captured Nambu. He was wearing sandals cut from tires and shorts cut from some-one's pants and a long-sleeved shirt that once belonged to the Philippine Constabulary. But the thing that struck me most about Juan Olmos was he didn't give a damn about us. All of us go around thinking we are the center of the world, stars of the show, and this is a part Americans in the Philippines had gotten used to playing. When you walked into the middle of a group

of Filipinos, they stopped talking among themselves, stopped
what they were doing. You were the center of things. Your
problem was top of the list, your schedule, your pleasure. But
Olmos stayed right where he was, fussing with that gun. We
weren't all that important to him.

"It wasn't until Felipe—Flash—walked over and said something that he ever bothered to give us a glance. Flash motioned
for me to come over. About time, I thought. I guessed we'd
shake hands, share plans. I'd thank him for helping us out and
commend him for the fine job he was doing. He'd be glad to
hear that. He'd ask whether he could be of any further service.
So I thought. But by the time I came over, Olmos had gotten
up and walked away. That was all the welcome we got.

"Well, we left the village behind and took a trail that went
uphill, through meadows, through burned-off clearings planted
with beans and sweet potatoes. Then we were in the rain forest,
walking among chest-high ferns, under trees that blocked out
the sky. We started passing sentries and people carrying sacks
of rice, and once we had to step aside and open the trail for a
column of armed men going downhill. They filed by without a
word. At last, and not a moment too soon, we came to Olmos's
headquarters on top of Mount Arayat. There were tents and
nipa huts and some other buildings that were wood and tin.
There were supply sheds, meeting rooms, commissary, armory,
hospital. There were blackboards, a printing press. It was quite
an operation.

"All the way up, they'd never stopped, they'd never even
asked if we were tired. By the time we arrived, we were
finished. Flash led us toward some nipa huts and a woman
brought us some rice with bits of meat, goat meat, and then
there was the doctor who cleaned Vernon Waters's leg wound
and rewrapped it and gave him some antibiotics. He didn't say
a word, though: it was as though someone had ordered the silent
treatment.

"I went out and sat on the steps of the nipa hut. No one was
guarding us, but I knew that they were watching. Fair enough.
I watched back. Even at night there was lots to see: sentries
changing, a group of men coming up the mountain, and a meeting going on inside one of the wood-and-tin buildings. I couldn't

hear much, but from the way they took turns speaking, and from the way they stood, it looked like a sort of self-criticism session. Then Felipe stood up and gave what sounded like a lecture on world events, the fighting in the Pacific and Europe, plus what sounded like local news. He was quite a speaker, I could see, and I was interested in how Juan Olmos would follow an act like that. But then I saw that Juan Olmos wasn't about to oblige. He wasn't among the speakers or the listeners. I spotted him squatting by a fire, smoking, fussing with a gun. As soon as I saw him, he glanced up at me, stared. He looked right through me.

"The next morning, Felipe Olmos woke me while it was still dark. His brother was about to leave, he said, and if I wanted to talk to him, now was the only time. I stumbled across the clearing, dipped my head in a barrel of rainwater, woke myself up, and waited while Flash went inside. A couple of guerrillas came out of the meeting room. Then it was my turn. Juan Olmos was sitting at a desk, eating lumps of sticky rice out of a soup bowl, eating with his fingers, taking on food like it was fuel.

" 'My brother says you are good,' he said. 'Yes?'

"I said I hoped I was, without knowing what that meant to him. I said I hoped that we could find our way to other groups of Americans, and get organized, and prepare for MacArthur's return.

" 'No Americans here,' Olmos said. He got up and stretched, like an animal that's been curled up sleeping. A stretch, a yawn, a shrug. 'No Americans here.'

" 'But we'll be back,' I said.

"I've never gone around talking slogans, but there was something in Olmos that provoked them. The way he talked of Americans, he might have been talking about Indians. No Indians around here anymore. We chased them off. Try the mountains . . .

" 'When the Americans come back, we'll fight together,' I said. And then I added two words I'd used before. They'd always worked. I said, 'I promise.'

"I can still see Juan Olmos standing there, giving me the same look his brother had given me in Baguio, only ten times harder: what kind of American are you?

" 'I promise,' I repeated. That was it.

"The men Olmos provided—guides, guards, stretcher bearers —took us across Tarlac and Nueva Ecija. This was Huk-land. Every village was organized, food and weapons and hiding places, people to scout ahead of us when we walked, sentinels for when we slept. I'd never seen anything like it. And—I say this mostly in self-criticism—I'd never thought such a thing possible in the Philippines. I didn't think they had it in them.

"Eventually, we made contact with the guerrillas of the United States Armed Forces Far East (USAFFE) of northern Luzon, an organized network in contact with General MacArthur's headquarters in Australia. The unit we found was holed up in a lumber mill outside of Baguio. I remember the morning we walked in. The way they looked at us. Not like stragglers, not like survivors, but as miracle men. Do you understand? *They knew who I was.*

"How'd it happen? Some of it was Harrison Wingfield's doing. He really talked us up, in Corregidor, later down in Australia. He beat the drum for us. And poor Meade had given us another kind of boost, shouting 'MacArthur's Ghosts' when he shot up that film crew. So there you have it. America needed heroes, Japan wanted enemies, the Filipinos loved to talk, and bingo, we were famous. It should have been plural: MacArthur's Ghosts. But Meade was dead, Sudul and Polshanski too, and Charley, well, he stayed Charley. He stayed put with the USAFFE boys. So it all came down to me. I was MacArthur's Ghost. Singular. One and only.

"Being an American, although a civilian, I had a connection with the USAFFE network on Luzon. Those are the stories everybody knows, the ones in the public domain, and mostly true. Stories about fighting off the Japanese patrols that boiled up into the mountains in October 1942. Or our raid into Manila, robbing medical supplies from a storehouse on the Pasig River, racing through town at night. Or cursing moonlight on the Lingayen Gulf, waiting for that first submarine to answer our signal light.

"But there's more. Griffin, by now maybe you know that the guerrilla effort wasn't the heroic underground our movie will show. The wartime Philippines was a mess. The guerrillas fought the Japanese and they fought each other. Imagine the Civil War, the Indian wars, a Mafia showdown, the Russian Revolution, and the Hatfield-McCoy feud. Imagine them all at once. That should give you an idea. There were USAFFE outfits, there were landlord armies, there were gangs, bands, bandits, ROTC units, there were Huks, Moros, headhunters. And there was me.

"Now one of the dirty little secrets of those years is that, though they fought when they had to, a lot of the guerrilla outfits, especially the USAFFE units, often weren't up to much. That was the "lie-low policy" that came up from MacArthur. It meant surviving, recruiting, building up a network, doing intelligence work. But it was a policy that avoided confrontation. Maybe that's why I kept going back to Mount Arayat. I felt like I was proving something. That I kept my promises. That I came to fight.

"If I traveled with anyone during those years, it was usually with Connie, the young Filipino who'd hooked up with us on Bataan. He knew the languages I didn't know. He handled the rice lands, the provincial capitals, the barrios, the way I managed the mountains. I was the one who foraged roots and fruits and wild things; he could promote a hot meal and a change of clothing, a warm and often not-so-lonely bed. We were a pair. Together, there was no place we couldn't go.

"Connie was a school principal's son, from the town of Tarlac in the province of the same name. He had the good looks and charm, the romantic streak and the life-long boyishness that lots of Filipinos have, but there was something else too: the sort of hustle you notice, or used to notice, in immigrants to the United States. Maybe he thought that's what he was, an American in the making. Once, near Malolos, we practically walked into a Japanese patrol. We never had a closer call, we were two men hiding behind a bush that couldn't have concealed a cat, and our lives depended on the fact that of three Japanese, not one looked left instead of right. After it was over, and the Japanese were dead, I asked him what on earth he was doing walking around with me and he answered, straight-faced, 'Improving my English.' He meant it. And what a flypaper mind he had! Once Camper and I were talking about autumn in America and

Camper mentioned that the foliage season moves south at twenty miles a day. No reason for Connie to care about elms and maples, but he never forgot that. Twenty miles became a figure of speech, a unit of measure, 'moving with the leaves.'

"Olmos and the Huks made him nervous, though. Connie's ambitions were conventional, but here was an army of peasants, dirt poor, aiming to turn the world upside down. He admired them and he worried about them, worried about the guns, the lectures, the drills, the theories, and most of all, he worried about the anger he saw in Olmos's eyes. One other thing. Though there were women among the Huks, Mount Arayat was about the only place in the Philippines where he couldn't get laid.

"The first time we came back, we walked into a celebration. The Huks, who were always busy, had just finished a three-day scrap. The Japanese and the Filipino cops—the "puppet constabulary," they were called—had gone into the rice lands at harvest time, down around a place called San Leandro. They wanted the crops and they even brought some landlords out from Manila to enforce their claims, so what followed wasn't just about Japan, it was about landlords, cops, and crops. It was Juan Olmos's kind of fight, a nasty, running battle, burning fields, blocking roads, ambushing trucks, and when the Huks were done, there was roast pig on the mountain.

" 'You came back,' Juan Olmos said to me matter-of-factly. But that one sentence was worth the trip, to me.

" 'I promised I'd be back,' I said.

" 'MacArthur's Ghost. You said that someday we would all fight together, Americans and Filipinos.' Then Juan Olmos said something else, said it while he was chewing on a rib, finishing the sentence and his bone at the same time, wiping the grease off his face with his sleeve, walking away laughing.

" 'We can't wait that long.'

"After that, Felipe Olmos sat with us a while. It can be as disconcerting as it is flattering, when someone just sees you and decides that you're going to be friends. But that's what he'd decided.

"So we were sitting chatting, when there was a commotion on the edge of the camp. Juan Olmos and some of the others came out of the woods leading a prisoner, but the prisoner was one of their own men. I remembered him from my first visit, a teenager whom Felipe called 'El Bandito de Para de Niño,' the baby-faced bandit. He was one of the friendly ones, a mimic and a clown. He was proud of the fact he could recite the names of all the U.S. presidents. It was something he must have learned in school or around a civil servant's household, something he did for tips and favors from his . . . I was going to say masters. It was a song-and-dance bit: Washing-tone, Adam, Jeffer-sone, Madi-sone, Mon-row, Adam. The second Adam made him stop, as if he'd lost his way, and then he picked up with Jackson, repeated the same hesitation with Grover Cleveland and the Roosevelts. Tonight he was in real trouble, though. They'd gone out and caught him sleeping on his watch. It wasn't the first time, I gathered, and Felipe Olmos looked worried. They took him inside the meeting room, and everyone filed inside. It looked grim. But not as grim as it got. They heard him out: another exercise in self-criticism. His last. They marched him outside, into the woods. As he passed by, the baby-faced bandit was walking briskly, as if this whole execution thing was his idea, and as he passed, he looked back and waved, waved to me, and then I heard him reciting the names of the presidents, like a rosary, and the farther away he marched, the louder he got, and faster, so fast that names started overlapping: Buchan-Lincoln-John-Grant. They killed him at McKinley. McKinley was the president who sent U.S. troops to the Philippines at the time of the Spanish-American War, and I wondered if that wasn't Juan Olmos's idea, ending his life right then. I also wondered if Juan Olmos hadn't stalked that kid the way he went after Japs, and whether the whole thing would have happened if I hadn't been there. Some of the execution detail came back crying. Not Juan Olmos. His mind was where it always was: on the next thing.

" 'I liked him,' I said, supposedly to Connie, but loud enough for everyone in the firing squad to hear. 'I liked that boy. I'm sorry he's dead. And I'll remember him.'

"Juan Olmos turned around as though I'd shouted 'about face' and marched right for me. That was when I discovered his English was as good as he wanted it to be.

" 'And I liked him, too,' he said. 'And I am sorry he is dead. And I will remember him.'

"He said it loud, like an announcement for the whole camp to hear.

" 'You come here to make friends,' he said. 'I come here to make army. Two hundred revolts in Philippine history so far. Two hundred! And not one winner. We fall. We fail. We divide. We sleep. Not this time. You remember my word, MacArthur Ghost. Not this time.'

"Then he was gone and the camp fell silent and all I could hear was Connie whispering. 'Sir,' he said. 'These people scare me.'

"In May 1943, during the rainy season, a submarine landed some weapons on the Lingayen coast. Pretty much on my own, I decided that a few of those M-1's should go to the Huks. They were sure to use them. After the war, the Huks claimed to have killed twenty thousand Japanese soldiers, puppet cops, collaborationists. (They didn't separate the three categories, you notice. Juan Olmos knew his enemies when he saw them and that was that.)

"Divert. I by God diverted two dozen M-1's into a farmhouse just off the coast and sent word to Olmos that he could come and get them. He sent some men whom I accompanied back to Mount Arayat, mainly to see whether I could get Juan Olmos to say thank you. He left that for the others. A lot of the men had gotten used to me and that M-1 delivery really raised my stock. That night, Felipe Olmos made a speech in my honor. We were sitting in darkness because there were Japanese in the area, and a fire might betray us.

"He spoke, stopping to translate his own words, which were about friendship, democracy, cooperation. Then he called on me to speak. I forget the exact words. But I'll never forget the scene: me standing in the middle of that clearing and, around me on the ground, more than a hundred Huk guerrillas, squatting in moonlight, listening, hardly moving. They were like a herd in the field at night, a cough here, the flare of a match there. For a moment, I choked up. What was I doing here? What was I promising? Who did I think I was? Well, they answered for me when I was done: 'MacArthur's Ghost. MacArthur's Ghost!' And there was Juan Olmos, raising the rifle I'd stolen for him, shouting, 'MacArthur's Ghost! MacArthur's Ghost.'

* * *

"Griffin, I'm sorry. It's way late and I have to stop soon. I want
to be out of here by first light. You know how I feel about the
morning. Already I've covered a lot of ground. The ending
comes closer all the time. I know the ending and you don't and
I wonder which of us to envy.

"October 1944. We had picked up the survivors of a U.S.
plane that got downed in Bulacan, a pilot named Barber, badly
wounded, and a wisecracking photo-reconnaisance cameraman
named Eddie Richter, Jr. Richter said that the Americans were
coming back, though they were hitting Leyte before Luzon.
The end was coming and I wanted to share it with Juan Olmos.
Connie and I arrived to find there was a meeting on Mount
Arayat, leaders of dozens of Huk squadrons meeting all night to
decide what next, now that the Americans were coming back.

"Years later, people asked me, What did I know about the
politics of the group? They asked, the same way they ask, Didn't
you *know* he drinks? Couldn't you *see* they were sleeping together? Didn't you *know* they were Reds? As if they'd been
there all along and known better than me since the beginning:
'Well, of course they're Communists.' And they would leave me
feeling—well, never mind how they left me feeling. They saw
what they wanted to see. I saw what I saw. I saw Felipe Olmos.
You could call him a socialist, a populist, a Communist, a labor
leader, an agrarian reformer, depending on the time of day. He
was political, but he was also beyond politics. So was Juan
Olmos, but in a different way. What he was about was anger.
Anger was his fuel, his fire, his guiding light. Other than these
two, I saw dozens of peasants who wanted lower interest on
loans, and a larger share of the harvest, and a little more of the
land, plus maybe a fair count on election day. They were the
ones who did the killing and the dying, who cheered MacArthur's Ghost.

"Juan Olmos was the first out of the meeting hall, like a pent-
up kid bursting into a schoolyard at recess. He stretched,
stamped his feet, saw me, and walked right over.

" 'You want to fight?' he asked.

" 'Fight?' I couldn't tell whether it was an offer or a challenge.

" 'You say, someday maybe we fight together.'

" 'Yes.'

" 'Today. You come . . .'

"That was how I got to San Leandro the first time. Juan Olmos had a score to settle there, lots of scores, and time running out to settle them. The first thing I learned was that the Japanese had concentrated there and were stockpiling everything they could lay their hands on. But there was more. Some time before, a Huk messenger had been caught there—betrayed probably. The local police chief, a man named Sylvester Olivares, had turned the man over to the Japanese, who beheaded him. There was still more. In and out of uniform, on and off duty, this same Olivares had served for years as the local landlords' enforcer. More than one labor organizer had disappeared while in Olivares's custody. That was what they told me as we headed down the mountain. I'm sure there was more. There always is.

"We came in from the west at dusk, moving out of the rice fields and onto the banks of a river, which, if we followed it, would lead us straight into San Leandro. We could see the town ahead of us, at just that time of day when the last sunlight came in from the west, so rich and golden it makes the poorest village on earth look like El Dorado. We sat on the riverbank and rested. I remember how we looked, that time, how that sun made us golden. The farmers at the water's edge, washing up. Felipe Olmos sitting alone on a field of grass. His brother pointing this way and that, dividing us into groups. Eddie Richter, who 'wouldn't miss this for the world,' loading his camera, and Connie, improving his English on a Huk woman who looked like she was saving her last bullet for him. And we were golden. All of us. And a golden city across the fields, birds flying around the church tower. And a golden army in the fields. Then the sun was gone, darkness came on, and we went in.

"I wonder, how did the Japanese feel when the phones went out? When the lights all died? When the bell started ringing in the cathedral? When the Chinese merchant slammed down the shutters of his little dry goods store? Or when they saw men with guns and bolos on the outskirts of town? Did they know they were dead? I think they did, the way they rushed out of their barracks and were shot. The ones who didn't die in the town square died on the bridge leading out of town. Others hopped into a jeep and raced south, Manila-bound, right into a firing squad that was waiting for them; they died in a ditch. A handful got out into the fields and were hunted down like rabbits, and they squealed like rabbits when they died. But the puppet constabulary who holed up in the municipal building were another matter. They wanted to live. They returned our fire, shot for shot. We lost men and all they lost was windows and plaster. It looked like a standoff to me. Juan Olmos didn't have the artillery to reduce the building and he didn't have the time for a siege: the next Japanese convoy to come up the road would put an end to that. The night drew on and nothing changed. Sometimes there'd be half an hour of silence. Then one side or the other would start in and it would build up to a racket, then subside, with nothing changed.

"I could see Olmos was boiling. And I could see why. The lights had come back on—on his orders, I suppose—and the whole population stood behind us in the streets that led off the square. They'd already done well, these people, rice and cooking oil and seed and canned goods distributed among them, and they had the Huks to thank for that. But this was about more than rice. It was about whether Juan Olmos could finish off one crappy, unimportant, three-story municipal building in a medium-to-small provincial town called San Leandro. One ugly building decked out with banners and slogans I couldn't make out and with a ring of what looked like Christmas lights running around the top, don't ask me why, and a gun or two in every window.

" 'What now?' Eddie Richter, Jr., asked me. 'What gives?'

"Eddie was like a race-track character hanging around stables, pumping jockeys and trainers for some inside information. He had a camera out of his shot-down plane; now, he said, he was aiming for *Life*.

" 'I think we ought to leave,' I said.

" 'Sure,' Eddie said. 'But I don't think we're leaving.'

"He eyed the lit-up square, open and empty, like an arena ready for action, killing, fucking, any kind of a show. Then he gestured toward the guerrillas forming up for attack.

" 'I think some people are going to die,' he said. 'Lots of people.'

" 'That's stupid,' I said.

"I walked over to where Juan Olmos was huddling with his lieutenants. One man I called the Birdwatcher, because he wore taped-together glasses with lenses thick as beer bottles. Another, always in black, was the Hangman. And, Birdwatcher, Pirate, Hangman, I could see they were uncomfortable with what was coming: it wasn't their kind of fight.

" 'This is stupid,' I said. It was the wrong thing to say, of course, and the wrong time to say it. Juan Olmos spun around and glared. Felipe put an arm on my shoulder, as if to lead me away.

" 'I said it was stupid,' I repeated. 'You got the Japanese . . .'

" 'This isn't about the Japanese,' Felipe said.

" 'It's about suicide,' I shouted. 'You go against that building, you'll lose half your men. What is it? Do you believe in heaven? Are you counting on a place in the history books? A statue in the square here? A shrine? Do you believe in that?'

" 'Mr. Harding, you don't understand,' Felipe said.

" 'All right! You want the building?' I brushed Felipe off and kneeled down right in front of Juan. 'Is that what matters? Do you want the building? Yes or no?'

"I snapped at him. I was talking the way you talked to a servant. We both knew it.

" 'Yes,' he answered.

" 'Okay,' I said. 'Come with me.'

"The bell tower smelled of bird shit and from it Juan Olmos and I and another man—the Pirate—could see all of San Leandro. On the north was the river and the bridge across it, and the road toward the mountains. To the south, the same road, straight as an arrow, toward Manila. Down below was the square, part cobblestone, part tar, part dirt. It wasn't much of a town.

"The Pirate stayed in the bell tower while Juan and I climbed out, slid over the tiled roof, down to the eaves. From there it was a five-foot jump and a dozen-foot drop to the roof of the municipal building. As soon as we were ready to jump, the Pirate started ringing the bells and that told the men below to open fire on the building. We jumped onto the roof and scrambled to the back of the building, away from the square. Then came the moment I dreaded, when I lowered myself over the edge, down toward a third-floor window. This was the moment I couldn't control. Either there was someone at the window or there wasn't. If there was, the only question was whether he'd shoot me when he saw my legs, my stomach, chest, or face: Washington, Lincoln, or McKinley.

But there was no one in the window; they'd all gone to the front, facing the square. In a minute we were inside, working our way from floor to floor, room to room, sneaking down hallways, slipping into rooms where one or two men were at the windows. They never saw us coming, never knew what hit them. Not until the first floor. Maybe they heard us upstairs. Or maybe it was the silence that told them the building had gone dead above their heads. They were ready: but not ready enough. They died turning to face us, raising rifles toward us, or raising hands to surrender, it didn't matter. A last few defenders ran out of the building, out into the square and the poor bastards mistook the cheer that went up at their appearance as a welcome. I can see them looking at each other, kind of puzzled, until they realized that the people rushing toward them were going to kill them and then they folded down onto their knees and died.

"Olivares, the police chief, had gotten away. The worst ones always do. Olmos went looking for him from room to room and when they were empty, he took it out on the building. Everything went out the window: books, chairs, tables, local records, court cases, debts, deaths, births. A real bonfire. I watched from down in the square. There were shot and beaten-to-death men still lying there, but everyone was merry, and I had a hard time with that, with all this celebration so soon after the dying. It bothered me. You couldn't miss the looks on peoples' faces. Juan Olmos had given them something they'd been waiting for, jubilee and judgment, revolution and kingdom come. And Eddie Richter wondered why I wasn't more in the spirit of things.

" 'You're famous in this town, Mr. Harding,' he said. 'They'll never forget you around here. Is it true you're called MacArthur's Ghost?'

" 'Used to be,' I said. 'Now MacArthur's back himself, who needs ghosts?'

"Eddie Richter stared at me. He couldn't figure it out. Then he stopped trying. It was no night for moping. They were starting history over here, he said. They'd erased the past, this was Day One. A hell of a thing, he thought, and he'd never seen anything like it. The guerrillas were great guys, Felipe Olmos had a very interesting mind, and that brother Juan was a real pistol. I was pretty hot stuff myself, because it took a special kind of American to win the trust and friendship these people were showing me.

" 'If I were you, I wouldn't be so quick to forget MacArthur's Ghost,' Eddie Richter, Jr., said. 'The people in San Leandro sure won't.'

"We left at dawn and I could see Richter was right. People came up to me to shake my hand, mumble thanks. Some of them just wanted to touch me. I'd never felt so strange. Those looks and touches: it was like communion. They followed us out into the fields, a whole procession, and then, group by group, they peeled off and went to their farms. A little later, looking back from the foothills of Mount Arayat, I could see columns of dark smoke from half a dozen different places, and I asked if they were burning off the fields. I asked Juan Olmos. Yes, they were burning off the fields all right. They had torched their landlords' houses. Eddie Richter, Jr., was right again. From this morning they were starting fresh.

"Eddie Richter decided he'd like to hang around a while. Felipe Olmos welcomed him. They were both talkers. I wanted to go, just slip away and be alone. My old problem, the problem of the *I,* the *we,* the *they* had raised up again; it needed sorting out. But as you might guess, this was one time Juan Olmos noticed my departure. He followed me several hundred yards down the trail, past the last sentries. Even then he looked around to make sure no one was listening. He said thanks. Just that. He turned back up the trail before I could respond. Then he stopped and added something. 'We're not finished yet.'

" 'I know,' I said.

"That was 1944. This is 1982. He was right, though. We're not finished yet. Sorry, Griffin. The sun's coming up and I have to go. I really have to go. Maybe I'll see you in the mountains."

Part Eight

★ ★ ★
★ ★

CADILLAC BILL

37

Cadillac Bill's Hangar was a nightclub that copied and parodied the nearby air force base at Clark Field. On stage there were cavernous openings that were hangars, each with a dancer inside, but the women were aircraft, bombers, fighters, tankers, seaplanes, whirlybirds. The bars were laid out like ramps and runways, and the customers were targets, willing targets for the girls in the hangars who swung through the air on acrobatic parachutes, sometimes high overhead, sometimes within stroking distance of the crew cuts down below. "Make love *and* war" was the slogan of the place, and Cadillac Bill's Hangar seemed to achieve a funny mixture of the two, a union that was also a reversal, because the women, the LBFM-PBR's, Little Brown Fucking Machines Powered By Rice, were the ones out to search and destroy American boys, who hunkered behind San Miguel bottles like pioneers cowering behind a circle of Conestoga wagons.

"Cadillac Bill?"

"Yes, Mr. Griffin."

"You designed this place?"

"Yes, sir. I did the best I could."

"I think you're a genius."

"Sometimes I think, what if I could franchise places like this all across the U.S., in everybody's hometown? I guess the country would never be the same."

"Is there someplace we can talk?"

"Sure. Come on." Cadillac Bill led Griffin back outside, onto the main street. "Gonna be a good night, I can feel it," Cadillac Bill predicted. He glanced up and down, waving and nodding, pointing at his softball T-shirt and flashing a V-for-victory.

"Christ I love it here. There's no place like this. You really think the Filipinos ever gonna make us leave? Close the bases and pack up?"

"I don't know."

"Not unless they can come with us when we leave," Cadillac Bill said. "That's what I think."

"They said the same thing in Havana, maybe," Griffin suggested. "They had nightclubs there, you know, and wild parties, and guys who stood around saying how much they loved it."

"Don't depress me, Mr. Griffin. I hate that kind of talk."

"Sorry."

"I hope it never comes to that. Anyway, I think old Uncle Sam learned a couple things since Cuba. Since Vietnam."

"And the Philippines gets the benefit of all that hard-earned wisdom? That it?"

"I don't know about that, Mr. Griffin. But I read a lot and I keep my ears open. And everything we say comes down to three little words. And it ain't I love you. It's keep the bases."

He unlocked a door that led into another part of the same building that housed all his other enterprises. WAR MUSEUM, the sign said.

"Stay where you are till I hit the light," Cadillac Bill warned. "You're standing in a mine field."

He was right. As the lights came on, Griffin saw mines, and a tank, a jeep, a zero fighter. He saw rifles, bayonets, pistols, helmets, all set in a sort of diorama, as if an actual World War II battle had been arrested at its peak and preserved forever.

"Now watch this," Cadillac Bill called out. The place darkened but now you sensed that you were on a battlefield at night. There were all sorts of sounds: distant gunfire, overhead bombing, artillery and mortars and, from nearer by, movement, shouts, passwords, obscenities, screams, and moans. There were random blasts of light, explosions, lightning, searchlights, tracer bullets. There were smells, too, smells of the jungle after rain, of cordite, coffee, shit, and gasoline, and finally—where did he find such an essence and how did he keep it?—the sweet, sickening smell of death. Slowly, darkness faded into false dawn and then there was sunlight in the room, and it lit up the skeletons Cadillac Bill had arranged in one corner—uniformed, helmet-wearing skeletons with guns and flags.

"How'd you like the show?" Cadillac Bill asked, motioning Griffin into an office that was also a sort of projection booth, a cluttered closet-size cubicle with newspapers, record jackets, and paper plates mulching on the floor, books and photos on the walls, and Cadillac Bill sitting on a pile of papers on his desk, the papers forming themselves around his ass, the way nests take the shape of animals that build them.

"Museum cost me a mint, ain't earned a cent," he said. "A labor of love. Everything's real. Skeletons included. I was hoping I could show this place to Colonel Harding."

"That's all he needs," Griffin said.

"He is sort of standoffish, isn't he? Not that he's a snob exactly. A loner."

"He is that. And now he's really alone."

"I heard about that. Got the army, navy and air force out looking for him. Thing I don't understand is, who curtsyed, who bowed? Was he looking for the NPA or what?"

"I don't know for sure what he's after. I'm after him. I think I know where he was headed. He left a letter for me."

"Where's he headed?"

"Kiangen. The place where the war ended. Yamashita's surrender site. I thought you might be interested in going there with me."

"Sure, I'll go with you," Cadillac Bill said. "It sounds interesting. We'll leave tonight. After the fish fights."

The fish fights.

Griffin sat in Cadillac Bill's office, lights out, peeking through a window at a small stage, carpeted with pink shag and flooded with orange light. Around the stage it was standing room only, elbow to brawny elbow, beer bottle to beer bottle. Then the woman appeared. She wasn't the fine-featured Spanish type, like Cecilia Santos, or, for that matter, Imelda Marcos. This was an earthier beauty, Malaysian stock, brown-skinned, round and ample. Not for this woman the frivolities of go-go, or the spurious suspense of striptease. Naked as Eve, and as unashamed, she stepped to the very edge of the stage. The raucous crowd of flyboys hushed. The woman reached down for a bottle of baby oil—Johnson & Johnson's—and proceeded to oil her body from head to toe, a gorgeous gleaming anointment. Griffin was squirming now; the office felt like a peep-show booth. After she oiled herself she paced about the stage a while, stretching luxuriously, yawning. Then she took an interest in the audience, an interest that was both critical and friendly. She studied one man, then another, and there was lots of elbowing and guffawing as her stare moved from subject to subject. Then it stopped: a cheer arose as a blond-haired California boy was pulled up onstage, which suddenly went dark.

When the lights came up again the flyboy, naked, lay atop the woman, conventional missionary position, and from the way he bucked and moved, he'd clearly been admitted. "Hold on, Kevin," someone shouted, and "Don't lose it," and "Ride 'em, cowboy." It sounded like a rodeo. Then it was showtime and the woman, while retaining contact with her partner, was off the floor, on top, moving urgently, and then she was sideways, lying beside him, first one side then another, and Griffin remembered Charley Camper's sexual-historical view of America and the Philippines, a man and a woman, changing positions but staying in touch, copulating forever.

"How do you like the fish fights, Mr. Griffin?" Cadillac Bill entered the booth and stood beside him. "You get the idea, don't you? She's got more different positions than Baskin Robbins got flavors. Forty-two of them, and she never loses hold through all forty-two, and there's never been a man who got to twenty without shooting off . . ."

He glanced past Griffin toward the stage, where the flyboy was straddling the woman from behind, ordinarily a male-dominant position, but he was holding on for dear life because there was nothing formal or perfunctory about the woman. Each position was a new challenge in an act that went beyond pornography, beyond obscenity, beyond sex itself. It was the mechanical bull from *Urban Cowboy*, the boxing ring from *Rocky*, and the Russian roulette in *The Deer Hunter*. It was a living ritual.

". . . and I don't believe we'll see the record broke tonight."

Griffin couldn't keep his eyes off the stage. The woman was astride the flyboy now, on top, only she was rotating like a helicopter, a human whirlybird, and her victim—for it was hard not to think of him as such—was in agony, face red, veins popping in his neck, eyes rolling backward in his head, clenched fists pounding the carpet like an about-to-be-pinned wrestler.

"I think she's got him!" Cadillac Bill said.

And she did. Moving high and low, wheeling slowly and quickly: the center did not hold. The flyboy emitted a primal groan and his conqueror leapt off him in shocking haste, in time for everyone to see the American boy ejaculate on his thighs, and belly, and carpet. The woman looked down at her defeated not-quite mate. A saucy, contemptuous grin played on her face. Then she walked away. As the house lights came up and the crowd filed toward the exits, the wilting flyboy lay there, soiled and beaten.

"That girl's got a brother, went to the University of the Philippines for a while. Then he took off to the mountains for the revolution. What I think is that *she's* the real revolutionary. She's the one who puts it on the line. And she's done more to fuck with the minds of the military than the NPA ever will. You ready now? The car's outside."

"Whose side are you on?" Griffin wondered aloud.

"There are no sides in the Philippines," Cadillac Bill answered. "There's only angles."

38

Sometimes history plays a game of spin the globe and randomly plants a finger on an obscure place, Appomattox Court House, say, and it all comes together for a day. Then the world rolls on. Such a place was General Yamashita's surrender site, Kiangen, accustomed to receiving occasional visitors, puzzled about what to do with them. The two Americans found a store owner who accepted guests in front rooms on the second story of his home. The front porch had a view of the mountains where Harry Harding had gone. Now that he saw those mountains, Griffin thought it more and more unlikely that the old man would ever come out of them. Griffin and Cadillac walked to the far side of town, where there was a war memorial, an elaborate, ecumenical shrine financed by the promiscuously repentant Japanese, who had also speared the lawn with a thicket of smaller markers, flowers and papers deposited at their base.

"Have you ever been here?" Griffin asked Cadillac Bill.

"Nope," he said. "I know the name though. I know *all* the names."

"Tell me about this place."

"How far back do you want me to go? Corregidor? Pearl Harbor? The Russo-Japanese War?"

"Start with when MacArthur landed down on Leyte," Griffin said. "That's where Harding stopped."

"Stopped? He didn't get no further than that?"

"No," Griffin admitted.

"Sounds to me—I'm not a writer—but it sounds to me like you got a story with no ending."

"That's what we're waiting for, Cadillac. And while we wait . . ."

"Okay. But if he don't show up, you're shit out of luck."

* * *

"He who defends everything defends nothing." Frederick the Great said it. Cadillac Bill quoted it. General Tomoyuki Yamashita knew it. Arriving in the Philippines only weeks before MacArthur waded ashore at Leyte, Yamashita realized what MacArthur had failed to grasp two years before: that not all of the Philippines, not even all of Luzon, could be defended. In early 1945 he led his army into the mountains. At first, he aimed to hold airfields in the Cagayan Valley, denying them to the Americans, who were then attacking Okinawa. He wanted to retain the northern port of Aparri; he still hoped to be relieved. And he wished to hold Baguio as well: he liked the climate. Fate whittled away at these designs. Hard-pressed by Americans and guerrillas, Yamashita abandoned Baguio in April. At the same time he realized that Okinawa had been lost, so there was no point in holding onto airfields or ports. Running low on medical supplies and clothing, but still equipped with small arms and ample ammunition, Yamashita led sixty-five thousand troops into the mountainous area between Routes 4 and 11, a last-ditch redoubt that became known as the Kiangen Pocket. There he stayed, in the last phase of a rear-guard action that even his enemies acknowledged was successful and impressive. Though Kiangen itself was captured in July, the last weeks of the war saw some of the harshest mountain fighting yet; slow or no progress in wretched, rainy weather through the sort of terrain where a few men could hold off an army almost forever. In the last month of the war, the Americans advanced only three miles into the mountains beyond Kiangen. And then, on August 15, 1945, General Tomoyuki Yamashita surrendered. He walked out of the mountains, down the trail to Kiangen, into the arms of his enemies, his captors, judges, executioners. And Harry Roberts Harding, MacArthur's Ghost, was at his side . . .

During the week that followed in Kiangen, Griffin spent so much time looking at the mountains, he felt like one of those morbid tourists who used to sit on sunny Alpine terraces, pointing their binoculars at the North Wall of the Eiger to catch a glimpse of climbers scaling, or hanging from, the deadly peak.

And as soon as he thought of that, something else came to mind: the realization that these mountains weren't like the Alps and Rockies; they weren't mountains at all, just higher piles of weeds and brush and trees. You could climb to the top and still not see the sky. And then Griffin came to with a start. Who said that? Whose voice intruded? Oh, yes, it was "Mean" Meade on Bataan, forty years ago. Another echo of an unfinished story. Which didn't have an ending. Even Cadillac Bill knew that.

"You're shit out of luck." That was Cadillac Bill's opinion. Clifford Lerner put it differently. He'd said George wasn't a writer, wasn't a reporter. He was a stenographer. He wasn't telling a story. He was being told—waiting to be told—one. Lerner was tough. He'd have done a week of homework before he sat down with Harding. He'd have books, Xeroxes, depositions. He'd check and cross-check. He'd interrupt a lot, circle around a touchy subject, double back to it, until he was satisfied. He'd know what it was about before he started—the themes, the mysteries, the questions and answers. He'd have the ending before he started. And he'd be busy, always busy, never waiting the way Griffin was waiting, waiting and wondering how much longer to wait.

Cadillac Bill was busy too. He had Kiangen organized in no time, kids and old-timers scouring the mountains for war memorabilia that he could use in his museum. Anthropologist, historian, showman, and entrepreneur, he turned an ordinary day into an occasion and—by himself—restored to Kiangen a sense of its historic importance. The area around town had been pretty well "picked over," Cadillac acknowledged: the Japanese were diligent about their fallen soldiers. So Cadillac and his people went farther and farther into the mountains, into "virgin territory," searching for a camp or cave, a rumored hideout or headquarters. In midafternoon he came home, bruised, muddy, exhilarated, weighed down with the catch of the day: canteens, helmets, sake bottles, first-aid kits. Mortar shells. A light machine gun. A burlap sack of bones, two skulls. Every morning he went farther out and every afternoon he came back later, "picking the Kiangen Pocket."

Meanwhile, there were sightings. A group of U.S. airmen out dirt-bike racing had given MacArthur's Ghost a ride through

Pampangas. An encampment of Rizalistas—worshipers of José Rizal—had seen him on the trail that led up Mount Arayat. A groundskeeper at the Philippines Military Academy in Baguio glimpsed him on the golf course at dawn. Down on Leyte, on Tacloban beach, a fisherman had seen Harding standing next to the life-size statue of MacArthur wading ashore. A busload of Canadian tourists were held up by gunmen near the Banaue rice terraces: they saw Harry Roberts Harding running things. There were more reports every day. And the last and least of them was this: that George Griffin, MacArthur's Ghost's ghost, had also disappeared. It was unclear why. It was increasingly unclear to Griffin himself.

Griffin sat having coffee with Cadillac Bill, watching rain cascade off the roof, bounce off an already-full catchment barrel, splash to earth and begin the long, ill-advised journey to Manila Bay. Then there was a catlike scratching at the screen window: a bunch of kids were out there in the rain, a bunch of Cadillac's playmates, vendors of bullets and bones.

"Sir," one of them said to Cadillac Bill, "you come."

"Not in this weather," Cadillac Bill replied. He pointed up at the rain. "Too much. No go."

"Sir," one of the kids insisted, a wide-eyed kid in a striped polo shirt and brown shorts, the leader of the pack. He reminded Griffin of the kid who had dogged him his first morning in Manila. There was an awful solemnity behind his playfulness. You felt he could watch a hanging and not be moved. Young Juan Olmos must have looked like that. The kid stayed right against the screen. Out in the rain. "Sir, you come."

"Insistent little bugger," Cadillac Bill said.

"Sir, you come."

"What you got?" Cadillac Bill asked.

"Sir, I got a whole one."

"A whole one . . ." Cadillac Bill was impressed. "Whole one" was part of the morbid idiom he'd worked out with the kids who climbed into once-fortified caves or burnt-out tanks and came out to report what they had found, remnants and fragments for the most part, but sometimes a whole one, an intact, mint-condition, boots-to-helmet skeleton. "You sure you got a whole one?"

"Yes, sir, I got."

"This better be good." He glanced at Griffin. "You want to come? Maybe get a column out of it. If this book of yours don't come off, you'll be trading in columns."

"Oh, all right," Griffin said. He'd turned down Cadillac Bill's invitations all week long. At the end, he might as well go along, just once. Get a column out of it. Sure. Along with the sex queen at the fish fights and the dart man in Manila. And the burlap sack of bones. And the dog beating in Tondo, people living in culverts, hanging garbage bags out to dry like fish nets. Great stuff.

It wasn't the sort of rain you negotiated with. As soon as you stepped out, you were soaked. Some of the kids laughed at the rain, played in it. They turned grassy banks into playground slides. But the kid in the lead, the one who'd summoned them, wasn't playing. He shushed the other kids away, scared them off, and led the two Americans toward the treasure—the "whole one"—he had found and was determined not to share. He took them out toward the war memorial, a forlorn place this morning, like a cemetary between funerals, with the rain spattering down on plastic flowers the Japanese had left behind.

"You stay!" the kid commanded, pointing them toward the shelter of the main shrine. As soon as the Americans obeyed, he scooted out through the wooden memorial markers and disappeared in the woods.

"Cadillac?"

"Yeah, Mr. Griffin?"

"I'm ready to leave Kiangen. After today."

"I'm not rushing you. Stay another week, it's okay with me."

"I just get the feeling this story wasn't meant to have an ending. Harding wanders into the mountains and becomes a ghost again. And that . . . that's all she wrote. No ending."

"You think so?" Cadillac Bill sighted past Griffin, out across the grass. "Well, there's your ending."

Beyond the markers, beyond the fields, a procession was winding its way out of the mountains, on the very trail that Yamashita had taken forty years before, a trail that ended on the gallows at Los Banos. And the man who accompanied him then on the trail was walking it again: Colonel Harry Roberts Harding, MacArthur's Ghost.

Griffin rushed down the monument steps. The NPA men were already fading back toward the mountains. Harding stood alone. He looked more gaunt and angular than ever. The bones showed through his face, a skull stirring to shed its mask of flesh. A white beard was on his face, a corpse's stubble.

"Colonel?" Harding had changed. "Colonel? It's me."

"Hello, son."

They walked back to the village in the rain, Griffin holding the Colonel by the elbow, while behind him Cadillac Bill and the kid were still at it.

"You give me one hundred pesos!"

"For what? For *that*?"

"Whole one! Mr. Cadillac!"

"What good is he to me? What am I supposed to do with him? No helmet, no gun, no souvenir . . ."

"Whole one!"

"Okay, okay. I'll tell you what I'm gonna do . . ."

The rains stayed all day. Nothing came up or down the mountain road. So after they sat Harding in a tub of hot water, after they handed him towels and wrapped him in blankets, fed him soup, tucked him in, Cadillac Bill and George Griffin sat up and watched him sleep. An unlikely pair of nurses, and an unlikely sickroom. MacArthur's Ghost lay in Cadillac Bill's bed, a pile of helmets and bayonets at the foot, a sack of bones at the head.

"Guardian angels watch to keep," Griffin reflected.

"He looks like something I'd put in a corner of my museum," Cadillac Bill said. "MacArthur's Ghost resting on a field of honor."

"He's not about to lead you to any treasure," Griffin said. "You or me. I'm sorry about that."

"I'm not so sure," Cadillac Bill said, his eyes on Colonel Harding. Vague and disoriented while awake, the old man wheezed and rattled when he slept. Once he had a coughing fit that sounded as though it would land his lungs in his lap. "There's something buried there. Treasure or what, I don't know. But I'll tell you one thing. Either he gets it or it gets him."

That night, Cadillac volunteered to sleep in the back of his car. Maybe it was the end of the rain that awakened Harding, the sudden silence. Or maybe it was moonlight that followed, a silvery flood that poured into the room, magnificent stuff, burnishing Cadillac Bill's guns and bones.

He was out on the porch, standing still, staring out at the mountains, the moon and stars. When Griffin came out to join him, he saw there were tears running down his face. He decided it was better not to speak. On the street below, Cadillac Bill's car sat like a vehicle from another planet, its owner asleep inside. Leaves stirred slightly in the breeze, dipped in, dripping silver. Beyond them were the mountains, as though seen for the first time, like the imaginary mountains of a child's sketchbook, range piled on range, no telling where the mountains ended and the clouds began.

"A night like this," Harding said, "you could go anywhere from here. You could go all the way forward or way way back. Look at those mountains. In 1945 I was in and out of these mountains all the time. Fighting, scouting, sitting in on the surrender negotiations, finally escorting Yamashita toward the American lines, me on one side of him, Juan Olmos and Connie on the other. And I remember how the Japs—the Shobu group —sixty thousand men who were trapped, didn't want him to go with me. They cried. It was like we tore the heart right out of them. That's what I heard a minute ago. Them crying."

39

There was no disputing that Colonel Harry Roberts Harding's return to Manila was the climax of the most brilliant campaign Eddie Richter had ever seen. It was nothing Eddie took credit for; it wasn't his doing. He was just glad that he was around to see it and smart enough to appreciate a masterwork from beginning to end, from that first shrewdly awkward appearance at Corregidor, through those dangerous offhand remarks at Manila Memorial Cemetery, the against-odds triumph at the movie location in Baguio. All that was good in a conventional way, raising questions, stirring the pot, revving up the talk of war heroes, treasure, treason, "all that good stuff." But then you got to the point where talent ended and genius took over: Harding's disappearance, his capture by the NPA, and then his return to Manila, two days before scenes from *MacArthur's Ghost* were to be screened on the final night of the Imelda Marcos Manila Film Festival! Jesus, that was beautiful. It transcended all those boundaries, those stubborn distinctions that drive a PR man crazy. It was local, it was national, it was international. It was news, it was entertainment, and best of all, it wasn't over yet.

Eddie had taken the call that Griffin made from somewhere along the road, two hours out of town. He made those hours count. Given two days, he'd have had film crews and banners outside the Manila Hotel, he'd have had the whole movie cast along the driveway, and a billboard that said "MAC'S BACK—THE MOVIE'S GOT 'EM!" or something like that. But maybe short notice was just as well, because while Eddie was diligent, Harding was inspired. So Eddie contented himself with phone calls. Then he went over to the Manila Hotel, stood back, and watched it happen.

It was terrific when you didn't have to hire the hall and rent the band, hang bunting, plug in the applause sign, feed the press corps. You took a seat in that damned beautiful lobby and watched. At first, everything was normal: Jap tourists, Canadians, swimming trunks, whining kids. Then a sudden stir among the white-liveried security guards who frisked you as you entered, a manager appearing, conferring, sending one of the guards outside. The guard motioned for the taxis to back off a distance and so they did, slamming into reverse and playing "Yesterday" and "Let It Be" and the other songs the Manila taxis hummed when they backed up. Then, more taxis, reporters, and photographers. Let it be, let it be. Now the first film crews and that meant the usual intramural scrapping, wires, lights, people jostling for position. At last, jeeps and limousines, that Colonel Herrera from Contreras's staff and the brown-skinned lollapalooza from the U.S. embassy, her and her boss, and the producers, Wingfield and Beaumont, and the ice queen, Cecilia Santos. What's the program? Who's in charge? Eddie made like a hotel dick, hiding behind a newspaper. Let it be, let it be. Now a few anticlimactic teases: a busload of nuns, puzzled by all the attention, and an English businessman heading upstairs for "Funch" with a pretty boy.

And then, at last, the moment they'd been waiting for. Harding was incredible, pulling into that curving colonial driveway in a pink Caddy pimpmobile that had clear memories of Batista's Havana, pulling in with the top down, some aloha-shirted Okie for a driver and George Griffin, budding author, in the front seat.

"I'm back," Harding told the microphones. He looked way past ripe, but he pulled himself together okay. "I took a walk in the country that I love. I met some people, refreshed some memories, that's all."

"Did the NPA capture you?"

"No. We met in the mountains. It seems we were on the same trail. I was climbing down a mountain and they were headed up it."

There was a peculiar silence after that. Had the colonel meant what he said? Was there a signal hiding in that stuff about the mountain?

"I know my coming back here has raised a lot of questions," Harding continued. "Some things, I'll never know. Others, I've got sorted out. Tomorrow night, after the movie, maybe I'll say a few words. And then I'll go on home. Promise."

That's great, Eddie thought, watching Harding and Griffin step into the hotel. Great! Always leave them wanting more. Wingfield was having kittens. Headed his way, too.

"There you are, damn it," Wingfield said.

"Something wrong?"

"Something wrong? Who are you working for, Eddie? I can't even get upstairs to see him. No visitors, no calls. How'd this happen?"

"What happened is terrific, from where I sit," Richter said. "With the coverage you get tomorrow night, who needs advertising?"

"Listen, Richter. Tomorrow night we've got a gala dinner and a screening of selected scenes, rough cut. We've got the president of the Philippines coming. We've got the First Lady and the whole fucking film festival. And our featured speaker, all of a sudden, is a senile, self-invited, self-promoting—"

"He was a hero once," Eddie interrupted. "Never forget that. He was a hero."

"Forty years ago! But now—"

"Forty years is nothing," Eddie Richter said. "Take it from me."

MacArthur's Ghost was being difficult. As soon as they were in the MacArthur Suite together, as soon as Griffin suggested that maybe they should "go over" what Harding planned to say tomorrow night, the colonel waved him off.

"It's the most important part," Griffin protested. "You can't just wing it."

"I'm winging nothing, son," Harding said. "I've made that speech a hundred times."

"Where?"

"In here," Harding said, pointing to his heart. "And here." His head. "And here." His stomach.

"I'm not just asking for your sake, Colonel. I'm asking for me. I've got a book at stake here. I want to know how it ends."

"I think you know more than you realize," Harding said. "You know."

"Just a rehearsal then."

"Damn it, I don't need rehearsals!" Harding burst out angrily. It was the first time he'd lost his temper around Griffin. It surprised them both. He instantly caught himself. "Sorry, son."

"Me too."

"You don't get it, do you? Don't you see? When I came here I was hoping it would never get this far. Never come to where I had to stand up and—and say what I'm going to say. I thought something would happen to me. Someone would get me. I invited them. I exposed myself. I damn near begged them, and nobody obliged. I was a pain in the ass all right, but not worth capturing, not worth keeping. Not worth killing. Why kill a ghost? So I'm going to have to do what I dread. What terrifies me. Tomorrow night's going to be the worst night of my life. And you don't rehearse for something like that."

Griffin stared at the old man, who'd sunk into the same chair he'd been in when Griffin first came to call, when he was drinking beer with Charley Camper. Long ago. Before the war. He wanted to press him, he wanted to be ahead of the pack. But in the end, he backed off. Being ahead of the pack would also make him a part of it, a reporter among reporters, no more or less. Maybe that was what he should have been, from the start, but there was no changing now.

"When'll I see you?" he asked.

"Tomorrow night. You go out tonight and have some fun. There's that Imelda party for the film festival. Kick up your heels. I'll see you tomorrow."

"And after that?"

"All you want, if you want. I'll sneak on home. But anywhere I was, I'd be happy to see you. It would be . . . my pleasure."

Weary as he was, he lifted himself out of the chair and offered his hand. "See you tomorrow, my friend."

40

The film festival gala Imelda Marcos decreed inside old Fort Santiago was a party to remember, and regret: Persepolis and Oscar night, Perle Mesta and Marie Antoinette. There were candy-striped tents overflowing with champagne, enough for an infinity of toasting, and enough cakes for a thousand weddings and—in barbecue pits that looked like mass cremations—a menagerie of cattle, pigs, and four-month-old calves, slowly turning. Griffin wandered from one display of conspicuous consumption to another. You could justify your presence only so far, saying that you were a writer, or a spectator, or even a judge. It was too fine a distinction; this was too gross a display. You were in the same place as everyone else, the politicians and cronies, the Malacanang matrons, the perfectly dressed Filipina touch-me-nots, the visiting movie distributors who staggered around with magnums of Dom Perignon in their hands and prawns in their mouths. Shoot them all, he thought. God will sort it out.

"Hello, George." He felt guilty being recognized. He didn't want anyone at this party to know him. Then he saw that the person who knew him was Susan.

"Hello," Griffin responded.

"That's all?" she asked and he had to admire the puzzled look that crossed her face, as if she'd been snubbed, and the way she made a little joke of it, glancing over her dress as if there might be something wrong with what she was wearing when she perfectly well knew that what she wore worked as nicely as the body it covered. He had to admire that. And there was more: the way she moved from role to role, diplomat to lover and back again, diplomat to lover to betrayer. He could only be one thing at a time: MacArthur's Ghost's ghost. "What's the matter, George?"

"What's the matter?" he repeated. "What could be the matter? Great party, open bar, plenty of food, balmy, tropical evening, marvelous, swinging people. Your perfect Faraway Place."

"I've been wondering about you, George," she said.

"I don't know if I want you wondering, Susan. It scares me."

"Is that why you ran off? You were supposed to bring your tapes and papers to the Embassy. Next thing, you were gone."

"I got scared," Griffin said. "Or smart."

"Scared?"

"Of you. Your operation, Susan. The way you worked over poor Charley Camper. That bothered me. But that was just for openers. You were only warming up."

"What's that supposed to mean, George?"

"Clifford Lerner."

"Who?"

"Come on, Susan. The journalist I told you about. The one who was working his way down memory lane, Olmos to Contreras. I told you he was good. I told you he played around at the G-spot. The next thing, Contreras's boys catch him with his pants down. At the G-spot. Then he's gone."

"Ah. And you think that was my doing?"

"I've wondered."

"Wondered? It sounds like you've decided. What else have you decided? Have you decided I was assigned to you? 'Get close to that man Griffin, no matter what it takes.' You think that?"

"All right," George said. "Do me a favor. Tell me I'm wrong. Tell me that talk we had about Clifford Lerner never got repeated anywhere. Tell me that. Please."

"Oh, George," she said. "Grow up." And with that, she left him.

He found a San Miguel and headed across the lawn, into the shadows of the old fort. The place was a hodgepodge. Under the battlements, a row of stables was a kind of auto mausoleum, sheltering the limousines of every president from Quezon on. Elsewhere, there was a museum shrine dedicated to José Rizal, the martyred patriot who had been held here before his execution by the Spanish. There were Rizal paintings, clothing, furniture, manuscripts; life-size tableaux of the man's last moments. Outside Rizal's cell, Griffin spotted some steps that led up to the walls that circled the fort. From the top, he could see the arrival of the First Family: Marcos, simply dressed in barong tagalog and dark slacks, and Imelda Marcos in a white, high-shouldered Spanish gown. The flashbulbs caught her diamonds; it looked as though she'd showered in them and hadn't finished drying off around her neck and ears. Between the two Marcoses was their daughter, Imee, the Princeton-educated one. War hero and beauty queen and troubled daughter: a family out of Camelot, and if Camelot had turned way past ripe, who was to say that the same thing wouldn't have happened to Kennedy's Camelot, or anybody else's?

Just outside was the Pasig River, once a natural protective moat, now a viscous coliform fiesta. Across the river lay the old business district, then Chinatown, then Tondo. You had to wonder if they knew what the king was doing tonight, and, if they did, would they react with anger or with envy? Crash, or trash, the party? That was the only question.

Footsteps around him. A row of choirboys come up the ladder, acolytes with candles, distributing themselves at intervals, along the wall. And then, at the end of the procession, a voice.

"What are you doing up here, Mr. Griffin?" Cecilia Santos was no choirboy. She wore a black skirt and a black jacket with golden tinselly threads woven through it. And she was smiling at him.

"Looking for perspective," he said, gesturing at the party. A parade started winding through the fort, religious statues, all gold and silver and lit by hundreds of candles, alternating with beauty queens on lavish, flowered floats. Wow!

"For perspective you'll have to go farther away than here," Cecilia Santos commented. She drew a cigarette out of her purse and—before Griffin could move to light it—snapped her fingers at one of the choirboys who, after a brief moment of spiritual crisis, rushed over and held out his candle to her Benson and Hedges. "Where is your companion?"

"He's back at the hotel, resting."

"No, not that tiresome old man, not him. I mean that dark, gorgeous creature from the embassy. You brought her to my sister's house. I saw her a while ago. Is she with you?"

"No."

"Too bad. She's so beautiful . . . for her type. The heavy, full-bodied earth mother."

Griffin laughed at the faintness of the praise. Women were brutal.

"In the Philippines our women tend to be somewhat lighter, finer. Have you tried one?"

"No." Griffin wondered what was up. It was no good trying to figure out women like Cecilia Santos and Birdy Villanueva. You'd be calling time-out after every sentence, just to think. Better to let what would happen happen and save understanding for your old age.

"Please . . ." She walked over to the edge of the battlement, executed a turn that a ramp model would have envied, and came back toward him.

"I would like to propose a truce."

"A truce?"

"Between us, yes."

"Not an armistice. Not a treaty. We're not disarming or—God forbid—surrendering."

"A truce to start with," she said. She offered him her arm. "Perspective later. Party first."

With Cecilia Santos on his arm, Griffin was a star. Earlier, when he felt like a stranger, he rationalized that being a stranger behooved him: he was the sharp-eyed spectator, professionally detached. Now he wasn't so sure. Cecilia Santos was marvelous company, and with her beside him, it seemed Manila was full of people who were anxious to meet him, not just journalists and movie people, but businessmen, officials, boutique owners, stewardesses. They all wanted to know about the book and, the more they asked, the more it seemed the book was his. Colonel Harry Roberts Harding had lived it, but the living was over. So, almost, was the telling. Then Harding would be empty, gone, silent, and Griffin would remain in sole possession. He wasn't there yet, but he would be soon, and he was looking forward to the time when the partnership would be over and he would be sole proprietor. As the evening bubbled along, he did less and less to discourage the only slightly premature notion that the book was in the bag, story, secrets, ending, and all, that Marcos, MacArthur, Yamashita, and—but of course—the elusive General Contreras all played important parts.

It got better and better, and why not? He'd spent weeks putting up with Harry Roberts Harding and this was his reward. Attention, adulation, expectations, the sort of flurry that Harding couldn't cope with, but why should Griffin deny himself? He was entitled. Was the book finished? "All but the writing," he answered with a smile that implied the true magic was still to come. *His* magic.

"My little sister!" Birdy Villanueva embraced Cecilia. "Hello, Mr. Griffin."

"Good evening. Where's Jun?"

"In the States by now, I hope."

"Is there a problem?"

"I hope not. Our daughter's graduating from Sweetbriar. How goes your book?"

"Very well," Griffin said. He noticed that Birdy glanced at her sister, as though the question about the book was something that Cecilia might be able to answer. In fact, Cecilia did answer, nodding slightly.

"I can't wait!" Birdy cried. "You must send me an advance copy. Mark the dirt! The section on General Contreras!"

"Birdy!" Cecilia cautioned.

"Well, why not?" Birdy asked. "We have a right to know about our leaders." She paused and laughed. "And I want to be the first to know!"

"My sister . . ." Cecilia sighed.

"Off with you," Birdy said. "I must leave. This time Imelda has really gone too far."

Birdy was the first important guest to leave, but not long afterward Ferdinand Marcos followed, departing with the air of a man who was anxious not to miss the last half of Monday Night Football. His wife and daughter lingered. Imee stepped out with Jeremy Irons. Imelda saved a dance for George Hamilton. And Cecilia Santos was George Griffin's partner.

"What if I cut in on the First Lady?" Griffin wondered aloud.

He thought he was whispering suavely, but Cecilia Santos put a finger over his lips. It wasn't the last part of her his lips would touch. He was feeling lucky.

"Cut in on her? And leave me?"

"Unthinkable," he said. On the dance floor Griffin attempted as little as possible during the upbeat tunes and Cecilia Santos appreciated his restraint. His reward came with the slow music. His lips were right against her ear.

"I feel good about tonight," he said. Turning slowly to "Stranger in Paradise," he could see the crowd of people surrounding the dance floor, hangers-on, bodyguards, gawkers. Outside the walls was a larger crowd, the uninvited millions. Well, who ever said life was fair? While they were still dancing, the Marcos women left, departing in the usual flurry of flashbulbs. The dance-floor mood was broken. Cecilia Santos pulled away abruptly, in mid-dance, as if something invisible had cut in on her. She didn't consult with Griffin. "I can drop you off at your hotel."

"All right," Griffin said. There was a perfect line out there. Maybe he'd think of it tomorrow. And use it on the next girl. This one was headed for the exit.

In the car, Griffin estimated the drive back to the Manila Hotel wouldn't take more than two minutes. He realized he'd have to move fast to have any chance at Cecilia Santos. What made it hard was that she'd fallen silent. It was as though she was waiting for him to make his move. He even thought he detected a faint smile of anticipation on her face, a curiosity about what he'd come up with. He leaned toward her just when she decided to light a cigarette. Her match flared, just long enough to light up, and just as Griffin moved toward her, his hand already on her shoulder, turning her toward him, he saw the look in her eyes, which wasn't amusement and wasn't longing. It was contempt. There was no mistaking it. He removed his hand and sat back in his seat and let a few hundred yards of Manila pass them by.

"You came on to me," he said after a while. "What was that about?"

"I needed to know about the book. Where it was. How far along."

"Why?"

"You wouldn't understand."

"Maybe not. I'm sure it's complicated. Try me."

"I was doing my job."

"Miss Santos, I wasn't going to accuse you of doing anything for the fun of it. What's your job? Who are you working for? Imelda Marcos? Larry Wingfield? Birdy and Jun Villanueva?"

"Everybody. Nobody. Myself."

"That's what whores say," Griffin fired back and before he had a chance to regret it, Cecilia Santos delivered a sharp slap across his mouth.

"Fast hands!"

"You're bleeding."

"It's your damn jewelry. Cut my lip."

"Why don't you apologize?"

"I was going to. I'm sorry. All right? I guess everybody has reasons for the things they do."

"Stop here," Cecilia Santos called out to the driver.

They were on Roxas Boulevard, right near Luneta Park, just before the turn that led to the Manila Hotel. At first he thought she was going to dump him at the curb and let him walk the rest of the way. But she made no move toward excusing him. They sat together and said nothing. Across the park, two Philippine marines stood guard at Rizal's floodlit statue.

"I don't know why I'm telling you this," Cecilia Santos said.

Traffic came up behind them. A panel truck loaded with religious statues from the party, some Virgin Mary or other calling it a night. Cecilia Santos signaled for the driver to pull around to the Quirino Bandstand. She told the driver to take a walk, then opened the door to let some air in. She breathed deeply as if she were about to start a speech. Then she laughed. Nothing to do with him, nothing he could share, but still a laugh.

"I don't even know where to start," she said.

"The movie," Griffin prompted. "Your sister. And Imelda Marcos."

"That was to be expected. The producers—Beaumont and Wingfield—came along with an attractive project. Both women wanted to be part of it. Birdy got there first. But there was no denying Imelda. They compete. They always compete. That was where I came in. I was acceptable to both sides. Never mind why."

Griffin hadn't even meant to ask. Looking at her, he knew why. She was like them. If Birdy Villanueva was a current challenger to Imelda Marcos, Cecilia Santos could replace either or both of them. Griffin reminded himself to try to figure out why it was that this most macho and chauvinistic of countries, this hothouse of sexual innuendo and pro-forma infidelity, produced such strong women. Was it a paradox or a consequence? The men, affable, clubby little philanderers, strutted and stroked while the women they played with played for higher stakes.

"But the competition became disorderly when your Colonel Harding returned. And then your book compounded things. Because people started to see that this wasn't just a glamorous project or a convenient investment. It had to do with history. And history had to do with us. It had to do especially with President Marcos, who revels in history, and dreams and mourns it. It had to do with General Contreras. This was a chance to put pressure on him . . ."

"Why? What is it about Contreras?"

"He frightens people. He's so outside of things, so aloof, so distant. This is a place where everybody who matters knows everybody else who matters. Marcos knows Villanueva. He knows Aquino. He knows Laurel. Birdy knows Imelda. They call themselves enemies, they may even believe it. But the worst enemy—they would all agree on this—is the man they don't know. That's Nestor Contreras."

"I see," Griffin said. But it was only half true. His book was going to let a lot of people down: Harding had nothing to say about Contreras.

"There have always been rumors about Contreras's past. Things that happened during the war. So when Colonel Harding remembered his name on Corregidor and, then, when he announced a whole book of memories, well, people saw a chance to apply pressure. They saw a chance to hit a nerve. And they were right. You saw what happened to your friend Lerner. It could happen to you. I suggest you go someplace far away to finish your book. With the movie company departing, I won't be able to protect you."

"You protected me? *You?*"

"Every mile you drove. Every meeting. The people I work for wanted you to finish the book."

"I thought you hated the thing."

"That was an act, an act that happened to reflect my personal thoughts."

"Cecilia Santos," he said. "Forgive me. Your personal thoughts? What are they? It's the last I'll ask you. Then I'm gone."

"Promise?" She laughed. A woman of private humors. Private everything. "You won't be gone. There are always more Americans coming to visit. To learn, to be shocked and titillated. To have adventures. A war adventure or a woman adventure. Or both. That's my answer, by the way, my personal thoughts. I'm tired of Americans coming here and telling us what things mean and what they meant and I'm tired of us waiting to hear what they say. Tired of memories and monuments and movies. *I don't care . . .*"

When she finished she looked at him to see what impact her words had. Griffin took a finger of his hand, kissed it, and reached out and put the finger on her lips.

"You're terrific," he said. "I wonder where on earth you'll get to."

She shrugged. "I'm not worried."

"I should hope not." He hated tearing himself away, but it was time to go.

"I'd like to run into you again sometime," he said. "And start all over."

"Now why would I want to do a thing like that?" she asked.

"You're terrific," he repeated, walking away.

"Mr. Griffin," she called out. "About Contreras . . . what did Harding say? What is it all about?"

"Nothing," Griffin confessed. "Not a word. The joke's on me."

"The joke's on all of us." Delicious laughter trailed behind her departing limousine.

The hour before dawn, supposedly the darkest, saw an odd commotion in the lobby of the Manila Hotel. Griffin wondered whether a group of tourists might be checking out at an ungodly hour. Then he saw reporters camping out, and cameramen. What was this? Had the old man pulled another surprise? He stepped into the lobby, toward the registration desk. Susan Hayes intercepted him.

"I've been waiting for you for hours," she said. She looked as though she'd been on an all-night vigil, a cup of coffee in her hand.

"What's the matter? He didn't go wandering off?"

"Yes he did," she said, and there it was again, that green-eyed look he thought he'd left behind. "I thought I should be the one to tell you."

"You mean—"

"He died around midnight."

Part Nine

★ ★ ★
★ ★

FINDING CONNIE

41

"What's the big deal about San Leandro?" Cadillac Bill asked. Elbow out the window, cigar in mouth, six-pack of road beer in the driver's seat, he steered through the broad, wet reaches of Nueva Ecija, the road a dusty causeway between fields of mud. "I been through that town a time or two. It's a dump."

"Colonel Harding was pointed there," Griffin replied. "He even gave me a picture. He said it was taken before the second Battle of San Leandro."

"Yeah. So?"

"He told me about the first battle. Not the second."

"That's not much."

"He said we'd find our ending there. He said it would be our last chapter."

"Christ, George, you spend more time looking for endings."

While Cadillac Bill drove on, Griffin closed his eyes, feigning sleep. He thought back to Harding's funeral. The death MacArthur's Ghost had sought in the mountains had been waiting for him in the Manila Hotel's best suite, right in bed, like a room-service hooker. Now he'd joined all the other ghosts whose company he and Griffin had been sharing. He rested under the funeral ground he'd trod so nonchalantly, wreath in hand, a few weeks before. And it was left to Griffin to travel to the place that had terrified him.

The Cadillac was hot, even with the windows down, and the sleep he was faking crept up on him. He found himself thinking of Susan. How she'd been there in the hotel lobby, waiting for him. "I thought I should be the one to tell you." How she'd walked with him out across Rizal Park, through the children's playground at the edge of the bay, strolling between slides and

swings and sandboxes that were like memories of uncom-
plicated life. How she'd gestured for a cab and taken him to her
home in Paranaque and sat next to him, not saying a word, as
if the silence was something perfect they were building and, the
longer it lasted, the better it was. And how she'd led him inside,
upstairs, and had made love to him, beginning with a gentleness
he appreciated, being in mourning. "That was for us," she said
when they finished. And how, all of a sudden, when Susan said
us, he was back with Harry Roberts Harding, dead one day, and
this was part of his legacy, wondering about *I* and *we* and *they.*
"For us," he repeated after her.

"Oh, shit!" Cadillac Bill's shout jarred Griffin awake. He saw
it was dusk, that there were rice fields left and right, and that
the road ahead was blocked by a row of oil barrels that were
painted like barber poles.

"What's this?" asked Griffin.

"A pain in the ass is what it is," Cadillac Bill replied, pumping
the brakes. Weaving through the barrels, the Cadillac was
forced to a crawl. "And that's the excitement of the Philippines.
You never know who's blocking the road."

Griffin saw some men behind the barricade of oil barrels. For
a moment, he was back with Harding, in a white Packard roadster, coming up on Japanese sentries at a trestle bridge over a
river that led to the South China Sea: "Mean" Meade at the
wheel.

"They've got rifles," Griffin said.

"So? Is a bear Catholic? Does the pope shit in the woods?"

"And uniforms. It must be the army."

"That's not exactly cause for celebration. They're a tribe,
that's all. A tribe among tribes. Got it?"

A half dozen soldiers moved toward the car, walked around
it appraisingly, like customers in a showroom. Cadillac rolled
down the window.

"Howdy, gents," he called out. Nervous as he was, he slipped
nicely into the role of an affable yokel. "What's cooking?"

They laughed—at him or with him, you couldn't say. It was
one of those two-edged moments that could end in a party or
a spray of bullets. They'd been drinking, Griffin saw. A couple
of San Mig cases were stacked at the side of the road, like some

sort of last-ditch stockade. They were casual about casualties out here and scrupulous about empties.

"Where are you going?" one of the soldiers asked. A white strip over his chest pocket identified him as DEL CAMPO, M., LT.

"San Leandro," Cadillac Bill said.

"Why?"

"My girl's got family there. Her mother's sick."

"Where is your girl?"

"Ca-li-for-ni-a," Cadillac Bill responded. "Visiting my mother. It's crazy, isn't it?"

Lieutenant Del Campo leaned down and peered into the back seat, capacious and leathery and lightly powdered with dust.

"You get plenty girls back there?" Del Campo asked. "You open the door and they jump right in, no?" He translated for the other soldiers, who laughed appreciatively. "You screw them in the pussy and the ass and in the mouth and then you drop them on the road and drive off in your pussywagon. You got passports?"

"Yeah."

"What kind?"

"American."

"Let me see." He sat down on a case of empty beer bottles and read every page. Next he took a piss. Then he walked over and returned their passports, staring hard at Griffin. "You travel too much."

42

The cathedral was still there, birds circling the spire as the sun slanted downward in the west: everything was briefly golden. San Leandro was as Harding described it, the square, the schoolyard, and the municipal building, which he and Juan Olmos had conquered for a night forty years before. *"For a little while, we owned the world."* The municipal hall was as stolid and ugly as he said it was, a banner across the door proclaiming that its imminent renovation was a personal project of First Lady Imelda Marcos, head of the Human Settlements Ministry. Cadillac parked the car right in front and sat behind the wheel, like a taxi driver waiting for a customer to decide where next.

"Welcome to San Leandro, jewel of the rice lands," he said. "What now?"

Griffin wasn't sure. How do you go looking for ghosts? Or finish a dead man's story? Yet there was something different about this town, a sullen reserve that distinguished it from the dozen places he and Harding had walked through together. Where were the radios, the tape players, the musical racket? Where was the rickety movie house, the lazy barbershop? Where were the kids who swarmed around the pink Cadillac in every other town, the ones who made every American feel like Santa Claus? The town held back. Why? On one corner, a group of men sat drinking beer and holding fighting cocks in their hands. Except for the swig of a beer bottle or the stroke of a plumed neck, they were motionless.

"What's our strategy?" Cadillac Bill asked.

"I'm not sure," Griffin said. "Could we just walk around?"

"Sure," Cadillac rejoindered. "Real natural like, huh, pardner? Hey, I've got news. Americans don't come to a place like this and take walks."

"We will."

"Correction: you will. I'll stay with the car. This town gives me the willies."

The square was part pavement, part cobblestones, part mud, just as the old man had said. The nipa huts were gone, at least from around the square. Wooden houses with tin roofs had replaced them, plus a few cement-block structures. Walking in the square gave Griffin a surrounded feeling, as if he was on the inside of a livestock pen. He nodded at the cluster of men in front of the store. They watched his every step. Their eyes were like the eyes in trick medieval paintings, following you as you passed in front of them. The men's eyes, and the roosters'.

The schoolyard was off one end of the square, oddly luxuriant and grassy, and some kids were kicking a ball around, playing a kind of volleyball that permitted players to use both hands and feet to keep the ball aloft. Griffin lingered in the shadows, watching, which was a relief after so much being watched. But when he moved, they saw him. The ball dropped to the grass and rolled off, and the kids stopped and stared at him, just like the men at the store.

He followed the road north, to the trestle bridge that spanned the river. Some Japanese troops had died here. They'd died in the square as well, and in a ditch on the other side of town, and one by one out in the cane fields, squealing like rabbits. That was the first Battle of San Leandro. It had left no marks behind, no monuments. But what about the second battle? How to recover a battle that was nothing louder than a dead man's whisper? Might as well ask the cobblestones to speak, or the birds, or the river Juan Olmos had followed into town.

"You got some mail," Cadillac Bill said, handing him an envelope.

"*Mail?*"

"A kid come running to the car, run off again before I could talk to him. Didn't even stick out his hand for a peso. This town is strange."

Griffin's name was on the envelope. That was hard enough to accept, in a town where no one knew him. What was inside was more incredible still. The note said that it was necessary for him to drive two kilometers on the road north and to turn left on a dirt track through the sugar fields, to drive as far as it was possible and then to wait—if he wanted to meet Juan Olmos.

"I'm telling you," Cadillac Bill said, "it's those soldiers, man. They saw your name on the passport. Man, we're sailing right into it. One pink pussywagon and two dead tourists . . ."

"The soldiers don't know about Juan Olmos though," Griffin reminded him. That stopped Cadillac Bill, but not for long.

"I'm supposed to feel better because of that? Hey, come on, Mr. Griffin! You tell me. You're driving around Detroit, let's say, and some kid hands you a note and it says, Hi, I'm dying to meet you in the park at midnight and tell you all my secrets, signed yours truly, Jimmy Hoffa. You jump right at that, do you? Is that the way you go about it? There's our left."

"Where?"

"There," he said, pointing at a barely noticeable gap in the fields of sugarcane. "Where there's a sign, an arrow, says this way to the ambush. Shit, I don't believe this!"

The road was made for carts and carabao. Cadillac Bill's machine touched the ranks of cane on either side, a constant brushing and snapping sound, like driving through a slightly kinky car wash. Cadillac Bill snapped on his headlights.

"Just thought I'd give 'em something to aim between," he said.

At the end, the road rose slightly. Suddenly they were out of the cane fields in a clearing. Down below, far away, they could see the few lights that betrayed the presence of San Leandro— no more than on a ship at sea—a display of lights that was mocked by the countless stars above.

"Well, no one's here so I guess we can go," Cadillac Bill said, mock hopefully.

"I see some old buildings over there." Griffin pointed toward some rafter beams silhouetted against the night sky, a broken wall below, and overgrown bushes that were left from someone's garden.

"Some old estate, probably. Lot of them that were destroyed during the war never got rebuilt. The owners stayed in Manila and ran things from there. It was more fun being absentee landlords, I guess."

Griffin got out and walked toward the ruin, wondering if this was one of the plumes of smoke that Harry Roberts Harding had

seen, looking down from Mount Arayat after the first Battle of
San Leandro. Juan Olmos had made a joke about it, a rare joke,
coming from him. The peasants, he said, were "burning off the
fields."

Gravel crunched underfoot: he was walking on someone's
driveway, a graceful loop that led to the front steps, fine and
wide. All around him was charred wood and broken masonry
and shrubs, hibiscus and bougainvillea, that closed over the
house the way the sea engulfs a sunken ship.

"George, goddamn it, there's something coming up the
road," Cadillac Bill shouted from behind. "Shit, it's a jeep! I told
you it was the army. Christ, we're in for it now. A tribe, George.
A tribe among tribes . . ."

Griffin watched the headlights light up the cane fields, scat-
tering beams high and low as they took the bumps. The jeep
pulled into the clearing and stopped in front of the Cadillac. It
was full of the same merry company that had manned the road-
block.

"Howdy!" Lieutenant Del Campo shouted. "What are you
doing out here in the dark?"

"We heard there was a square dance."

"You got some pussy in your Cadillac?"

It was getting ridiculous, Griffin thought, a gang of pistoleros
right out of *Treasure of the Sierra Madre.* Eddie Richter was
right. This was where the old movies went to die.

"I guess we'll be going," Cadillac Bill said, opening the car
door with exaggerated nonchalance. "We didn't mean to tres-
pass or anything."

Lieutenant Del Campo's response was direct. He drew out his
pistol and shot out Cadillac Bill's right front tire. The air seeped
out with a hiss and the Cadillac settled onto the ground, violated
and deflated.

"You stay," Del Campo said. "You wait."

"What for?" Griffin asked.

"Your friend. Juan Olmos."

The helicopter came in from the west, searching for the signal
fires that Del Campo had his men build. A searchlight pointed

down as the helicopter hovered overhead. It lit up the old ruin
and Griffin saw things that he'd missed before: a tile-bottomed
fish pond, some broken lawn furniture, a ghostly, overgrown
gazebo, and what must once have been a tennis court. Every
turn of the helicopter lit up another corner of the past. But
when the helicopter landed it wasn't the past that came walking
out. It was the distinctly contemporary figure Griffin had last
seen in Phil Robinson's office at the U.S. embassy: Major Herrera.

"Very good, Mr. Griffin." Herrera stopped to light a cigarette,
one of the clove-scented cigarettes that people smoked in In-
donesia. "I made a bet with someone that you would never get
to San Leandro. I underestimated you."

"Who was the bet with?"

"General Contreras. He's a very poor loser."

"Jesus," Cadillac Bill moaned. "Contreras. We're in the deep-
est possible shit."

"And this is Cadillac Bill. The famous Cadillac Bill. And his
famous Cadillac. 'Viva Las Vegas.' Did you have a chance to look
around? This was quite a place once. It belonged to Harrison
Wingfield."

"He lived here?"

"He lived in lots of places. It's been many years now, but
people remember him. The great American. You must talk
about him with General Contreras."

"Must we?" Cadillac Bill asked.

"Shall we go?"

"Hey, Major," Cadillac Bill protested. "I'm just a taxi driver."

"The helicopter. Please."

"My car!"

"These gallant soldiers will need the keys," Herrera said.
"Well, actually they don't need the keys. They're all accomplished car thieves. But it would be helpful. I'll have one of these
fellows drive it to Angeles City. I'll have *all* of them drive it."

"Christ."

"Gentlemen? Shall we?"

43

DAVAO IMPERIAL RESORT. Set in a nest of birds of paradise, shrewdly illuminated by a spotlight hidden among ferns, the sign recalled Griffin's adventures on the Faraway Places beat. So did the driveway, winding through a tropical garden that was floodlit like a stage set, *Midsummer Night's Dream,* maybe, with pastel beams hitting orchids and ginger blossoms. Just as they slowed to take a speed bump, they were spattered by an errant lawn sprinkler.

"It never fails," Major Herrera sighed. "They put more water on the driveway than on the garden."

"What is this place?"

"Our newest five-star hotel-casino. Not yet open to the public."

Griffin had expected a tent encampment in the mountains or a ramshackle military headquarters near one of the fenced, fortified "strategic hamlets" the Philippine army had been hammering together to win hearts and minds in Mindanao. Mindanao was the Philippines' wild west, Siberia and the Amazon all in one; island of gold, lumber, pineapple, sugar, and bananas, island of stone-age tribes, twentieth-century pirates, Moslem separatists, NPA rebels, lost commands.

They stepped into a lounge, just off a not-yet opened casino, with rows of one-armed bandits still in packing cases. The place was jammed with men in uniforms and hostesses, as though the military had volunteered for a not-so-dry run that would give the new resort a chance to test the act that would lure high rollers from Thailand and Macao. The evening's entertainment was a Las Vegas lounge act, a road company Tony Bennett with an overlay of Latin charmer, Fernando Llamas or Ricardo Montalban. "Thank you, thank you very much. For my next song . . ."

Major Herrera led Griffin and Cadillac Bill to a VIP table in the back of the room, with a good view of both stage and audience.

"Where's your boss?" Griffin asked.

"My boss?" Herrera returned. "Don't you know? That's him onstage."

General Nestor Contreras, boy partisan, U.S.-trained junior officer, leader of the Philippines Vietnam contingent, shadowy master of guerrilla warfare, possible heir apparent to the presidency, was challenging his troops to a version of "Name That Tune."

"Come on, ladies and germs, just give me the name of a woman, any kind of a name. Hey! Any kind of a woman . . ."

"Donna!" someone shouted. Immediately, General Nestor Contreras whispered something to the leader of a trio that looked as if it was minutes from a firing squad and launched right into a version of the old Paul Anka tune. "Maria," and he was Tony from *West Side Story.* "Mary," and he was Jimmy Cagney as George M. Cohan, shuffling and smiling as he lauded the virtues of an old-fashioned, simple girl. "Lucille," and he was Little Richard. On and on. He was Buddy Holly singing "Peggy Sue," Maurice Chevalier singing "Gigi." Filipinos had been around Americans a long time and they were famous, also infamous, for their ability to copy. They were a nation, or a not-quite nation, of talented imitators. That's what Contreras was doing, but he did it with a vengeance. Depending on the song, he was a fifties rock-and-roller, a savvy song-and-dance man, a red-neck minstrel, a well-traveled crooner. He could do it all, his performance declared, do it just as well as the originals, but there was an anger in each of his impersonations, as if he were working his way through all the different kinds of persons Americans could be, the whole national gallery, mastering their manner, learning their music, and moving on. Come on, come on, he exhorted his captive audience. Lola. Sheila. Donna. Lili Marlene. Finally he was done. He headed toward them.

"Who's who?" he asked Herrera.

"This one is Griffin," Herrera answered. "And this is called Cadillac Bill."

Contreras sat down. "The men in the glass suits. Name your name. Mr. Johnny Walker. Mr. Haig and Mr. Haig. Mr. Jack Daniels. Mr. Jim Beam."

Griffin could see how people might find Contreras dashing. He had matinee-idol looks and, though a touch of silver streaked his hair, he was a youthful Kennedyesque figure nonetheless, a fiftyish playboy-general. But there was something else, a certain recklessness, a take-it-to-the-limits manner that made him volatile and unpredictable. He was one of those men who could go either way, a lover or a killer. You could see why people talked about him. And why they worried.

"Out," Contreras said to Major Herrera. "The men, the girls, the band, the waiters. Everybody out."

Contreras sat back and watched the crowd disperse. Two bottles of scotch and a bucket of ice arrived. In a minute they had the place to themselves, an empty stage, tables covered with glasses and bottles, the smell of new carpets and old cigarettes hanging in the air.

"What did he say about me?" Contreras asked.

"Not a word," Griffin answered.

"You're lying," Contreras snapped. "You're scared and you're lying. Reconsider."

"I heard your name on Corregidor, when he arrived. Since then, I've heard your name from other people. Everyone's been asking what he had to say about you."

"I'm not surprised."

"But he never mentioned you, I swear to God."

For a moment, Contreras seemed disappointed, like a poet who found he was too inoffensive to have his book burned or a gangster who found the police weren't even interested in him.

"I know that man. I really know him. I know he'd never forget me. Never . . ."

"I'm sorry."

"He mentioned me on Corregidor. That was like a signal. 'I'm back. I'm coming. I don't care about the cost to either of us, Connie.' "

"Hold it! Did you say Connie?"

"Yes. I wasn't a General then. I was . . . Connie."

"Connie as in 'just improving my English'?"

"That's me!" Contreras whooped.

"Connie, who could never get laid on Mount Arayat?"

"Never! The only place—"

"Quick, Connie, how fast do autumn colors move south?"

"Twenty miles, Mr. Griffin. Twenty miles. You've got me!"
For a moment, it was like a reunion, old buddies, comrades in
arms, Livingstone and Stanley. Then Contreras drained his glass
and winced, as if he'd been reminded of some bad news. "Now
what am I going to do with you?"

"Why do anything?" Cadillac Bill asked. "We're just fine on
our own, thanks."

"It's this way," Contreras said. "Major Herrera represents me
in Manila. As you know, I rarely go there. I build my base here,
in the army, in the mountains. I let Manila be Manila. Herrera
is my ambassador to that place. He looks after my interests.
When my name comes up in a speech on Corregidor, I hear
about it from him. When a certain journalist starts investigating
my past, I hear about it, too. When I learn that a book associated
with a certain movie can be counted upon to embarrass me and
that my enemies are pressing for its completion, I hear about it
from him. He advises me to avoid Harry Roberts Harding. I do
so. It hurts, but I do so. He advises me that Clifford Lerner's visit
to the Philippines should be ended. I agree. And he also advises
me that if a certain book writer gets within five miles of a town
named San Leandro, I should act. *Act?* Why be obscure? I
should have you killed."

"Why?"

"Because you would find what Colonel Harding wanted you
to find. What killed him, I think. Knowledge that kills."

"Now, whoa, whoa, slow down, hold up," Cadillac Bill protested, motioning with his hands as though he was reining in a
team of runaway horses. "This conversation is getting way out
of hand. Now, General, just give a listen. I'm not as dumb as I
look. That's good news. But I got better. George Griffin here
ain't quite as bright as he looks. The fact is, General, what he
knows couldn't blow the lid off a dixie cup. He got some war
stories is all, old harmless shit. Harding was spinning his yarn
real slow and he croaked before he got to whatever the hell
happened at San Leandro. Get it? *Before.*"

"If that is so—"

"It is so, it is, it is! We don't know diddly, General, and that's all right with me! We can walk out of here this minute and no harm done."

"Interesting," Contreras mused. "True?"

"Yes," Griffin acknowledged. "Colonel Harding had gotten past what he called the first Battle of San Leandro. The first. But there was a second battle. Something awful that happened in that place. It terrified him."

"Ah. And if I let you leave, right now, I suppose you would be prepared to promise me that you would never go back to San Leandro? Never seek Juan Olmos? Never wonder about Yamashita's treasure?"

"Sure thing," Cadillac Bill responded. "Me you put in a car, Griffin you put on a plane, and you got a deal."

"No," Griffin said. "No promise."

"What, are you crazy!" Cadillac Bill shouted. "You got a death wish? You want to fly home freight?"

"No promise."

Contreras smiled at him. "I like that. If you had promised I'd have known you were lying. And that would make me angry."

"I want to know how it ended," Griffin said.

"You want to hear it, then?" Contreras asked. "Even though—"

"Yes," Griffin answered. "I want to hear it. I made a promise to a man."

"Not me!" Cadillac Bill cried. He put his hands over his ears, like a pair of earmuffs. He looked like a hear-no-evil monkey. "I don't hear nothin' now. My ears are tighter than a crab's ass, which is watertight."

"Shut up, Cadillac," Griffin said.

"Say what? I can't hear you."

"I want to hear it," Griffin repeated. "And you know something else, Connie? I think you want to tell it."

"I do," Contreras nodded. He poured himself a tumbler full of scotch and glanced around the nightclub. A single spotlight hit the stage, a single candle burned at their table. It felt like a confessional. "I do indeed."

* * *

"I was young. I was ambitious. I was smart. Not as smart as I thought I was. Not as smart as I was going to be. But smart. I was good-looking. I was charming. Does it sound like boasting? Actually, I'm apologizing. You'll see."

He drained another scotch, opened the second bottle, refilled his glass. Abruptly, he stood up, drink in hand, and started pacing. He looked as though he'd been called upon to deliver a toast. Master of ceremonies in a room full of ghosts.

"It was hard knowing Colonel Harding was here, searching for me. He would have found his way to me, eventually. Sure as shooting."

He laughed at the phrase and repeated it, savoring the sound. He cast a malicious glance at Cadillac Bill, made a gun out of his fist and his finger, pointed it and pulled the trigger.

"Sure as shooting." Then the joke passed and his mood recaptured him. "Yes, he'd find me. And when he found me—that was going to be hard. A problem. An embarrassment. Or worse. I dreaded that reunion. And I wanted it with all my heart. I was waiting for him to come. He kept me waiting . . ."

"Because he was telling the story his way," Griffin suggested. "In order."

"That was part of it," Connie agreed. "But only part. He wanted *me* to come to *him*. He wanted the past to touch him. He invited it. He'd come so far already. Now he wanted me to come a little way myself. And I couldn't do that. So I sit here thinking about him. Picturing. Remembering. About when we were young and owned the world."

"Go ahead," Griffin urged him softly.

"In May of 1944, three weeks after what you call the first Battle of San Leandro, I accompanied my . . . friend to Baguio. For a reunion. We arrived in the morning. My friend was nervous. He saw the old man Wingfield right away, cutting branches in his rose garden, a cane in one hand and a pair of clippers in the other, and a couple of Filipino boys weeding and turning soil. A perfect colonial scene, no? Not just a return. A restoration. He looked across the grass at us, squinting, not seeing, his face all wrinkled. 'Who is it?' he called out, as though a loud voice could make up for his poor eyes. 'It's me, Uncle Harrison,' my friend called out. 'You? Harry?' 'Me,' my friend repeated, and he ran to the old man and held him in his arms, and held him. 'Welcome home,' Harding said. And the old man answered, 'Welcome home to you, my boy.' After a moment, Harding remembered I was there. I stepped forward smartly to be introduced. Did I say introduced? To be *presented*. Harding made much of me. It mattered to him that Uncle Harrison accept me. And he did. That he did. 'Any friend of Harry's is a friend of mine.' Hah! How are you doing, Cadillac Bill?"

Cadillac Bill had dropped his hands from his ears. He listened disconsolately, every syllable a death sentence.

"No treasure. No killing. Not much of a story so far. Not the sort of story you want to get your ass shot off for, is it, buckaroo?"

"No story's worth that," Cadillac Bill replied, sending a look George Griffin's way. "No story."

"It gets better, cowboy," Contreras said. "All right. Harrison Wingfield. A big, broken, slow-moving, sad kind of man. You know who reminds me of him? That English actor who came to Imelda's festival. The Englishman with the Russian name."

"Ustinov? Peter Ustinov?"

"Yes. Older, sicker, but the same kind of man. Fat. Delicate. Angry. Cunning. Lonely. Wingfield looked around his garden. 'They tore everything out,' he said. 'They dug latrines. They parked trucks. But I'll have it back the way it was. You should see the house. They burned books in the fireplace. They shat on the carpets and carved their initials on the wall. But they're gone now. And I'm back.' He had returned just one week before, and he was camping out on a cot in the kitchen. The rest of the house was as the Japanese had left it although, frankly, it seemed to me that some of the damage might have come from local people.

"He led us out to the front porch, once grand, but the front steps had vanished and some floorboards were torn up and the pickets on the railing around the porch were loose, like knocked-in teeth. Still, he made a point of going out on the porch and sitting on a chair. Then he looked at Harding. 'See,' he said. 'I told them I'd be back. You heard me.' And Harding answered, 'Yes, sir, I remember.' "

Contreras sat, poured, drank, smoked a cigarette, resting on a chair like a boxer between rounds. Then he resumed.

"For two days, we helped patch and carpenter and repair. It was easy for me to see that the old man thought of Harding as his prince. I also could see that this made Harding uncomfortable. I think I enjoyed myself with the old man more than Harding did. He fascinated me. His brains. His power. And something else. His passion. His feeling for everything he owned, everything—it seemed to me—that he wanted to pass on to Harding. Harding was the young prince, I was the prince's friend. He accepted that and he cultivated me: I was a bright, game boy, and he liked bright, game boys. The old man knew what Harding had been up to. He knew about our adventures. And because he was a smart man, he found the—what?—the fly in the ointment, the cloud on the horizon, the . . . Wake up Cadillac Bill! . . . The pubic hair between his teeth."

"Huh?"

"Getting warm now," Contreras promised. "The old man pressed me about the Olmos brothers and the Huks. How many times had Harding visited them? A half dozen I said. Is it true that he'd obtained weapons for them, USAFFE weapons landed on the coast and diverted from their rightful owners? Yes. Accompanied the Huks on missions? Yes. Actually participated in combat? Combat against the Philippine Constabulary as well as the Japanese? Yes. And had he been the witness to the destruction of public records? Yes. And the burning of public property, ranches, haciendas, and such? Yes, again. He knew everything, it seemed. Well, almost everything. He didn't know about Harding's woman, but apart from that—"

"His *what*?" Griffin exclaimed. There was no concealing his surprise.

"Shit!" Cadillac Bill exploded. "What'd I tell you, General? This man's no threat to anybody. You could tell him somebody stole a rope, he wouldn't spot the cow at the end of it!"

"I was the one who couldn't get laid on Mount Arayat. My friend fared better. Don't be upset that he didn't tell you. I know why."

He drained the middle third out of the second bottle of scotch. This time, instead of gulping the drink, he studied it, shook it, so that the ice cubes clinked together.

"Isn't it strange?" Contreras asked. "Harding died just yesterday. His woman has been dead for thirty-five years. Think about it! That's half a lifetime. And yet, they were a couple once."

"Tell me about her," Griffin said. It felt as though he was prying.

"Not so fast," Contreras said. "I have a question. Did Harding ever mention any other woman?"

"No."

"In his later life?"

"None he mentioned."

"I keep telling you," Cadillac Bill interrupted. "George ain't fought his way out of the jungles yet. The way he goes at a story, it's like watching somebody trying to drain Lake Erie with an eyedropper."

"Shut up," Griffin said, turning back to Contreras. "There was no one he mentioned."

"That was Harding. One woman. And then a lifetime of regret."

"Who was she?"

"Her name was Loretta and she worked with Felipe Olmos. Teaching, propagandizing and—what I remember—struggling with some hopeless mimeograph machine that Harding helped her repair."

"Do you remember what she looked like?"

"George! You old fox! Aren't you something, once you get the scent. The colonel shoots his gun off thirty-five years ago and, wow, you're off like a shot."

"She looked like a million other Filipinas," Contreras said. "Dark skin, brown eyes, long hair." The way he talked, it was as though he was filling out a form, not remembering a person.

"That's all?" Griffin asked. "Nothing else?"

"There was," Contreras said. "I hardly ever saw it. She dismissed me at a glance. She saw an opportunist. Which I was. But she had a smile that was . . ."

Contreras paused, groping, seeing that smile, struggling to describe it. He shrugged and gave up, but it was all right. Griffin knew the smile, just as Harding had. The smile from the Baguio postcard, the wise and waiting smile. For once in his life, he'd caught up with it, for a while. Then the distance had opened up again, and it stretched out forever.

"And you told Harrison Wingfield about her," Griffin said.

"Is that a question?"

"It's a statement."

"A statement? You live dangerously, Mr. Griffin."

"And you were improving your English."

"All the time, my friend, all the time. Yes, I told him. I wanted to impress him. He was a powerful man. I wanted him to mark me as a comer. I wanted to tell him something he didn't know."

"And he blew up?"

"He was smarter than that. He gave us a good supper and he sent us on our way back to Kiangen. And it was there, three months later, Harrison Wingfield made his move. In the last day of the war. The last day of that war, anyway. . . . Excuse me."

He walked away. From a room where the door was marked CABALLEROS, they heard the sound of vomiting and flushing water.

"Talk about spilling your guts," Cadillac Bill said. "We're in for it now. You think you got a great story, Mr. Griffin. I think you do. I think you got the greatest story never told. And you, sure as shit, won't never tell it."

"He didn't mention a woman," Griffin reflected. "Not out here. Maybe there was someone in the States, after the war."

"Griffin! The more you know, the worse off you are, ain't you figured that out yet? 'Ye shall know the truth and the truth will make you dead.' Lincoln."

"I wonder what became of her . . ."

"Hey, I don't wonder a bit. Screw her, I say. I say screw him. He's dead."

"*Screw him? He's dead?*" Contreras had overheard. "We can do better than that, Cadillac Bill. Screw the living. Then make them dead. Your slogan, no? 'Make love and war.' "

"How did you know that?"

"Your fame precedes you. Subic Bay will mourn you. Angeles City will be inconsolable."

"Sure they will. I can see it now. A moment of silence before they start the fish fights."

"Why so glum, chum?" Contreras baited him. "We're getting to the good part."

* * *

" *'Where were you when the war ended?'* The old question. For me, for Harding, for Juan Olmos, for some others, the answer is: we were fighting for our lives. We were scratching a hundred yards a day on mountain trails, crawling through rockfalls and mud slides. What we thought about was whether we would be the last to die, the war's last victim. Others were conspiring. Making lists, they were, and checking them twice.

"It was Harding's idea that Juan Olmos and a handful of the other Huks go with us to Kiangen. It was the same sort of impulse that had led him to take me to meet Uncle Harrison in Baguio. He wanted them to be represented among all the other units, the army, the USAFFE groups, the brass, the glory hounds and trophy hunters who gathered for the kill. Ah, but the killing went very slowly. Cut off from sea and air support, without hope of relief, Yamashita and his men fought on and on. A whole empire reduced to a rainy mountain kingdom, ten miles by thirty. We went out in the mornings to test the bars of the cage that held them in, that held us out, and the animal inside— thinner and wilder each day—flung himself against the cage. And we returned to our camp, wondering how long it would go on, until one night they told us that the war was over. Harrison Wingfield told us. Uncle Harrison was waiting for us on the last day of the war."

Contreras was up out of his chair, making his way back to the stage where he'd performed a few hours ago. This was the late show, the after-hours special, invitation only.

"You've done great things, son. And you've made some foolish mistakes. Alliances and attachments that won't hold up. I understand. After all there was a war on."

Contreras was a brilliant mimic, taking the low, stentorian schoolroom voice, which Griffin knew was exactly how Harrison Wingfield must have sounded. He even looked a little like him, his hands hooked into his belt, his stomach puffed out. "But the war's over now. This is a new phase. You have a new role to play. Rebuilding, reorganizing, reconstructing. This has to do with law and order, with respect for property, with the restoration of government to its proper function."

Now Contreras walked to the other side of the stage, almost into the shadows. Now he was lanky and awkward as Harding must have been. When he spoke his voice was halting, reverent, and stubborn.

"What was the war about, Uncle Harrison? Putting rich people back in touch with their fortunes? Putting the cop back on the beat? Business as usual?"

And Harrison Wingfield again, raising his hand; he'd heard it all before.

"Business as usual, son. That's exactly right."

"Hearing you talk, it sounds like I fought a war without knowing what it was about."

"Happens all the time. Happens to millions. It's simple. Wars are fought to save the world. Not to change it. That's a revolution. And believe me, son, there won't be any revolution here. It's been tried before. It's not in the cards."

"Elections every couple years. Carnival elections with 98 percent of the people pretending to choose which people from the other two percent get a chance to screw them for the next four years?"

"A silly exercise. I admit it. But they've gotten attached to it. It's a changing of the guard, that's all."

"I can't accept that. I made promises."

"You made promises no one can keep. Extravagant, foolish promises. Your friends are poison. You think they were fighting against the Japanese?"

"I know they were. I was there. They were fighting when no one else was."

"They were fighting for themselves, fighting against authority and property and law. They'll keep fighting. And I'm warning you: they won't win. I'm warning you. As one American to another."

Harding shrugged.

"As friend to friend."

Another shrug, love mingling with conviction, Harding's resolve bending but not breaking.

And old Wingfield. "I'm warning you . . . as a father to a son."

Contreras stood onstage, walked slowly to Harding's side. Then, in a lost, lonely, little boy voice.

"No."

"Yes!"

* * *

"I'm tired," Contreras said. He stepped past the table and parted some heavy drapes that covered the window. Outside, black had turned to gray. "Another morning."

"Was he really Harding's father?" Griffin asked.

"Who knows?" Contreras answered, yawning. "Or cares? He said he was. I think he felt he was. Perhaps he'd screwed the woman. Perhaps he was a desperate old man staking a claim. He was always staking claims."

"Jesus," Griffin sighed. "Poor Harding."

"Hold it," Cadillac Bill said. "That's it? That's the story?"

"Not hardly, Cadillac Bill. I'm just warming up the audience. Now is star time." Outside, he ordered them into the back of a truck that Major Herrera was set to drive. "Promises, promises," Contreras sighed. "Colonel Harding made promises. Harrison Wingfield kept promises. And I perfected my English."

The last they saw of him, he was walking across the resort lawn, over a little bow bridge across a carp pond, toward a cottage on the edge of a new golf course. He was whistling. They heard the whistling, after the blindfolds slipped over their heads.

They were at the end of a road that had twisted twenty miles, crossing streams, cutting around mountains the way a knife cuts into a perfectly peeled apple, so that the skin comes off in one, long, spiraling strip. They hadn't seen the journey. They felt it, the way a condemned man feels every step that leads him to his execution. They felt the bumps and turns and splashes, they heard the slurp of mud, tasted clouds of dust, detected muted voices as they went past roadblocks, winced at the slap of branches against the jeep. And at the end, they smelled wood from campfires. They were led out of the truck. It drove away. Around them, men were talking. A firing squad forming up? Movements, whispers. They felt the sun; they were sweating. They were faint. Then there were hands on their shoulders, pushing them to the ground, to their knees, position for prayer or confession or beheading. At last, they felt a pistol against their temples, cool and metallic. They were that close. Then the blindfolds were yanked away.

Squinting into sunlight, brushing away sweat, they saw a dozen men in semimilitary uniforms, khaki pants, boots, odd uniform parts, guerrilla garb. T-shirts and motorcycle jackets, black with pink lettering. An army or a softball team? The lettering said: FUN BUNCH. Cadillac Bill gasped. "I think you found your ending, George." Some were young, like the NPA. Others were Negrito-looking tribesmen, aborigines. Others were old, grizzled warriors, two- or three-time losers. One had a Mohican haircut. Another had a mouth of gold teeth. A third had painted his nails red. FUN BUNCH. And then a man came out of the woods, a tall, gaunt Filipino who walked directly toward them. He towered over them, appraising, and Griffin recognized the anger in his eyes, the anger that Harding had said was his fuel, his fire, his guiding light.

"My name is Juan Olmos," the man said.

Part Ten

★ ★ ★
★ ★

HOW THE WAR ENDED

44

Action!

Tall and handsome, surrounded by men who loved him, MacArthur's Ghost, Colonel Harry Roberts Harding, scanned Corregidor's burned-off jungle and bombed-out buildings, the barracks, the post movie theater, the commandant's residence. They had asked—no, they insisted—that he say a few words. So, while generals and politicians, guerrillas and soldiers, stood silent, and the only noise was the low whirring of newsreel cameras, the gaunt, awkward missionary boy who united and redeemed a conquered nation stepped forward with a Bible in his hands. Looking around, he could see old comrades like Charley Camper, who had been with him since the beginning, and true friends like Nestor Contreras, whom he'd met along the way, doughty fighters like Juan Olmos, sage counselors like Harrison Wingfield, living symbol of America's return. And yes, somewhere in the ranks was the woman Harding had loved in the mountains, the passionate guerrillera. He saw them all. They were all together because he—the man who kept his promises—had brought them together. Other men had already spoken of history and patriotism, loyalty and sacrifice, the hallowed friendship between democratic nations, America and the Philippines. It was left to Harry Roberts Harding to find a simpler text.

"To everything there is a season," he intoned, "and a time to every purpose under the heaven.

"A time to be born and a time to die; a time to plant and a time to pluck up that which is planted.

"A time to kill and a time to heal; a time to break down and . . ."

*   *   *

It was clever of Palm Tree Productions to schedule its last day
of filming on Corregidor. This was not the Corregidor that was
starved and hammered to death in 1942; this was the Corregidor of 1944, recaptured in a brilliant airborne strike that seized
the island in days. That was as it should have been. And there
was MacArthur's Ghost, as he should have been: the young hero
in the hour of his glory.

"Hey, George!" And here was Eddie Richter, smoking a cigar,
wearing a blazing aloha shirt, his fingers tweaking Griffin's ear-
lobe. "So how's the budding author?"

"Blooming," Griffin replied. "Are they ready?"

"Ready as they'll ever be, kid. Beaumont and Wingfield and
Miss Fire and Ice. Also, that embassy woman. It's a regular fan
club."

"I want you there too."

"Hey, I don't count. I'm a throw-in."

"You're more than that, Eddie, a lot more," Griffin said. "And
you know it."

"Do I now?"

"Yes."

"And this is what this high-level conference is all about?"

"Yes."

"Well then. What are we waiting for?"

45

"Hello, everybody," Griffin began. "You hired me to accompany Colonel Harding on his return to the Philippines. And that's what I did. I left him once when I shouldn't have. And he left me. I'm sorry about that."

Beaumont nodded and ran a hand over a beefy forearm that was sunburned. Wingfield glanced over a clipboard full of invoices and plane tickets: both men were ready to leave. Whatever emotions had brought them here were gone. Cecilia Santos was staying, though for how much longer it was hard to say. Her departure was a certainty. So was the departure of Susan Hayes, outward and upward bound. An ambitious bunch.

"And then there was the book. The book was a by-product. But it mattered to me. And after a while, I saw that it mattered to Colonel Harding too. He got me to do it his way, starting at the beginning, everything in order. He made me promise I'd finish it, a solemn oath. At the time I thought he was hamming it up. The speeches, the hints, the disappearance—it all smacked of self-dramatization. But he died. Maybe he was hamming it up then, too. Anyway, I've got this book under way. I thought you might be interested in how it ended, the last chapter, which is more or less the speech he never gave. It's up to you. You can hear it now or you can wait for the book."

"I'd rather hear it than read it," Wingfield said, glancing at Beaumont.

"Sure," Beaumont agreed. He stepped to the edge of the tent, opened the flap. They were wading through Ecclesiastes again, stopping at the same verse, like a needle stuck in a groove. Or —Griffin thought—history refusing to move on.

". . . a time to get and a time to lose," MacArthur's Ghost announced. "A time to keep silence and a time to speak."

* * *

First he gave them a cast of characters, Hollywood style. Their star was Harry Roberts Harding. They knew him, or they thought they did; at least they'd seen him, toward the end, so all that Griffin did was give them a sense of the younger Harding, the gawky, idealistic, lonely kid who built his reputation on keeping promises, reconciling opposites, holding things together. He hoped that the people he trusted and who trusted him would therefore trust each other. That was what it came to: a recipe for martyrdom, when you thought about it. Still, there were people who trusted him and no one else. Juan Olmos was one of them. Scourge of landlords, cops, soldiers, tax assessors, missionaries, foreigners, you name it. Yet he trusted Harry Roberts Harding enough to accompany him to Kiangen. You can spot Juan Olmos in some of the pictures they took the day Yamashita surrendered. Oh, there were lots of people crowding in front of the camera—it was a historic occasion—and Olmos moved, or got moved to the edge of things, shunted toward the margins, a tall, dark man with the angry stare of an Apache scout. He had reason to be angry, for it had already begun, the drift from patriotic resistance fighter to left-wing guerrilla to mountain bandit to ghost and bogeyman and legend. While other guerrilla groups were recognized and rewarded, the Huks were disarmed and discredited, hunted down; America had made the inconvenient discovery that many of the staunchest anti-Japanese guerrillas hadn't fought the war to protect private property and foreign investments. So the hunt was on. And Harrison Wingfield, third in the cast of characters, was the master of the hunt.

"My uncle," Larry Wingfield volunteered. He didn't want Griffin to think he'd been thrown off-balance.

"A fabulous character," Griffin said. "Did you ever meet him?"

"How could I?" Wingfield fired back. He died . . . when? In 1950, I think. I was four."

"He died April 29, 1949," Griffin said. "I'll be getting to that."

"So?"

"A fabulous character. I guess I said that. Remember how, in the histories of the Old West, they describe the advance of civilization? First the explorer, then the missionary, the fur trapper, the prospector, rancher, farmer, and so forth? Well, Harrison Wingfield was all of them. And more. Because when he found that Harding had developed a dangerous connection to the soon-to-be-outlawed Hukbalahap guerrillas, when he came to Kiangen and saw that this included a friendship with his personal enemy, Juan Olmos, and when Harding's companion, an ambitious Filipino kid named Nestor Contreras, tipped him that Harding was in love with a Huk guerrilla . . ."

Griffin paused for breath, and saw Beaumont glancing over at Wingfield, who shrugged as if to say, We've put up with extras who smile in the middle of battle scenes. We put up with bribes, commissions, water shortages, power outages, hookers, starlets, and paternity suits. We put up with Mrs. Marcos. We'll handle this.

"In love with a Huk guerrilla," Griffin repeated. "That made him a traitor to nationality. To class. And to family. Because Wingfield—Uncle Harrison—was more than Uncle. In Harding's case he was, or said he was, father."

Wingfield looked up in alarm, ready to let fly, but Beaumont intervened in the nick of time. He put a hand on Wingfield's arm as if to say, I'll handle this.

"Well," Beaumont said, "I guess we were making a home movie and we didn't know it. Uncles and cousins all over the place. That's damn interesting. But it doesn't change anything, Griffin, does it?"

"Maybe not," Griffin said. "But I wasn't finished. This was just the cast of characters. Harry Roberts Harding. Juan Olmos. Harrison Wingfield. Those are the leads. Now you've got the featured players. A bookish, talky intellectual named Felipe Olmos. An ambitious kid named Nestor Contreras. Featured players. Now a bit player. A cameo, short but pungent, by a fellow named Eddie Richter. Couldn't have made it without him."

He patted his pocket, pulled out a manuscript that was the length of a long letter, written in longhand on Cadillac Bill's "Make Love and War" stationery. "Here's your ending . . ."

46

"Are the reporters coming?" Harry Roberts Harding asked Nestor Contreras. It was August 17, 1945, and the two men were in a jeep headed down a mountain road to San Leandro, a town of no particular importance in the province of Nueva Ecija.

"They said they were coming," Connie replied.

"You were supposed to confirm. You have to stay on those guys. I promised I'd bring reporters."

"Yes," Connie answered. "I confirmed."

"Maybe we should wait for them," Harding said, glancing back up the road to Kiangen. "Why don't we stop and wait?"

"They said they were coming," Connie assured him. "I wouldn't worry. Some of them left before we did."

"You saw? How many?"

"Three jeeps full. They are probably waiting for us now in San Leandro."

"All right!" Harding exulted. "I was worried. You know what did it? What hooked them? The treasure! Yamashita's treasure!"

"Would you mind telling me?" Connie asked. "I've heard talk about it."

"Not at all."

As they drove, Harding told Contreras how he felt about Juan Olmos and the Huks from Mount Arayat. Sure, they were scary, a harsh, disciplined bunch who didn't care what side of the law they walked on. Olmos wanted to stay in the mountains forever: Japanese or Americans, cops or landlords, foreign soldiers or domestic, it made no more difference to him than a change of season to a hunter, from duck to deer to rabbit. But Harding had decided it was time they came out of the mountains. He told Juan Olmos there had to be an end to fighting, time to lay down weapons—swords into plowshares—and place his hopes in a peaceful future. It was a future Harding promised to share; their fate would be his. He would be with them when they put down their guns—and he would see to it that it was an honorable ceremony, with medals, speeches, photographers, and press. They'd have the same pensions and benefits the more respectable (and lethargic) USAFFE units were claiming. He set it up: he was MacArthur's Ghost. But Juan Olmos wanted more. He wanted some insurance. That was when Harding thought of Yamashita's treasure. It was the sort of rumor that comes out of every war: czarist jewels, Napoleonic bullion. Harding's inspiration was to take these wildfire reports and add something else. Blackmail. He concocted a rumor that, during those otherwise dreary, stalemated weeks around Kiangen, Olmos and his men had come into possession of another treasure: a list of names, from Yamashita himself, of all the Filipinos who had collaborated with the Japanese, all the well-heeled, high-rolling, self-protecting, self-perpetuating elite who were now insinuating themselves back into power. That would be Olmos's insurance in time to come. Did it exist? Connie asked. Or was it as wishful as all the other treasures? Harding wouldn't say. "They know who they are. And if they touch us . . . we'll touch them. It's already working. You see how the reporters reacted."

But there were no reporters that morning in San Leandro. There were three U.S. Army trucks in the square and a half dozen American soldiers, under the command of a Lieutenant Carpenter. There were also about a dozen Filipino soldiers attached to the USAFFE forces. Otherwise the place was empty.

"Are you this Harry Roberts Harding?" Lieutenant Carpenter asked. "Where's your guerrillas? We're feeling stood up."

"They'll be here," Harding answered. "Where are the reporters? The photographers?"

"I don't know," Carpenter said.

"You said they left ahead of us," Harding said to Connie.

"Maybe they broke down."

"Then we'd have passed them on the road."

"Maybe they got lost."

"Maybe?"

"Maybe, maybe, maybe," Carpenter parroted. "I hear lots of

maybes. Are they coming or do we have to go out and get them? It's all the same to me."

"You go out looking for them," Harding retorted, "and it won't be all the same, I promise you. Wait. And if you get tired of waiting you can pass the time by praying. Pray that they come in to you."

Then, an hour or so later, a doughty, cocky little guy came strolling into town, a camera round his neck, a beard and mustache on his face, and the air of an outlaw scout who might be casing a ripe bank.

"Who are you?" Carpenter challenged.

"Eddie Richter, Jr. Airman."

"He's with the Huks," Harding explained.

"You forget how to salute, Richter?"

"Yes," Eddie Richter answered calmly. "Where's your party, Harding? Where's the welcome committee?"

"We're ready."

"What about the guys from the papers? The photographers and all? They couldn't make it?"

"Are your guys coming or not?" Carpenter asked.

"If I say so, they come," Richter snapped. "And if I don't say so, they don't come." He took in the square and didn't like what was there, or what was missing. "I haven't made up my mind yet."

"Tell them to come," Harding said. "It's all right. Tell them I said so."

"I don't know."

"It's all right," Harding repeated. "I'll be here. No harm will come to them. I promise."

"You sure? This town doesn't look so hot today." He nodded at Carpenter. "And I don't like the looks of him."

"It's all right," Harding said. "Bring them in. Tell them that I'm here."

"This little shitty pitchfork gang takes longer than Yamashita's army to come in," Carpenter complained, after another hour of waiting. Just then they saw the first of the guerrillas. They must have come in along the river and then, clambering up the banks, assembled on the far side of the trestle bridge, four lines of twenty-five men (and women) each. The regulars crossed over first, as if to demonstrate that this was a people's army. The leaders followed behind, Juan Olmos and some of the others, the man known as the Pirate, and the Birdwatcher, and the Hangman, and the woman known as Loretta, hair tucked under a cap. They marched past the schoolyard, past the shops, and stopped directly in front of the cathedral, where Harding and others stood next to the three canvas-topped trucks. They glanced toward the bullet-pocked municipal building they'd savaged a few months before. They surveyed the Japanese barracks, a wrecked shell that the locals had raided for wood and tin. They checked the Chinese shop, which was closed. They peered down the muddy lanes that led off the square, into the fields, and they were empty. They studied the schoolhouse and the yard in front, both deserted, and they squinted down the road to Manila, no traffic in sight.

"The sooner this is over with, the better," Carpenter remarked.

"You're right," Harding conceded. "Where's Eddie Richter?"

"Here," Eddie replied, stepping out of the ranks.

"I want you to photograph this," Harding said. "Lots of photographs."

A moment of comedy: Eddie Richter, reconnaissance cameraman, now yearbook photographer, jamming the ranks together, composing orderly rows, one sitting on the ground, one kneeling, one standing in back. "Remember, everybody. If you see the camera, the camera sees you." They saw the camera. But he couldn't get them to smile. Not even Harding smiled. When Richter nodded and backed away, Harding stepped in front.

"This is hard for all of us," he began. "After today, the war is over. I am not MacArthur's Ghost after today. And you will not be guerrillas. All of that will be in the past. But we won't forget the past. We'll remember. And we'll build on it. I want you to know that I'll never forget you. No one fought better. Or longer, Or harder. No one.

"You saved my life. Now I return the favor. I stand with you as you give up your guns and begin a new life. I'll stand with you today. I'll be with you tomorrow, wherever you are. Always. I'll accompany you to government offices, to courtrooms. I'll stand outside election booths. I'll speak. I'll write letters. I'll contribute. Anything to see that the victory you earned will never be denied . . . or forgotten."

Contreras remembered it was just then that Carpenter looked at one of the other Americans and mimed the sawing motion of a violinist and whispered sarcastically, "Could we put this to music?" And it was also then that he saw something else, something he would not have seen if he hadn't known to look for it: a cloud of dust from way down the Manila road, as from a truck, or a whole convoy of trucks, headed toward San Leandro.

"Now I want you to follow me," Harding said, strolling over to where the trucks were parked. "And, one by one, stack your weapons in front and permit me to shake your hands and give you my thanks and my blessing . . ."

"Blessing!" Carpenter whispered. "I don't believe this man. What's he do? Walk on water? He a miracle man?"

"No," Connie answered. "No miracles." At any moment, he expected the Huks to run for it, to fire their weapons and race out of the square, back toward the rice fields and the mountains. The whole thing was so fragile, bound together by the frailest of bonds, ties of trust and friendship and belief, and yet there was a miracle. One last miracle. One by one, the Huks came forward, unstrapped their revolvers and pistols, sidearms captured from the Japanese, and stacked their rifles—a collection of Nambus, Arisakas, Springfields, Enfields, Mausers—which were a residue of all the armies they had ever fought. They dropped them off and shook Harding's hands. Juan Olmos was the last.

Then it happened. Sleepy, empty San Leandro came to life. Some trucks and jeeps came down the Manila road and piled into the square. On the other end of the town, an armored car sat on the trestle bridge. There were Filipino police and soldiers jogging down the alleys, popping out of the church, the schoolhouse, and the battered old municipio.

"What is this?" Harding asked Lieutenant Carpenter. He didn't answer. He turned to Connie. "What's going on?" Connie didn't answer either. He was looking at the municipio, at the front steps, where Harrison Wingfield was standing next to a white-suited, middle-aged Filipino whom Contreras later learned was Sylvester Olivares, San Leandro's chief of police.

"What is this?" Harding cried out again. But Wingfield didn't answer until the trap had fully sprung, until there were cops and soldiers all around the square, rifles and machine guns pointed inward. Then Wingfield nodded at Lieutenant Carpenter. Carpenter and half a dozen others went into the truck and brought out shovels, dozens of shovels, which they dropped in front of the Huks. For a moment, it looked like the surrender ceremony had been embellished with a symbolic trade of guns for shovels, swords into plowshares. Then the troops closed in, gesturing and shouting, forcing the Huks to pick up the shovels, then herding them toward the schoolyard just off the square. Harding rushed toward Harrison Wingfield, screaming. He was tackled and handcuffed before he reached the steps. "What is this?"

"This is about murder and theft and arson," Uncle Harrison said. "This is about terror, banditry, and insurrection. This is about . . . keeping promises."

Harrison Wingfield's moment. Give credit where credit is due. He paused and looked past the guerrillas, who were prodded and taunted as they were led away. He looked past the town, over the fields, toward the mountains, and he quoted a poem Harding had first heard on the eve of the war.

". . . for the angel of death spread his wings on the blast/And breathed in the face of the foe as he passed . . ."

Harding turned and faced Connie, whose hands were free. "You knew?"

"He said *arrest*," Connie answered sheepishly.

"Arrest?" asked Uncle Harrison Wingfield. "Arrest means *stop*. I'm stopping them, all right. I'm putting them in the ground."

Thus, the second Battle of San Leandro. Swords into plowshares, war into peace. In the midday sun, surrounded by police and soldiers, affable Filipinos, American boys, the Huks cut through the sod, their brand-new shovels glinting in the light.

When they were done they stood around, waiting for something —a sentence, a curse, perhaps a prayer. But sentence had long since been pronounced. The first fusillade of shots was light, casual, almost affectionate, like spray from a garden sprinkler, like water on dust, like a handful of rice tossed at a new bride. Though some fell dead, many many more were only wounded, grazed, winged, lamed, bleeding, screaming.

And now, just as Harding's surrender had been turned into something else by Uncle Harrison, now Uncle Harrison saw his own ritual transformed by police chief Olivares. A believer in the personal touch, he joined his men on the playground picking up shovels and using them against the wounded, swords into plowshares and plowshares into what it had all always been about: clubs. They walked across the playground from side to side, across and back, practicing reverse triage, attacking the most lightly wounded first, then dispatching the mortally wounded, and lastly mutilating the safely dead. And that was the second Battle of San Leandro, Harry Roberts Harding's last battle, which he didn't fight at all, and fought a thousand times, and died fighting, the battle that summed up all the battles before it and promised more battles to come, the battle that ended everything and nothing, that changed things forever and guaranteed that nothing would change at all.

47

"... a time to get, and a time to lose; a time to keep silence and a time to speak; a time to love, and a time to hate; a time of war, and a time of peace ..."

"That's it!" someone shouted. "A print. And a wrap!" Cast and crew cheered. The movie was in the can. Griffin looked around the tent. He hadn't expected applause when he finished reading; it wasn't that kind of text. And he wasn't expecting Larry Wingfield to shake his hand or Cecilia Santos to melt into his arms. Silence was the most he could have asked for. And silence they gave him.

"So what about Yamashita's treasure?" Hugh Beaumont asked eventually.

"That was Harding's attempt to buy some insurance for Olmos and his men. A list of collaborators. It wasn't such a clever idea. If anything, it backfired. It made them that much more dangerous. It condemned them. Then again, they were already condemned."

"No gold, no silver, no jewels, no gems, no art? No secret weapons? No drugs?"

"Not in this story."

"We went with a gold Buddha from Burma," Beaumont offered, as though they were comparing notes. "They have it, they lose it, they get it back, they lose it for good in a swamp, in a patch of quicksand. One of the bad guys rides the statue down into the mud, a Jap officer. They sink together, the gold statue and the man. Glug, glug, glug, slurp, slurp, slurp. Terrific. Better than your story."

"Yes."

"Yours is so goddamned sad."

"So goddamned true. There's more . . ."

"No thanks," Larry Wingfield said. "I've heard enough of this."

"You sure? Want to know how your uncle died? April 29, 1949. Aurora Quezon, widow of late president Manuel Quezon, is riding through the province of Bulacan to dedicate a monument in her husband's birthplace, the city of Baler. It's a twelve-car convoy. They let her car go well in front to avoid the dust that kicked up off the road. The rest of the convoy fell back. About a hundred Huks opened up on the lead car, killing Mrs. Quezon and several others. It was a shocker. And puzzling. In many ways it marked the deterioration of the movement, a revolution going bad, turning sour, random, nasty. But Mrs. Quezon wasn't the prime target. Someone else was riding with her that day. It was Harrison Wingfield they wanted. And got. It took him years, but Juan Olmos evened the score. Not that the score is ever evened. One man's even is always another man's odd . . ."

"Hold it," Hugh Beaumont interrupted. "Didn't I just hear you say Olmos was in the group that was executed at San Leandro?"

"He was. He went down wounded, shot in the arm. He crawled to the edge of the schoolyard, near the schoolhouse . . ."

"And got away?"

"And waited for one of the cops to come along for the coup de grace. People were screaming all around him. Blood. Brains. Teeth. He waited. Then someone came over. Olmos had his bolo ready. The cop went down, sliced ear to ear, and Olmos was up, acting like a cop, walking past the dead and dying, his own men . . . and women. Then he was into the schoolhouse and out into the rice fields. He was gone . . ."

"Fascinating," Wingfield snapped. "I'm leaving." He was almost out of the tent before he wheeled around. "So what! Harding fell in love with a bunch of Communist guerrillas. You really think this would have been a better place if they won it back then? Or now? You'd want to live in the People's Republic of the Philippines? Hey! You like Pol Pot? You'd love the Olmos brothers. I don't know, Griffin, maybe you expected me to break out hankies over some damn obscure, mini–My Lai in a war everybody's forgot. What did you think? That you could rub our nose in shit and get thanked for it? I've got news. You make me feel better about this movie all the time. Because the bottom line is, while we were losing China and getting ready to screw up in Korea, this is one place we won one. I like that. It suits me fine. It's my kind of story. My kind of film. Film? Scratch that. It's not a film. It's a movie, an American movie. It's got lots of killing and chasing around in exotic locations and it's got some exotic fucking too. It's a movie—"

"So you've got your movie, Larry. I've got the book. Mine's true."

"Honest, Griffin, I'm not losing a minute of sleep over that one. Not a minute. Assume you find a publisher for this . . . sob story. You'll still be riding on our backs. Piggybacking. The 'real story.' The story behind the film. Okay, you're published. You sell well. So how well is real well? Thirty thousand? Fifty thousand? That's one small town. Get it? *You're* San Leandro. *I'm* Manila. We're going to open in twelve hundred theaters. We'll do better on our first night than your book ever does. Got it? It's a democracy, Griffin, and I love it. Because I've got the votes. Ciao."

Next it was Hugh Beaumont's turn. "Well, I don't blame you, Griffin. I don't mind your telling it the way it was. But I have just one small bone to pick with you."

"What's that?" Griffin asked. He liked Hugh Beaumont without knowing why. An overweight oilman in a lime-green jump suit, a fat and happy Texas Republican who admitted that he hadn't read a book since *Kon Tiki*.

"I saw Harry Roberts Harding in Baguio in May 1944. He was on his way to Kiangen. There was no reason for him to remember me. I just saw him walking through the Baguio market one day, and I saw how people came up to him, kids and hags and wounded soldiers, nuns, cripples, amputees, internees, how the whole world crowded in on him, for a look-see, a touch, a word. And I said to myself, this is something to remember. This is what we were fighting for. That kind of feeling. I'm not too sentimental, Griffin. But he was like nobody I ever saw. I've always had a feeling for him. Now, are you telling me I was wrong?"

"No. I'm not saying that."

"Of course you're not. You're just saying there was more going on than I knew about. That it wasn't so simple. That a grown up man like me, and rich besides, ought to know better. And I can't deny you. But you know something? I *like* my version better."

"I prefer Mr. Griffin's version," Cecilia Santos said. She was leaning forward, smiling. "Tell me, George, are you saying that you found Juan Olmos?"

"He found me."

"Incredible."

"Or rather, an associate of his did. General Nestor Contreras."

God, you're beautiful when you're shocked, Griffin thought. If I could give you a surprise like this each night you'd be mine. But I'll never have enough surprises for you. Just this. "Let me tell you about Juan Olmos . . ."

Who keeps score for the losing side? Who'll remember the shifts and turns of a war that was fought in a hundred obscure places? Who can be relied upon to keep track of skirmishes, ambushes, betrayals beyond number? Who'll maintain rosters of the names of men who were killed and dumped in unmarked graves, if buried at all, put under the ground or left to join it from above? Who except a thin, gaunt, middle-aged man who never forgave and never forgot?

For Juan Olmos's brother, Felipe, the ending came quickly, when six Huk-backed congressmen elected in 1946 were denied their seats: their "no" votes would have jeopardized passage of the Bell Trade Act, a package of privilege and concessions the United States insisted upon as a condition of the Philippines' already highly conditional independence. Felipe's belief in elections had kept him from San Leandro—he'd been in Manila, organizing the campaign. It gained him very little else. Later he returned to the hills, an ineffectual warrior who surrendered, at his own brother's urging, in 1950. Juan Olmos kept fighting, but by the early fifties he was fighting not to win, but to survive. He still maintained—he always would—that if the war had been wholly civil, it might have ended otherwise.

The Americans made the difference, supplying weapons, vehicles, airplanes, breaking the previously ineffectual Filipino forces into small mobile units that held what they captured, denied the Huks the towns, probed their mountain hideaways. The Huks were hunted, penetrated, betrayed. Olmos remembered all the men who never arrived at destinations, the rendezvous that were never kept, the once friendly villages turning sullen, the men, good men, who surrendered, induced by amnesty and promises of land in Mindanao. Bribes, ploys, dirty tricks. Dead Huk soldiers, drained of blood, left out to intimidate peasants who were scared of vampires. Slowly, the shadow government, the magnificent underground network, broke into a thousand bleeding pieces and it was only pride that kept Juan Olmos fighting. And then, in 1954, he received an unexpected message from one of his most determined hunters. Colonel—later, General—Nestor Contreras sought a meeting with him, alone, on Mount Arayat. That was where, and then was when, Juan Olmos and Nestor Contreras formed their strange entente. The two men had one thing in common: neither one, it turned out, had forgotten San Leandro. And in Florida, sitting outside a motel office, up all night with his memories, there was a third man who never forgot.

"You mean," Hugh Beaumont said, "General Nestor Contreras has this red terror tucked away in Mindanao?"

"His conscience. His idol. His dirty little secret. I don't know." And then it came to him. "His ghost."

"So someday Contreras maybe follows Marcos. And America says, okay, a sonofabitch but our sonofabitch, he speaks our language, we can do business with him."

"And he might turn out to be like every other man who ever made it to the top out here," Griffin said. "Then again, maybe not."

"One question, George." It was Cecilia. "After you were done with Juan Olmos, you were returned to General Contreras. Right?"

"Yes."

"And he let you go?"

"That was Cadillac Bill's doing."

"Cadillac Bill?"

"Wait a minute," Griffin said. He stepped outside and surveyed the party Palm Tree Productions had ordered up to thank its local hosts. He caught the smell of barbecued meat, heard music, glimpsed what looked like a hydrofoil full of del Pilar Street girls. It took a loud shout and a vigorous wave to detach Cadillac Bill from a cornered guerrilla beauty whose surrender he had been negotiating.

"Howdy," Cadillac Bill said, stepping into the tent. "You folks are missing all the fun."

"I want you to tell these people how you saved my life."

"Oh. That."

"When Griffin and me got back from seeing Juan Olmos, General Contreras was waiting for us at the spiffy new hotel he uses for headquarters. He had flunkies all around him, and bar girls, and bottles. I don't know about the bar girls, but he sure as hell had gotten into the bottles. He was looking meaner than cat shit.

" 'You've seen Juan Olmos,' he says. 'You know my secret. You know that General Nestor Contreras, heir apparent to President Marcos, has a massacre in his past.'

" 'You didn't set it up,' says Griffin. He sounds half assed and wishy-washy to me. 'Besides, you were young . . .'

" '. . . and ambitious and charming,' Contreras fires back. 'Just an eager-to-please Filipino lad who wanted to improve his English. No I didn't set it up. No, I didn't shoot anybody. All I did was betray my best friend. All I did was listen to Wingfield's plans. I knew it was coming and I watched it come. I watched some of the best fighters this country's ever had be butchered. Don't dance around the truth, Mr. Griffin. Don't tell me what's been bothering me these years shouldn't bother me at all.'

" 'I think you wanted to tell this story,' Griffin says. 'I think you always wanted to tell it.'

" 'So? So what?' Contreras isn't exactly flattered by George's sensitive understanding of his need to get things off his chest. 'I told you. That doesn't mean I want you to tell the world. No. I think I'm going to have to put you in the ground.'

" 'Just a damn minute,' I say. It was my turn now. 'I know I don't count for nothing here, but when I see a pissing contest turn into forty days and forty nights of rain, I get worried. What's all this about, General? Forty years ago you helped put some Reds away. Maybe they were good men. So what? You think that's gonna hurt you with America? *This* America? Shit, we're talking Communists! Enemies of our way of life, yours and mine. Enemies of . . .'

"I wave at the golf course, the gardens, the bottles, the bar girls, the new casino-hotel that would be needing customers.

" '. . . enemies of all this. They're gonna love you in the States. You saved the Philippines back then. You made it safe for democracy and elections and tourists and military bases and our whole way of life. You did it once and you by God can do it again, that's what they'll think. You're a hands-on, shirt-sleeves-up, can-do, no-bullshit, wham-bam-thank-you-ma'am kind of guy . . .'

" 'You think so?' Contreras said. That's when I knew we had him. All it took was a little common sense.

" 'I know so. Take my word for it, General. You got nothing to apologize for. You're a winner. Winners don't need to apologize to losers. Winners don't apologize to anybody . . .'

"Contreras looks at Griffin, looks at me. He pours a drink, raises it to his lips, halfway swallows it, and busts into a laughing fit that sprays George and me with a fine mist of ice and Johnny Walker scotch. He flushes beet red. He chokes. He jumps out of his chair and dances. He keeps laughing. Finally he turns and he says, 'Get out of here.' Which we gladly do."

48

There was nothing left to say. No thanks or congratulations, no verdicts, no applause. What had happened had happened and then it was time for the ones who knew, Griffin and the rest, to join the ones who didn't know or care, the people who were partying out on the Corregidor parade ground. Cadillac Bill resumed pursuit of his guerrilla extra: her torn uniform excited him. Hugh Beaumont had a plane to catch and Larry Wingfield needed to make some long-distance phone calls. Cecilia Santos looked as though she might have lingered, but Eddie Richter swept her off to meet a party of newcomers, Italian film producers interested in a project that had Vietnam MIA's imprisoned by South China Sea pirates. Griffin watched her, the way she held herself while being introduced: Miss Fire and Ice. Welcome to the Philippines. And even as he stared at her, Cecilia Santos looked back at him and rolled her eyes as if to say, Here we go again. She was terrific. And so—in her own way—was Susan Hayes, standing at the edge of the party.

"Waiting for me?" Griffin asked.

"Or my car. Whichever came first."

"Susan? Thanks for coming."

"Congratulations. You worked hard, George, and it shows. If I helped you out, I'm happy. And if I slowed you down at all, well, I'm sorry."

"The helping went much further than the other stuff."

"How will the book do?"

"You mean, do I think it's a best seller? Will I ever have to work again?"

"I wouldn't put it quite as crassly but . . ."

"I aim to keep working. See, Susan, I'm like you."

She smiled and nodded and Griffin felt that something connected them now. Then she glanced at her watch. "I've got to go," she said.

"Now? Tonight?"

"There's something in the air at the embassy. Involving me."

"Something good?"

"I think so."

"That can't wait until tomorrow? Come on, Susan."

"*It* can wait," she said. "But I can't."

He watched her climb into a movie company car that would take her down to the hydrofoil dock. He wondered if he would ever get to know her. Then he realized he already had.

At the end, it came down to Eddie Richter. It ended where it began and that was further proof—as if any were needed—that endings and beginnings were illusions: everything went on forever. It came down to Eddie and George walking through the party, past the bombed-out movie theater and the commandant's ruined house, out to the Pacific War Memorial, where all —well, some—of the war's great battles were carved in stone. The place was deserted, shining in moonlight. They walked straight to the edge, and moonlight was all over the sea too.

"You never let go of him, did you Eddie? Not from the morning you took that photograph in San Leandro . . . not from then till now."

"You picked up on that, huh?"

"Why? Did you love him? Did you hate him?"

"I could never decide about Harding. After I took that group picture, I wandered around, trying different things. Remember, I was going to be a famous photographer. I was behind the school when I saw the troops coming up. I saw it all. I saw Wingfield standing there . . ."

Eddie stopped. He covered his face with his hands.

"I heard Wingfield got upset when the shooting turned to beating," said Griffin. "He even objected."

"Sure, sure," Eddie countered bitterly. "What'd he do, the grand old man? Belch?"

"Sorry."

"I saw Harding standing there. MacArthur's Ghost. The man who made promises. Well, his men were being killed in front of him. I don't mean killed. I mean stomped and kicked and gouged. Tortured. Shat on. Laughed at. And his woman was out there too, don't forget. And there he stood, tied up, tugging, screaming, vomiting. But you know what? It wasn't enough."

"What—what did you want?"

"I wanted him to remember. For one thing. Remember the promises he made. His buddies got put in the fucking ground. I'm not saying we should have handed the Philippines over. But to kill them, no way, kid. They deserved to live. They deserved to be a part of whatever happened, win, lose, or draw. They deserved a future. You know me, George. I don't care about politics. I don't have any recipes for this place. But I hate what happened that day. And you know something? Those people who died, they're the real ghosts. From that day on, this became a spooked country. Because they can hold all the elections they want, they can rotate presidents in and out of Malacanang, change one sonofabitch for another, but it's a hollow game. I know it. You know it. Contreras, too, I guess."

"And Harding. Right, Eddie?"

"They came in because of him. They put down their guns on his account. They got butchered and put in the ground. That was Wingfield's phrase. 'Put in the ground.'"

"And you never forgot that."

"Never," Eddie said. "I'm not saying I thought about them every day, or even every week. That was all right. I'd made a promise. It's not just big shots who make promises, George. 'I shall return.' Not just them. Sometimes a squirt like me makes a promise while nobody's listening and he keeps the promise while nobody's watching. It just takes a while longer. Life gets in the way. But the older you get, you concentrate on what matters. When I retired down to Florida, selling condo time shares, I got busy. Beaumont and Wingfield think this movie was their idea. I got news."

"So you brought them Harding."

"Yeah. I'd kept in touch with him, on and off. Just praying he wouldn't die before I got my act together."

"What do you think of him now?"

"I think . . . oh hell!" Eddie Richter broke off and looked away, as if he'd just gotton interested in something out to sea. "I think I'm losing touch. Ten years ago, I could've told you exactly what I thought of him. A snappy answer. . ."

"And now?"

"Okay. He had a memory. And a conscience. And a heart. Which—alright, already!—got broken. You want me to come right out and say it? He was a better man than I thought he was. And now we're passing out medals, I might as well say it: so were you."

"And you, Eddie."

"Oh, cut it out. So we're all splendid guys. Tell me, does it make a difference, with assholes running the world? Did it ever make a difference?"

"We'll see," Griffin said. "It keeps coming back to me. Something Felipe Olmos said. Things die down. They don't die out."

"You believe it?"

"I think I do."

"Well. They can do a lot of things to you. They can make you do a lot of things. But they can't make you forget. And if enough people remember, well . . ." The tanned old-timer reached up and tweaked Griffin's ear. He threw a haymaker at the sky. He stared out across the Pacific. "Maybe we're all immortal."